Verena Berger,
Miya Komori (Eds.)

Polyglot Cinema

2-NIGHT LOAN

Due Back
Anytime on the third day

Fine for Late Return
£2.50 per day

Short Loan Items
... cannot be renewed or reserved
... are not due back at the weekend

Opening Hours
Email
Telephone

Beiträge zur europäischen Theater-, Film- und Medienwissenschaft

herausgegeben von

Verena Berger, Andrea B. Braidt
und Daniel Winkler

Band 2

LIT

POLYGLOT CINEMA

Migration and Transcultural Narration
in France, Italy, Portugal and Spain

edited by

Verena Berger and Miya Komori

LIT

Cover Picture: *Turm zu Babel* (*Tower of Babel*) – MICHAEL LASSEL
(Artist and painter, www.lassel-michael.de)

This publication has been funded with support from the
Austrian Federal Ministry for Science and Research (BMWF)

Bibliographic information published by the Deutsche Nationalbibliothek
The Deutsche Nationalbibliothek lists this publication in the Deutsche
Nationalbibliografie; detailed bibliographic data are available in the Internet at
http://dnb.d-nb.de.

ISBN 978-3-643-50226-1

A catalogue record for this book is available from the British Library

©LIT VERLAG GmbH & Co. KG Wien 2010
Krotenthallergasse 10/8
A-1080 Wien
Tel. +43 (0) 1-409 56 61
Fax +43 (0) 1-409 56 97
e-Mail: wien@lit-verlag.at
http://www.lit-verlag.at

LIT VERLAG Dr. W. Hopf
Berlin 2010
Fresnostr. 2
D-48159 Münster
Tel. +49 (0) 2 51-620 320
Fax +49 (0) 2 51-922 60 99
e-Mail: lit@lit-verlag.de
http://www.lit-verlag.de

Distribution:
In Germany: LIT Verlag Fresnostr. 2, D-48159 Münster
Tel. +49 (0) 2 51-620 32 22, Fax +49 (0) 2 51-922 60 99, e-mail: vertrieb@lit-verlag.de

In Austria: Medienlogistik Pichler-ÖBZ, e-mail: mlo@medien-logistik.at

In Switzerland: B + M Buch- und Medienvertrieb, e-mail: order@buch-medien.ch

In the UK: Global Book Marketing, e-mail: mo@centralbooks.com

In North America by:

Transaction Publishers
New Brunswick (U.S.A.) and London (U.K.)

Transaction Publishers
Rutgers University
35 Berrue Circle
Piscataway, NJ 08854

Phone: +1 (732) 445 - 2280
Fax: + 1 (732) 445 - 3138
for orders (U. S. only):
toll free (888) 999 - 6778
e-mail: orders@transactionpub.com

Contents

IV. Post-Colonialism and Cultural Contact in French Migrant Cinema

V. Polyglot Fiction and Nonfiction: Narratives from Spain and Portugal

VI. Local and Global: Polyphony in Italian Cinema

Introduction: Moving Pictures
from a Modern Babel

Verena Berger/Miya Komori

As an allegory for a plurality of languages, the phrase 'the confusion of tongues', taken from the Old Testament story of the Tower of Babel, has found its way into popular imagery. In the biblical story, God recognises that 'if as one people speaking the same language they have begun to do this, then nothing they plan to do will be impossible for them' and 'confuses' their language to divide and scatter them over the earth (New International Version Gen. 11: 1–9). The popularity of the Babel myth and the resonance of the metaphor can be seen in the work of artists across time, genres and geographical borders, from the 16th-century Flemish paintings by Pieter Brueghel the Elder (1563) and Lucas van Valckenborch (1568; 1594/1595) to the Argentine writer Jorge Luis Borges' short story *La biblioteca de Babel*[1] (1941), Igor Stravinsky's cantata *Babel*, the Swiss writer Friedrich Dürrenmatt's play *Ein Engel kommt nach Babylon*[2] (1953), the 3D computer game *Indiana Jones and the Infernal Machine* (1999) or the film *Babel* (2006) directed by the Mexican Alejandro González Iñárritu. The latter is set in the USA, Morocco, Mexico and Japan and its protagonists express themselves in English, Spanish, Arabic, Japanese and sign language, not understanding each other both literally and figuratively. Subtitled in order to make it accessible to its audiences, *Babel* can be considered not only a modern cinematographic interpretation of the Babel metaphor, but also a representative example of polyglot cinema.

Polyglot, from the 'ancient Greek Πολύγλωττος many-tongued, in Hellenistic Greek also speaking many languages' can mean a person who 'speaks, writes, or understands a number of languages'; something 'written or uttered in a number of languages'; 'characterised by a multiplicity of (native) languages; involving the use of several languages, or elements of several languages'[3]. The title of this volume therefore refers to both the presence of a plurality of languages in cinema in general and the concept of a 'polyglot cinema' as proposed by Chris Wahl:

---

1 *The Library of Babel.*
2 *An Angel Comes to Babylon.*
3 See the definition of 'polyglot' in the Oxford English Dictionary.

[In] polyglot film [...] languages are used in the way they would be used in reality. They define geographical or political borders, 'visualise' the different social, personal or cultural levels of the characters and enrich their aura in conjunction with the voice. The complexity and variety of the character network and the intense singularity of each person which form the centre of the polyglot film render dubbing impossible without destroying the movie [...]. Polyglot films must be shown with subtitles (or without any aid) because they are anti-illusionist in the sense that they do not try to hide the diversity of human life behind the mask of a universal language. (Wahl 2005b)

One of the most significant characteristics of polyglot cinema is therefore the presence of bi- or plurilingual[4] dialogues. In contrast to the abolition of linguistic difference by dubbing, especially in films from Hollywood, polyglot cinema depicts the diversity of language use. Wahl not only offers one of the very few approaches to the topic (e.g. Mowitt 2005; Wahl 2005a; Bleichenbacher 2008; Abecassis 2008), but also proposes a classification of polyglot film into several subgenres: the episode film (*I Vinti* 1952, Michelangelo Antonioni; *Night On Earth* 1991, Jim Jarmusch), the alliance film (*Le Mépris* 1963, Jean-Luc Godard), the globalisation film (*Lisbon Story* 1994/95, Wim Wenders), the fraternisation film (*Kukushka* 2002, Aleksandr Rogozhkin), the colonial film (*Ava & Gabriel – Un historia di amor* 1992, Felix de Rooy), the existential film (*Um Film Falado* 2003, Manuel de Oliveira) and, finally, the immigrant film (*Solino* 2002, Fatih Akin) (Wahl 2005b; 2008: 340ff.).

Migration certainly offers an ideal setting for portraying bi- and plurilingual dialogues as well as culture contact and conflict on screen. With the exception of theatre, there are hardly any other media which can represent conversation in conjunction with an image as apparently realistically as film. While literature uses language in its written form, cinema and theatre have the advantage of allowing their audiences to experience language at an acoustic level. With regard to filmic style, the resulting transnational narratives imply a hybridity of aesthetics, settings, acting and languages. Hamid Naficy denominates this 'accented cinema' when referring to the aesthetics of films perceived as different from the mainstream or dominant modes of production (Naficy 2001: 24), which have traditionally been heavily influenced by Hollywood. In terms of language, this can be seen in the fact that after World War II, English became the 'vulgate of Anglo-American power' and everybody, from Madame Bovary to God, spoke in English (Shohat/Stam 2006: 108; 127–128). As a response to the cultural colonisation by the West in general and of the film industry by Hollywood in particular, there has been a marked, if not exactly mainstream,

4 The term 'plurilingualism' was chosen for the title of this collection in preference to the more common English term 'multilingualism' in accordance with the Council of Europe's *Common European Framework of Reference for Languages* (Byram 2007: 1) and the extension of the more precise terms from French and German as used by the European Language Council: '[...] both in French and German we use different words for referring, on the one hand, to an individual's ability to use several languages – *plurilinguisme/Mehrsprachigkeit* – and, on the other, to the multilingual nature of a given society – *multilinguisme/Vielsprachigkeit*' (Mackiewicz 2002: 1). Nevertheless, the editors have respected the terms and concepts preferred by the authors in their articles.

movement away from the homogenisation which characterised the post-war period. For instance, from as early as the 1970s, *Beur* cinema in France has portrayed topics such as racism, unemployment and immigration, themes that also appear in the younger *cinéma de banlieue* and *cinéma du métissage* (Seeßlen 2005; Tarr 2005; 2007; Bloom 2007).

While France has a relatively long tradition of immigration, other European countries, particularly in the Mediterranean region, have only recorded a large influx of migrants since the late 1980s/early 1990s. Formerly known as countries of emigration, the cinematic production of Italy (Capussotti 2009; Ponzanesi 2005; Winkler 2010), Portugal (Cardoso Marques 2002) and Spain (Castiello 2005; Moyano 2005; Santaolalla 2005) dealing with the issue of migration is correspondingly less developed than that of France. From the Spanish director Montxo Armendáriz' *Las cartas de Alou*[5] (1990) to the Italian Gianni Amelio's *Lamerica* (1994) and the Portuguese Teresa Villaverde's *Transe*[6] (2006), a number of film-makers have started to portray the figure of the migrant. As a consequence, the integration of migrant languages at the acoustic level has become a dominant strategy in the representation of the protagonists' everyday lives as well as questions of memory, homeland and identity.

The presence of two or more languages on screen augments the need for complex solutions to make the film accessible to its audiences. Like Wahl, Naficy argues that subtitling is the best way to maximise reception while respecting the individual voices, particularly when there is no single dominant or 'original' language (Naficy 2001: 122). Though not the only option, subtitling, along with dubbing, represents the most common method of translating the message (Reinart 2004: 74ff.). The most recent technical possibilities and the digital resources of a film's DVD allow its audiences to select audio and subtitling settings, theoretically enabling the protagonists to speak almost any language (Heiss 2004), and arguably fulfilling the ancient Babylonian dream of a universal language. Nevertheless, polyglot cinema does not claim to be understandable at all linguistic levels, but rather aims to depict the breadth of languages with which migrants are confronted. While subtitling and other forms of film translation can make this more accessible to its audiences, the central tenet of polyglot cinema is the representation of language diversity as its protagonists experience it.

The aim of this collection of essays is twofold. On the one hand, the articles analyse culture and language contact in films from a formal perspective, considering aspects such as linguistic interference, borrowings or code-switching. On the other, socio- and psycholinguistic aspects will be investigated to explore the impact of issues including the acquisition and rejection of the native or target language, linguistic integration or exclusion, and the role of identity and post-colonialism in the context of migration. The multifaceted nature of the topic requires a complex ap-

---

5   *Letters from Alou.*
6   *Trance.*

proach to the analysis of polyglot cinema which draws on several disciplines such as cultural, film and translation studies as well as linguistics.

The first section of the volume focuses on 'Cinema and Translation'. The TRAMA group, headed by Frederic Chaume (University of Alicante/Spain), offers an insight into different strategies used by film-makers when confronted with plurilingual scripts and domesticating or foreignising tendencies on the basis of a specially designed corpus. As the heading suggests, the following chapter, 'Polyphony and Translating the 'Other' in French and Spanish Cinema', considers the difficulties of translation at both a linguistic and a cultural level. Michaël Abecassis (University of Oxford/UK) looks back to pre-war French cinema to establish and outline the evolution of plurilingual cinema in France from the first silent films to the early talkies produced in several languages simultaneously, leading to the *Beur* and *banlieue* cinema of multicultural modern France. John Sanderson's (University of Alicante/ Spain) contribution on the representation of the Hispanic as the 'Other' highlights the issues arising when an audience recognises it as one of themselves, resulting in the necessity of *intra*-linguistic translation strategies.

The next two sections are dedicated to the depiction of migration in French-language cinema. The first focuses on 'Polyglot Narratives of Migrant Communities in France'. The common thread in these articles is community, whether it is cultural or familial, or even both, as illustrated by the first article, in which Alec Hargreaves and Leslie Kealhofer (Florida State University/USA) examine the use of language by second-generation North African-French film-makers. Their essay takes a sharp look at language contact and conflict between French and Arabic in the films and their cultural implications, either with reference to their parents, the first-generation immigrants, or for colonial subjects in Africa. With her particular focus on Thomas Gilou's *Raï* (1995), Cristina Johnston (University of Stirling/UK) highlights several themes running through *banlieue* film which are underlined by the use of language. Gaëlle Planchenault (Simon Fraser University/Canada) takes Yamina Benguigui's *Inch'Allah Dimanche* (2001) to analyse how language acquisition can empower female immigrants in their new communities. The chapter closes with an article about a rather less well-known community of immigrants in France as Salih Akin (University of Rouen/France) explores both inter- and intralingual language contact among the Kurdish community in *Vive la mariée... et la libération du Kurdistan*, shot in Paris in 1998 by the Kurdish migrant film-maker Hiner Saleem. The two articles comprising 'Post-Colonialism and Cultural Contact in French Migrant Cinema' offer a rather different perspective, focusing on films from former French colonies. Karine Blanchon's (Paris/France) essay on the cinema of Raymond Rajaonarivelo traces his relationship with the language and culture of both his homeland and its former coloniser, while Hélène Sicard-Cowan (Montreal/Canada) examines the development of language and identity in the Vietnamese film-maker Lâm Lê's' *Vingt nuits et un jour de pluie* (2006).

The two final chapters are devoted to cinema from Portugal, Spain and Italy. 'Polyglot Fiction and Nonfiction: Narratives from Spain and Portugal' begins with an overview of Hispanic immigration cinema by Cristina Martínez-Carazo (University of California/USA) and of plurilingualism and migration in Lusophone film by Carolin Overhoff Ferreira (University of São Paulo/Brasil). Miya Komori's (WU Vienna University of Economics and Business/Austria) essay analyses language contact and acquisition among migrants leaving Spain in the economic downturn of the late Franco period, while Verena Berger (University of Vienna/Austria) examines plurilingualism in the context of documentary cinema from Portugal and Spain. In the final section, 'Local and Global: Polyphony in Italian Cinema', Camille Gendrault (University of Bordeaux 3/France) rounds off the volume with an exploration of the inter- and intralingual language contact that characterises migration in Italy, where incomers not only have to deal with a foreign language but also a myriad of local dialects.

Our thanks go to all the authors participating in the collection and to Michael Lassel, who kindly allowed us to use his painting *Turm zu Babel*[7]. Finally, we also express our gratitude to Fritz Peter Kirsch, Daniel Winkler and Karl Ille for their comments as well as to Richard Kisling and LIT for the publication of this volume.

References

ABECASSIS, M. (ed.) (2008), *Pratiques langagières dans le cinéma francophone*, in: *Glottopol*, 12, URL: http://www.univ-rouen.fr/dyalang/glottopol/numero_12.htm (May 2010).

BLEICHENBACHER, L. (2008), *Multilingualism in the Movies: Hollywood Characters and Their Language Choices*, Tübingen: Francke.

BLOOM, P. (2007), 'Beur Cinema and the Politics of Location: French Immigration Politics and the Naming of a Film Movement', in: Ezra, E. & T. Rowden (eds.), *Transnational Cinema: The Film Reader*, London: Routledge, 131–142.

BYRAM, M. (2007), 'Plurilingualism in Europe: Its Implications', in: *Conference Report – Berlin Conference, 26–27 January 2007: Preparing for the World of Work – Language Education for the Future*, URL: www.britishcouncil.org/.../newsletter_-_sep_07_-_borrowed_from_-_plurilingualism.doc (09 May 2010).

CAPUSSOTTI, E. (2009), 'Moveable Identities: Migration, Subjectivity and Cinema in Contemporary Italy', in: *Modern Italy*, vol. 14:1, 55–68.

CARDOSO MARQUES, J.A. (2002), *Images de portugais en France: Immigration et cinéma*, Paris: L'Harmattan.

CASTIELLO, Ch. (2005), *Los parias de la tierra. Inmigrantes en el cine español*, Madrid: Talasa Ediciones S.L.

HEISS, C. (2004), 'Dubbing Multilingual Films: A New Challenge?', in: *Meta*, vol. 49:1, 208–220.

MACKIEWICZ, W. (2002), 'Plurilingualism in the European Knowledge Society'; Conference *Lingue e produzione del sapere*, Swiss Academy of Humanities and Social Sciences, Università della Svizzera italiana, 14 June 2002, URL: www.celelc.org/docs/speech_final_website_1.doc (09 May 2010).

---

7   *Tower of Babel.*

MOWITT, J. (2005), *Re-Takes. Postcoloniality and Foreign Film Languages*, Minneapolis: University of Minnesota Press.

MOYANO, E. (2005), *La memoria escondida. Emigración y cine*, Madrid: Tabla Rasa.

NAFICY, H. (2001), *An Accented Cinema. Exilic and Diasporic Filmmaking*, Princeton: Princeton U.P.

PONZANESI, S. (2005), 'Outlandish Cinema: Screening the Other in Italy', in: Ponzanesi, S. & D. Merolla (eds.), *Migrant Cartographies: New Cultural and Literary Spaces in Postcolonial Europe*, Lanham: Lexington Books, 267–280.

REINART, S. (2004), 'Zu Theorie und Praxis von Untertitelung und Synchronisation', in: Kohlmayer, R. & W. Pöckl (eds.), *Literarisches und mediales Übersetzen. Aufsätze zu Theorie und Praxis einer gelehrten Kunst*, Frankfurt/Main: Lang, 73–112.

SANTAOLALLA, I. (2005), *Los 'Otros'. Etnicidad y 'raza' en el cine español contemporáneo*, Madrid: Ocho y Medio.

SEESSLEN, G. (2000), 'Das Kino der doppelten Kulturen', in: *epd Film*, 12, URL: http://www.epd-archiv.de (03 June 2010).

SHOHAT, E. & R. STAM (2006), 'Cinema after Babel: Language, Difference, Power', in: Shohat, E., *Taboo Memories, Diasporic Voices*, Durham/London: Duke U.P., 106–138.

TARR, C. (2005), *Reframing Difference: 'Beur' and 'banlieue' Filmmaking in France*, Manchester: Manchester U.P.

TARR, C. (ed.) (2007), *Beur is Beautiful: Contemporary French-Maghrebi Cinema*, Special supplement, *Cineaste*, 33:1.

WAHL, Ch. (2005a), *Das Sprechen des Spielfilms. Über die Auswirkungen von hörbaren Dialogen auf Produktion und Rezeption, Ästhetik und Internationalität der siebten Kunst*, Trier: WVT.

WAHL, Ch. (2005b), 'Discovering a Genre: The Polyglot Film', in: *Cinemascope – Independent Film Journal*, 1, URL: http://www.cinemascope.it (28 April 2010).

WAHL, Ch. (2008), ' 'Du Deutscher, toi français, You English: Beautiful' – The Polyglot Film as a Genre', in: Christensen, M. & N. Erdŏgan (eds.), *Shifting Landscapes: Film and Media in European Context*, Newcastle: Cambridge Scholars Publishing, 334–350.

WINKLER, D. (2010), 'Sud Side Stori. Genretradition und -transformationen im sizilianischen Kino. Marco Bellocchio, Vincenzo Marra, Roberta Torre', in: Winkler, D. & B. Wagner (eds.), *Nuovo Cinema Italia. Der italienische Film meldet sich zurück*, Vienna: Böhlau (Maske und Kothurn, 56:1), 47–61.

I. CINEMA AND TRANSLATION

Linguistic Diversity in Spanish Immigration Films.
A Translational Approach

Juan José Martínez-Sierra, José Luis Martí-Ferriol, Irene de Higes-
Andino, Ana M. Prats-Rodríguez and Frederic Chaume

Polyglot Films and Translation

As Dirk Delabastita and Rainier Grutman explain, 'Back in the 1980s [...b]ilingual writers and multilingual texts were still very much frowned upon,' although '[i]n to-day's world, talk of multilingualism no longer raises eyebrows but is seen [...] as a sign of the times' (Delabastita/Grutman 2005: 11). But what is a multilingual text? According to these authors, the simplest possible way to define a multilingual text 'would be to say that such a text is worded in different languages' (Delabastita/Grut-man 2005: 15). It was precisely this sign of the times that called for an expansion of the concept of *multilingual text*, since multilingualism – or plurilingualism – is no longer limited to written texts and has progressively expanded into art forms such as cinema. It is in this context that we need to consider the advent of *multilingual* or *plurilingual audiovisual texts*. Yet multilingual films are not a new phenomenon. Indeed, they 'developed hand in hand with the coming of sound' (Dwyer 2005: 296). What is recent is their current function, since '[t]he polyglot film developed from a sheer tool to fight the problems of international film distribution after the coming of sound to a discrete mode of narrative and aesthetic expression' (Wahl 2008: 349). [1]

Multilingual films typically seem to be referred to as *polyglot films* (namely, films 'marked by the naturalistic presence of two or more languages at the level of dialogue and narrative', Dwyer 2005: 296), which, in addition, appear to be arche-typal of – but not restricted to – the 'European style of filmmaking' (Wahl 2008: 334). In fact, authors such as Dwyer (2005) or Wahl (2005; 2008) consider that this type of film constitutes a *genre*.

---

1   This study was funded by '3a convocatòria d'ajudes per a projectes d'investigació i formació *OPI-UJI: Migració i Interculturalitat*', a programme from Universitat Jaume I (Castelló/Spain) which supports research on migration and interculturality. It was also funded by the Spanish Ministry of Education and Science, by means of a research project called '*Estudio empírico y descriptivo de las normas profesionales de la traducción audiovisual en España*' (HUM2007–65518).

Polyglot films – or the polyglot genre – have been described by the above mentioned authors, who have also touched upon the relationship between multilingual texts/films and translation to varying extents. Additionally, other authors have dealt with polyglot audiovisual texts from the translational perspective. More specifically, the dubbing of such material has been addressed by authors such as Agost (2000), who focuses on the translation for dubbing of different audiovisual genres with more than one language in the source version; Heiss (2004), who advocates the use of multiple modes in the translation of polyglot films and perceives media formats like DVD as ideal for coping with the translation challenges of polyglot films; or Valdeón (2005), who centres his research on the analysis of dubbing in the television show *Frasier* – with special attention to the scenes in which different languages are used mainly to create humorous effects.

Polyglot films are becoming more and more widespread[2], and not surprisingly their translation is also gaining research ground at postgraduate levels. Of note in this vein is Montserrat Corrius' PhD thesis (2008), which studies the translation of the so-called *third language*, i.e. any language other than the source and the target language, within Zabalbeascoa's priorities/restrictions model (1993). Other future lines of research include that of Herrera, who lays the foundations for an analysis of the translation of the film *Babel* as an example of multilingual film translation and whose project description can be seen in Herrera (2007). The author argues that films of this nature should not be dubbed, since the richness and the evoked meaning of the mingle of languages is lost in a dubbing where all languages are translated into just one language. A further line of research is that of Bartoll (2006), who described the translation strategies found in the subtitling of some plurilingual films.

Research Objectives

Our main objective is to describe how plurilingualism is tackled in cinema productions by using a corpus of Spanish films belonging to the so-called *polyglot* genre. This article does not focus on film dubbing and subtitling, but on a previous step: the use of foreign languages and translation in Spanish immigration films or, to be more precise, Spanish films starring immigrant characters. We consider that this previous step is necessary in order to further analyse and discuss translation strategies in the dubbed and subtitled versions of these films. Thus, it is our intention to identify a set of possible solutions by which foreign languages in this genre are conveyed to the original Spanish audience; in other words, what *strategies* are used when these languages appear in the original film. Our research questions can be formulated in these terms: how are foreign languages represented in the original film and how are they conveyed to the Spanish audience? Are they translated? If so, are they dubbed, subtitled, or do they use voice-over? Why? If they are not translated, why not?

---

2   Even in countries such as the US, despite 'America's historical rejection of subtitling – and more
     general lack of interest in foreign-language films' (Dwyer 2005: 295–296).

This study will be briefly complemented by a second step – an examination of the translation (dubbing, subtitling, etc.) of these foreign language dialogues to other target languages, like French, Italian, English, or German. The present paper reports on the first stage of the study, which explores the issue of how foreign languages are translated in an original – not translated – product addressed to the *source* audience; in our case, Spanish films starring immigrant characters primarily addressed to a Spanish audience.

The utterances referred to in the study are formulated by characters who are immigrants, and who may either speak their own mother tongue or try to render their message in Spanish. If a foreign language is used, the message may be left as it is, or it may be subtitled, interpreted, or self-translated. When the immigrants speak Spanish, they may do so with an accent or not. These options – which we take as a starting point grounded on Bartoll's research (2006) and Corrius' PhD thesis (2008) – have been addressed from an empirical and descriptive standpoint in this research project.

Following the general description of the scope of the research project, its specific objectives are now established:

- To select a corpus of Spanish polyglot films released in Spain in the last two decades on DVD;
- To analyse these films from a micro-textual, descriptive point of view, by identifying all samples in which immigrants communicate;
- To generate a taxonomy of identified translation strategies, like self-translation, liaison interpreting, voice-over, subtitling and no-translation;
- To draw conclusions on the use of the various strategies employed, which may bring up additional considerations on the way in which plurilingualism is handled in Spanish polyglot films.

Hypotheses

One way to assess the importance plurilingualism may have in the Spanish film production scene is to quantify the number of films that can be considered as *polyglot* and that, at the same time, deal to some extent with the question of immigration. This number may also increase diachronically, since the migration phenomenon has become more widespread in Spain and the Western world over the last two decades. The first – quantitative – hypothesis of our research could therefore be posited as follows: the number of polyglot films that deal with immigration issues in Spain will show an upward trend over the last two decades.

The set of strategies identified during the empirical and descriptive phase of the project will be arranged according to their reception in the target culture. Some of the strategies will seek to make the message uttered in the foreign language understandable. Subtitles or self-translation are examples of this approach. Other strategies, however, may tend to leave the foreign language message as it is, thus scaling down the importance of the dialogues in the foreign language, but not necessarily the ideology behind the strategy of no-translation.

As Spain is a country with a strongly established dubbing culture, for both historical and traditional reasons (Chaume 2004), the target audience is used to accessing information in a fashion that can be easily understood. A second hypothesis, related to this question, could thus be postulated: more domesticating than foreignising strategies will be found in the translation of foreign languages in polyglot films dealing with the migration issue. We will have to draw both quantitative and qualitative conclusions, since the evaluation of the strategies found will depend on characters, situations, interaction, etc., and not only on the number of times one or another solution appears.

Methodology

This research project was developed using descriptive and empirical methodology. Although it only involves a case study, an effort was made to put the corpus size into perspective in relation to the total population of films released in Spain in the last two decades. Preliminary research was thus conducted by quantifying the total population of Spanish films (excluding co-productions, documentaries and animation films; see below) released from 1989 onwards. A further filter was applied to this list, namely, that only films in Spanish with a plot containing references to migration issues were considered. A final filter was introduced referring to the format: only films available on DVD were considered, since they allowed us to stop, rewind and select menu options as often as necessary. A corpus of 11 films was generated by this rigorous, iterative process. The corresponding section in this paper describes the corpus as such, but the film list could be termed 'Spanish polyglot films starring immigrant characters released on DVD in Spain in the last 20 years'. Observation and quantification of the corpus enable us to verify the validity of our first hypothesis.

The empirical phase of the project consisted of watching the films and selecting samples. Each time an immigrant character appeared on screen, the language selection was recorded, together with the associated strategy. The results are twofold: in the first place, a proposed taxonomy of identified strategies was created from the empirical observation process. In addition, data analysis enabled us to validate our second hypothesis. The final conclusions related to the hypotheses, as well as those required to meet the objectives listed above, are presented in the conclusion below.

Corpus

The corpus selected for this study consists of 11 Spanish fiction films released during the period 1989–2008 and containing at least one single line of dialogue spoken by a non-Spanish-speaking immigrant character, either in a leading or a supporting role. Wahl's classification of polyglot films distinguishes five subgenres – migration films, existential films, globalisation films, fraternisation films and colonial films (Wahl 2008: 340–346). According to his definition, the films in our corpus could be placed into the migration category[3], because they 'emphasise the process of adaptation or integration, whether successful or not, to a foreign society and language' (Wahl 2008: 340). Since this paper focuses on post-colonial migration and its role within globalisation, the films in our corpus portray only non-European Union characters coming from developing countries in Africa, Asia and the former Eastern bloc. Films containing immigrants from Spanish-speaking countries in Latin America have been left out because their main language of communication is Spanish, and therefore these films do not correspond to the plurilingual focus of this essay.

The total volume of Spanish-only fictional productions in this twenty-year period amounts to 863.[4] This global number includes all the films produced in Spain, regardless of the language – films shot in Basque, Catalan, Galician and Spanish were taken into account. Co-productions, documentaries and animation films were eliminated.[5] From these 863 Spanish-only films released in Madrid during the first semester of each year during that period, only 80 of them star an immigrant character. The choice of films is based on Argote (2003), Davies (2006), Villar-Hernández (2002) and Cantero (2008), whose research has been devoted to this subject. As stated before, our research was limited to productions shot in Spanish and available on DVD. As can be observed in Appendix 1, Spanish productions represent only a small fraction of the films released in Madrid annually, and Spanish films starring immigrants are still fewer. Due to this circumstance and to the fact that many of the titles initially proposed were not available on this format, exhaustive field work was required to find the films. This lack of availability forced us to reduce the number of items in our corpus from 56 films to just 11 – a low figure that prevented our research from being representative of the total population. Thus, ours can be considered a case study which offers a preliminary survey of plurilingual movies in the Spanish film industry.

The following films were included in our corpus: *Bajarse al moro* (Fernando Colomo, 1989) is a comedy portraying Chusa, a woman who smuggles drugs from Morocco to Spain, her cousin, who is a dealer, and her boyfriend Alberto, a policeman. *Las cartas de Alou* (Montxo Armendáriz, 1990) tells the story of an undocumented Senegalese youth who arrives in Spain in search of a job. The letters he sends home reflect his experiences within Spanish society. *Bwana* (Imanol Uribe, 1996) introduces us to Antonio, a Spanish taxi driver, and his family, who meet Ombasi, an undocumented African immigrant they find stranded on an Andalusian beach. *Pídele cuentas al rey* (José Antonio Quirós, 1999)

---

3   However, not all the films in our corpus deal specifically with the topic of migration. The appearance of immigrant characters in films such as *Bajarse al moro* or *Pídele cuentas al rey* is merely incidental.
4   This information was obtained from *Cine para leer*, a publication which only lists the films released in Madrid every semester (see Appendix 1).
5   We considered that co-productions might reflect the situation and attitudes of different countries (rather than those of just one), which would call for a more complex analysis that lies beyond the scope of this paper and that we suggest as a further research line. Similarly, our purpose was to focus on the *narrative* genre (more concretely, on films) and not on the *informative* genre (Agost 1999: 87), and for this reason documentaries were also excluded. Following Argote (2003: 2), we also decided to leave animation films for further research.

tells the story of Fidel, a miner who walks all the way from Asturias to Madrid with his family to seek an audience with the king. On his journey, he gets to know other people's situations, including those facing immigrants. *Salvajes* (Carlos Molinero, 2001) presents Berta, a middle-aged woman whose teenage nephews get involved with neo-Nazi groups. At the same time, she becomes romantically involved with Eduardo, a middle-aged policeman investigating the brutal beating of an immigrant. *Poniente* (Chus Gutiérrez, 2002) tells the story of Lucía, a teacher who returns to her Andalusian hometown to run her father's farm after his death. Lucía falls in love with Curro, the farm's accountant, and they both try to confront the racism of the townspeople. *A mi madre le gustan las mujeres* (Daniela Fejerman and Inés París, 2002) portrays the shock felt by Sofía's adult daughters after she introduces them to her new lover, who happens to be a Czech girl. *El traje* (Alberto Rodríguez, 2002) – the suit – is the present Patricio, a young Guinean immigrant, receives from a basketball star. As soon as he puts it on, he finds he is treated with greater respect. *Tapas* (José Corbacho and Juan Cruz, 2005) explores the different relationships between ordinary people of all ages living in a small city next to Barcelona, everyday people who tend to be left out of cinema stories. *El próximo Oriente* (Fernando Colomo, 2006) is a romantic comedy dealing with the inter-racial relationship between Caín and Aisha, a Bangladeshi girl who is pregnant by Caín's brother, Abel. *Fuerte Apache* (Jaume Mateu-Adrover, 2007) portrays Toni, a veteran disenchanted social educator who works at an internment centre. His attitude changes when Tarik, a homeless North African boy, is committed to the centre.

Data Analysis

After a close reading of all 11 films, we were able to define a taxonomy of translation strategies for foreign dialogues in the original films. This classification is as follows:

- self-translation
- liaison interpreting
- voice-over
- subtitling
- no-translation

Moreover, immigrants may also speak Spanish, either *standard Spanish*, or *non-standard immigrant Spanish* – that is to say, a social variety of Spanish including phonetic interference and poor syntax. Although in this case we cannot strictly speak about translation strategies, the choice of speaking Spanish – whether standard or not – is ideologically and socially significant, since it also represents the degree of linguistic insertion in the target culture. We therefore take it into account in our analysis.

The following sections provide examples of these strategies listed from the most domesticating to the most foreignising, according to the continuum in Figure 1:

Figure 1. A continuum of translation strategies in polyglot films

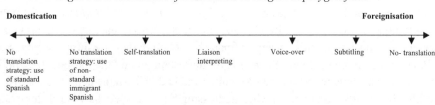

Use of Standard Spanish

Immigrant characters may express themselves in standard Spanish. This is the case with immigrants who have spent many years in Spain, or who have been brought up in Spanish. In *El próximo Oriente*, the Bangladeshi girl, Aisha, and her sisters speak standard Spanish, without any linguistic trace of their immigrant origin. As seen in the film, they have contact with Spaniards, so they were probably born in Spain or came as small children and studied in Spanish schools. *Salvajes* portrays the son of Omar, who has been brutally beaten, acting as an interpreter for his mother. He speaks standard Spanish. As he is a small child, he must go to school in Spain and might even have been born there. This seems to be the most domesticating strategy, since the audience easily understands all the dialogues and almost forgets that the character portrayed is an immigrant. Most of these characters are actually second generation immigrants, so the use of standard Spanish seems to show a greater level of integration.

Use of Non-Standard Immigrant Spanish

Immigrants can also be portrayed speaking non-standard immigrant Spanish. This strategy is generally used in the case of immigrants who have been in Spain for a short period of time and are still in a process of integration into Spanish society. This is the case in *Tapas*, where the Chinese immigrant, intentionally named Mao, always speaks Spanish with an overtly marked oriental accent. He is looking for a job as a cook, and is still not fully integrated into Spanish society. His fiancée is a Chinese girl too, a fact that confirms this assertion. At the end of the film, he has to socialise with the customers at the restaurant, and his gradual integration into society is seen. Nonetheless, he always speaks Spanish with a Chinese accent.

In *Fuerte Apache*, the North African immigrants speak non-standard Spanish every time they address a Spanish person (except for one occasion, in which an immigrant has an argument with a Spaniard and, at a given point, resorts to his mother tongue to express his irritation; no translation is provided). In fact, they speak fairly correct, fluent Spanish, which could be understood as a sign of integration if the unfolding of events did not prove otherwise. On the other hand, as we shall see, the situation changes when they address people from their own geographical origins. During his first encounter with the Spanish family, Ombasi, the undocumented African immigrant in *Bwana*, utters a few words in Spanish, probably learnt beforehand as some sort of code words to facilitate connection ('*¡Viva España!*' and '*Indurain*' – the name of a famous Spanish cyclist). In *El próximo Oriente*, Aisha's parents and the imam of the mosque also speak this variety of Spanish. Although they are fairly well integrated, as they have contact with Spaniards in the restaurant and the mosque, they probably came as adults from their home country and had to learn the language on arrival. While they mostly use Spanish when addressing Spaniards, Aisha's father, for example, also speaks Spanish to his daughters when they talk to him in Spanish – that is, when they want to show he does not live in Bangladesh anymore. The immigrant beaten up in *Salvajes* and his wife speak non-standard Spanish when talking to the husband's employer. Although they have been living in Spain for some time and are (to a certain extent) integrated in the country, they have not lost their accent. All the immigrants starring in *Pídele cuentas al rey* can speak Spanish. However, they always show non-native speech patterns and at times make mistakes, some of which are intentional. For example, a street vendor uses archetypical sentences, those Spaniards usually make fun of, as seen in the film. *Las cartas de Alou* follows Alou's progress as he learns Spanish. At the beginning of the film, he repeats only a few Spanish words taught to him by a friend. Later on, he uses Spanish to communicate both with Spaniards – his employers, his customers, his girlfriend and her father – and with immigrants who are not Senegalese. He also speaks Spanish with his fellow countryman Mulai when the latter's wife is present. In spite of his gradual integration into Spanish society, Alou never loses his strong accent, reflecting the fact that he will never be fully accepted into Spanish society, as illustrated by his ultimate deportation from Spain. Nevertheless, his desire to be accepted by Spain, even after being deported, is proven by his efforts to immerse himself in the language. In the films *Bajarse al moro*[6], *Poniente*, *A mi madre le gustan las mujeres* and *El traje* all the immigrant characters speak non-standard Spanish when speaking to Spaniards. Only in *El traje* do we find a slight variation, since Patricio also speaks Spanish with his African flatmates. This is a less domesticating strategy, though still at the end of the spectrum, since we cannot hear these characters speaking their own language. However, it is an integrating strategy as it shows immigrants interacting with local people.

Self-Translation

Self-translation takes place when an immigrant can speak both his or her native language and Spanish. He or she might be speaking with relatives or friends in their native language and then need to translate his or her dialogues to facilitate communication with Spanish characters. This third strategy exposes the audience to the foreign language, but immediately mitigates any possible shock by translating the dialogues into Spanish. At the same time, characters show that they are or can be

---

6   In this film, even the Moroccan characters who live in their own country speak non-standard immigrant Spanish when they address the Spanish protagonist.

proficient in both languages, thus trying to empathise with both the other Spanish characters in the film and the audience. *Fuerte Apache* includes a curious example. In a conversation between Tarik (the homeless child) and Toni (the social educator), Tarik mentions the word *baraka*. This is an Arabic word that can now be found in the Real Academia Spanish dictionary – although it is not commonly used –, a fact he is most likely unaware of and that makes him feel that a translation is needed so that communication is not impeded.[7] In *Las cartas de Alou*, Moucef says two Arabic proverbs when speaking to the protagonist, and then translates these sentences literally to non-standard immigrant Spanish so that his friend can understand him. It is interesting to note that, although none of these characters is Spanish, they use this language as their *lingua franca*. In the film *El traje*, Patricio tells Pan con Queso his name in Bube – a Bantu language spoken by the Bubi people in Equatorial Guinea – and immediately translates its meaning to his Spanish friend.

Liaison Interpreting

Liaison interpreting usually takes place when an immigrant can only speak his or her native language and then needs someone else to translate his or her lines of dialogue into Spanish. He or she might be speaking with relatives or friends in their native language and then someone else translates his or her lines to facilitate communication with Spanish characters. *Salvajes* presents a noteworthy example. Omar's wife does not want to talk to the policemen, so she pretends she cannot speak Spanish. Her son therefore acts as an interpreter during that conversation. Nevertheless, as noted above, she does speak non-standard immigrant Spanish. Migration is an important issue in this film and one scene portrays some immigrants who have just arrived in Spain. One of them asks for food in his mother tongue and another character translates his request into Spanish for the others to understand what he just said. The film *Poniente* contains a scene depicting a workers' assembly. The immigrants, who come from a range of countries, are discussing the demands they want to make to their boss. Among them there are three immigrants who speak Arabic, an unidentified Slavic language and an unidentified African language. These three people translate the contents of the meeting to and from Spanish, so that the rest of the workers can understand what is being said. This scene suggests that most of the immigrants who work and live in the fields of Almería are poorly integrated in their host society, because they cannot understand Spanish. This fourth strategy can therefore be placed at the foreignising end of the spectrum, since its use blatantly implies segregation, at least on a temporary level. It can also be said to underline the foreign origins of the character, to show that they are new arrivals in the country or, alternatively, less integrated. In the case of the latter, it may even serve to highlight the impossibility of their (ever) fitting into Spanish society.

---

7   Technically, this would be a case of what Jakobson (1984: 69) calls *intralingual translation*, since the word *baraka* is now also officially Spanish.

Voice-Over

This is quite an unusual strategy in fiction films in Spain and other countries with a dubbing tradition (although not in Poland, for example) since it implies breaking a sacred dubbing pact with the audience: actions, settings and dialogues must be credible, situations must be true-to-life and the whole film has to be believable. Verisimilitude can be damaged if the audience hears a voice-off translating foreign dialogues. No examples have been identified in our corpus, although the literature review indicates the existence of this strategy (Corrius 2008: 313).

Subtitling

Subtitles can be used to translate foreign language dialogues when immigrants speak among themselves and there are no Spanish characters in the scene, or there is no interpreter. Subtitles do not hide the intervention of the professional translator; they clearly depict immigrants as such and make explicit the need to translate their speech. In *El próximo Oriente*, when Aisha, her sisters or her parents talk in Bangla to each other, the foreign language is always subtitled. During Caín's conversion, the Arabic prayers repeated by the imam and by Caín himself are also subtitled. However, as we shall see below, subtitling is not the only strategy employed in the mosque. The narrative strategy of *Las cartas de Alou* relies upon the letters Alou writes to both his parents and his friend Mulai. At the beginning and the end of the film, Alou writes to Mulai about his plans to travel to Europe, and in the middle of the film he writes to his parents twice describing his life in Spain. In all these scenes, a voice-off reads what Alou is writing in his mother tongue. These narratives are subtitled so that the Spanish viewer can understand the feelings and experiences of an immigrant living in Europe. At one point in *Bwana* Ombasi dreams of his dead friend who tells him, in their unidentified mother tongue, not to trust white people. As the film unfolds, this message proves crucial to the story, and this is probably the reason it has been subtitled in Spanish; that is, for narrative purposes. We can thus conclude that immigrants usually keep their language in their family circle. However, the decision to subtitle some dialogues might not only be related to the desire to depict immigrants as such, but also to the narrative itself. If understanding their content is important to the development of the film, they will be subtitled.

No-Translation

No-translation lies at the foreignising end of the spectrum, a strategy which clearly seeks to depict immigrants as such. Any effort to make these characters understood is deliberately avoided. Film directors intentionally want the audience to feel at a loss when listening to these untranslated, foreign lines of dialogue. This can be seen in *Bwana*, for example. Ombasi, who arrives in Spain in search of a better life, uses his mother tongue throughout the film, a fact that increases his sense of alienation and of not belonging. We find another example in *Fuerte Apache*. As mentioned above, in this film the North African immigrants use their native language when talking to other immigrants, even in presence of a Spaniard, a fact that has certain implications in terms of group identification. In *El próximo Oriente*, on the one hand, some conversations among neighbours are not translated. The director might have wished to show the multiculturalism of the area. Similarly, prayers are also generally not translated either. On the other hand, as we saw above, they are translated where they play an important role in the development of the film's plot. Another example is found in *Pídele cuentas al rey*. As Fidel walks through Spain, he witnesses a police raid. Some of these undocumented immigrants speak in their language and viewers cannot understand what they say as it is not translated. This strategy and the fact they are arrested at that same moment highlight their feeling of not belonging. In *Las cartas de Alou*, most dialogues between immigrants are not translated, and neither are the prayers said in Arabic and the words pronounced at Lami's burial. When Alou finds his friend's dead body and he sings a Senegalese lament, no translation is provided – perhaps because none is really needed to understand what is being expressed. The same happens in *Poniente*: whenever there is a dialogue between two or more immigrants, no translation is given. This leads to some bizarre situations, like an extended scene inside Curro's car where four immigrants are having a conversation in Arabic and the viewer does not know what is going on. Other scenes without a translation show a North African youth insulting Miguel and a group of immigrants singing a song in Arabic at a party. In *A mi madre le gustan las mujeres*, Eliska only speaks Czech twice: when she talks to her family – one isolated scene – and when she says a Czech proverb to Sofía. Eliska's brother can only speak Czech, but he has very few lines and their content does not seem relevant. The use of Czech in this film is purely anecdotal, and does not affect the development of the plot, which is perhaps why no translation is provided.

Conclusion

Two different kinds of conclusion have been drawn from the present research: some resulting from the preliminary work on corpus selection and others related to the hypotheses postulated in the corresponding section of this paper. As far as corpus selection is concerned, empirical data are presented in the table and graph in Appendices 1 and 2. An analysis of these data enables us to conclude that:

-   The number of Spanish productions released in Madrid, as a percentage of the total number of productions released, is very low (863/6931, or 12.5 %) during the last two decades.
-   The percentage of films shot in Spanish and containing immigrant characters is also low (80/863, or 9.3 %) during the same period.
-   About 70 % (or 56/80) of the films in Spanish that deal with the immigration issue were subsequently released in DVD format, indicating some interest in films from this subgenre in the home entertainment market.

Below we put forward some conclusions related to the two main hypotheses presented in the hypotheses section. The graph in Appendix 2 shows a curve of the number of Spanish films related to immigration released in Madrid during the last two decades. The curve does not show a clear upward trend – in fact, if compared to the increasing number of Spanish films released, the amount of films dealing with immigration has decreased. On the basis of these empirical data our first hypothesis is therefore rejected, as it emerges that it was not scientifically sound.

The analysis of the translation strategies carried out in the data analysis section can shed some light on the second hypothesis, namely:

a) Three levels in the use of translation strategies can be distinguished on the basis of the number of films in which they appear:

   1. Use of non-standard immigrant Spanish (11 films) and no-translation (7 films)
   2. Subtitling (3 films), use of standard Spanish (2 films), self-translation (3 films) and liaison interpreting (2 films)
   3. Voice-over (no examples found in any of the films)

b) Although we hypothesised that domesticating strategies would be used more extensively than foreignising ones, empirical data show that the number of films using a rather domesticating strategy (use of non-standard immigrant Spanish) is similar to that of films which include the most foreignising strategy (no-translation).

We can therefore conclude that there is no clear trend in the use of translation strategies in Spanish polyglot films, as regards a domesticating or foreignising policy. This case study points to a number of potential areas for further investigation, such as the subtitling or dubbing of the same films into other languages and a similar case study on different film genres, such as documentaries or animation films. As far as translation strategies are concerned, we can conclude that the norm seems to be the use of two strategies: use of non-standard immigrant Spanish, a relatively domesticating strategy, and no translation, an absolutely foreignising strategy. Finally, voice-over is not used at all as a translation strategy. Therefore only six strategies were found.

Filmography

ARMENDÁRIZ, M. (1990), *Las cartas de Alou*, Spain.
COLOMO, F. (1989), *Bajarse al moro*, Spain.
COLOMO, F. (2006), *El próximo Oriente*, Spain
CORBACHO, J. & J. Cruz (2005), *Tapas*, Spain/Argentina/Mexico.
FEJERMAN, D. & I. PARÍS (2002), *A mi madre le gustan las mujeres*, Spain.
GUTIÉRREZ, Ch. (2002), *Poniente*, Spain.
MATEU-ADROVER, J. (2007), *Fuerte Apache*, Spain.
MOLINERO, C. (2001), *Salvajes*, Spain.

QUIRÓS, J.A. (1999), *Pídele cuentas al rey*, Spain.

RODRÍGUEZ, A. (2002), *El traje*, Spain.

URIBE, I. (1996), *Bwana*, Spain.

References

AGOST, R. (1999), *Traducción y doblaje: palabras, voces e imágenes*, Barcelona: Ariel.

AGOST, R. (2000), 'Traducción y diversidad de lenguas', in: Lourdes, L. & A. Mª Pereira (eds.), *Traducción subordinada (I) (inglés-español/galego)*, Vigo: Universidade de Vigo, 49–67.

ARGOTE, R. (2003), 'La mujer inmigrante en el cine español del inaugurado siglo XXI', in: *Imaginando a la mujer, Feminismo/s*, 2, 121–138, URL: http://www.mugak.eu/ef_etp_files/view/Rosabel_Argote_La_mujer_inmigrante_en_el_cine_espa%C3%B1ol.pdf?package_id=2392 (19 February 2009).

BARTOLL, E. (2006), 'Subtitling multilingual films', in: Carroll, M./Gerzymisch-Arbogast, H. & S. Nauert (eds.), *Proceedings of the Marie Curie Euroconferences MuTra: Audiovisual Translation Scenarios*, URL: www.euroconferences.info/proceedings/ 2006_Proceedings/ 2006_Bartoll_Eduard.pdf (28 February 2009).

CANTERO, M. (2008), 'La política de la intolerancia o el discurso del malestar de la interculturalidad en el cine español', in: *FILMHISTORIA Online*, Vol. XVIII, URL: http://www.pcb.ub.es/filmhistoria/ensayo_inmigracion _1.html (10 March 2009).

CHAUME, F. (2004), *Cine y traducción*, Madrid: Cátedra.

CORRIUS, M. (2008), *Translating Multilingual Audiovisual Texts. Priorities, Restrictions, Theoretical Implications*, unpublished Ph.D. thesis, Barcelona: Universitat Autònoma de Barcelona.

DAVIES, I. (2006),'Raza y etnicidad: desafíos de la inmigración en el cine español', in: *Letras Hispanas*, 3 (1), 98–112, URL: http://letrashispanas. unlv.edu/vol3iss1/davies.PDF (10 March 2009).

DELABASTITA, D. & R. GRUTMAN (eds.) (2005), *Fictionalising Translation and Multilingualism, Linguistica Antverpiensia*, 4, 11–34.

DWYER, T. (2005), 'Universally speaking: Lost in Translation and polyglot cinema', in: Delabastita, D. & R. Grutman (eds.), *Fictionalising Translation and Multilingualism, Linguistica Antverpiensia*, 4, 295–310.

EQUIPO RESEÑA (1990), *Cine para leer 1989*, Bilbao: Mensajero.

——— (1991), *Cine para leer 1990*, Bilbao: Mensajero.

——— (1992), *Cine para leer 1991*, Bilbao: Mensajero.

——— (1993), *Cine para leer 1992*, Bilbao: Mensajero.

——— (1994), *Cine para leer 1993*, Bilbao: Mensajero.

——— (1995), *Cine para leer 1994*, Bilbao: Mensajero.

——— (1996), *Cine para leer 1995*, Bilbao: Mensajero.

——— (1997), *Cine para leer 1996*, Bilbao: Mensajero.

——— (1998), *Cine para leer 1997*, Bilbao: Mensajero.

——— (1999), *Cine para leer 1998*, Bilbao: Mensajero.

——— (2000a), *Cine para leer 1999*, Bilbao: Mensajero.

——— (2000b), *Cine para leer. Enero-junio 2000*, Bilbao: Mensajero.

——— (2001a), *Cine para leer. Julio-diciembre 2000*, Bilbao: Mensajero.

——— (2001b), *Cine para leer. Enero-junio 2001*, Bilbao: Mensajero.

——— (2002a), *Cine para leer. Julio-diciembre 2001*, Bilbao: Mensajero.

——— (2002b), *Cine para leer. Enero-junio 2002*, Bilbao: Mensajero.

——— (2003a), *Cine para leer. Julio-diciembre 2002*, Bilbao: Mensajero.

——— (2003b), *Cine para leer. Enero-junio 2003*, Bilbao: Mensajero.

——— (2004a), *Cine para leer. Julio-diciembre 2003*, Bilbao: Mensajero.

——— (2004b), *Cine para leer. Enero-junio 2004*, Bilbao: Mensajero.

——— (2005a), *Cine para leer. Julio-diciembre 2004*, Bilbao: Mensajero.

——— (2005b), *Cine para leer. Enero-junio 2005*, Bilbao: Mensajero.

——— (2006a), *Cine para leer. Julio-diciembre 2005*, Bilbao: Mensajero.

——— (2006b), *Cine para leer. Enero-junio 2006*, Bilbao: Mensajero.

——— (2007a), *Cine para leer. Julio-diciembre 2006*, Bilbao: Mensajero.

——— (2007b), *Cine para leer. Enero-junio 2007*, Bilbao: Mensajero.

——— (2008a), *Cine para leer. Julio-diciembre 2007*, Bilbao: Mensajero.

——— (2008b), *Cine para leer. Enero-junio 2008*, Bilbao: Mensajero.

——— (2009), *Cine para leer. Julio-diciembre 2008*, Bilbao: Mensajero.

HEISS, C. (2004), 'Dubbing Multilingual Films: A New Challenge?', in: *Meta*, 49 (1), 208–220.

HERRERA, R. (2007), *El original multilingüe audiovisual y su traducción: el caso del doblaje al español de la película 'Babel'*, unpublished M.A. research project, Granada: University of Granada.

JAKOBSON, R. (1984), *Ensayos de lingüística general*, Barcelona: Ariel.

VALDEÓN, R. (2005), 'Asymmetric representations of languages in contact: uses and translations of French and Spanish in *Frasier*', in: Delabastita, D. & R. Grutman (eds.), *Fictionalising Translation and Multilingualism*, *Linguistica Antverpiensia*, 4, Antwerpen: Hogeschool Antwerpen, Hoger Instituut voor Vertalers en Tolken, 279–294.

VILLAR-HERNÁNDEZ, P. (2002), 'El Otro: conflictos de identidad en el cine español contemporáneo', in: *Working papers in Romance Languages and Literature*, Graduate Romanic Association, University of Pennsylvania, vol. 6, URL: http://ccat.sas.upenn.edu/romance/gra/WPs2002/paz_1.htm (10 March 2009).

WAHL, C. (2005), 'Discovering a Genre: The Polyglot Film', in: *Cinemascope,* 1, URL: http://www.madadayo.it/Cinemascope_archive/cinema-scope.net/articolo07_n1.html (6 March 2010).

WAHL, C. (2008), ' 'Du Deutscher, toi français, You English: Beautiful' – The Polyglot Film as a Genre', in: Christensen, M. & N. Erdŏgan (eds.), *Shifting Landscapes: Film and Media in European Context*, Newcastle: Cambridge Scholars Publishing, 334–350.

ZABALBEASCOA, P. (1993), *Developing Translation Studies to Better Account for Audiovisual Texts and Other New Forms of Text Production*, unpublished PhD Thesis, Lleida: University of Lleida.

Appendix 1

Time Period (1st Semester 1989–2008)	35mm Films Released in Madrid	35mm Spanish Films Released in Madrid	35mm Films in Spanish, Possibly Depicting Immigrants, Released in Madrid	Films in Spanish, Possibly Depicting Immigrants, Available on DVD
1989	268	31	3	2
1990	285	32	2	1
1991	256	26	2	1
1992	250	27	4	0
1993	239	27	3	2
1994	263	26	1	1
1995	283	37	1	0
1996	318	45	4	3
1997	368	49	3	1
1998	384	38	5	2
1999	209	36	2	2
2000	400	51	5	2
2001	387	53	5	4
2002	408	53	7	7
2003	412	51	3	3
2004	420	59	0	0
2005	417	52	7	5
2006	468	56	10	10
2007	482	64	5	3
2008	414	50	8	7
Total	6931	863	80	56

Appendix 2

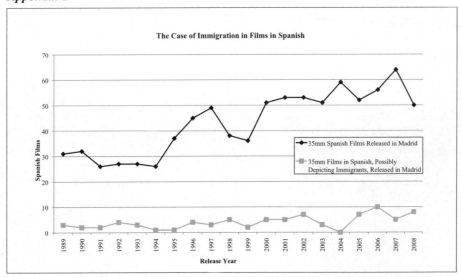

II. Polyphony and Translating the 'Other' in French and Spanish Cinema

The Voices of Pre-War French Cinema:
From Polyphony Towards Plurilingualism

Michaël Abecassis

Introduction

When France and most particularly Paris learnt to speak with the beginning of talk-ing pictures, it was the poetry of a whole city that was conveyed onto the screen. To film France speaking, film directors first voiced the accent of the streets often tinged with melancholy and that of its Parisian singers, the stars of the music-hall. The exhilaration as well as the inexperience that the transition to talkies brought made French a polyphony of sounds. The term 'polyphony' in music refers to the superpo-sition of two or more melodic lines: etymologically, the Greek *polyphōnia* signifies 'a variety of tones or voices, e.g. of birds and musical instruments' (Oxford English Dictionary). A polyphonic novel[1] by extension is one in which several voices inter-act. The film with its subtitles, intertitles, dialogues and voice-overs already appears as multiple layers of texts and subtexts, but the interaction of multi-accented voices is comparable to various melodies which are at the same time independent and harmo-niously linked. 'Plurilingualism' on the other hand expresses a diversity of languages within for instance the same community, but we will use the term in a broader sense to refer to the mingling of various accents. One would commonly distinguish socie-tal plurilingualism ('the social reasons for and manifestations of language contact') and its corollary individual plurilingualism, defined as 'an individual speaker's abil-ity to speak more than one language' (Bleichenbacher 2008: 9). The boundary be-tween polyphony and plurilingualism can overlap. Polyphony does not necessarily imply people are using the same language, but the emphasis is more on the harmoni-ous interweaving of voices than on the many languages that are spoken. However, the accented voices using the same language as a lingua franca not only convey a group identity, and identify someone regionally or socially, but are laden with cultural herit-age. Stress, intonation and the use of a particular vocabulary by a foreign character

---

1 The notion is introduced by Bakhtin in his analysis of Dostoevsky (Bakhtin 1978: 10) to refer to the plurality of voices (*raznorechie* in Russian literally means 'different speechness') and conscious-ness in a novel.

all contribute to making the film multilingual. Looking at contemporary films first and moving backwards to the beginning of sound in French films of the silent era to the 1930s, this article aims to establish the origin and function of plurilingualism in pre-war French cinema and to see how it has developed. Our argument is that at the beginning of the sound era, the films experimenting with the use of sound and music were in search of polyphony, both an aesthetics of sound and image[2], while later gradually moving towards a reflection on social and regional identity with plurilingual voices.

Plurilingualism in Today's French Cinema

A reference to plurilingualism in French cinema immediately brings to mind the 'cinéma de banlieue' which emerged in the mid-1990s with the depiction of multi-ethnic youth living in the working-class estates of Paris. Mathieu Kassovitz's *La Haine* (1990) was one of the most significant of *Beur* and *banlieue* films, but Mehdi Charef's *Le Thé au harem d'Archimède* (1984) can certainly be considered one of the precursors of the genre. Today, award-winning films by Abdelatif Kechiche such as *L'Esquive* (2005) and *La Graine et le mulet* (2007) show that the issue of ethnicity and plurilingualism in a multicultural society are central to contemporary French cinema. Since then there has been a growing number of films focusing on the daily lives of migrants from Maghreb, their sense of identity and nostalgia for the country they have left and their difficulties of integration.

From the linguistic point of view[3], it is striking to observe how the socio-linguistic situation has evolved. Consciously or unconsciously, film-makers incorporate facts as well as stereotypes which do not accurately represent the social classes but rather distort them and alienate them linguistically. As Barbéris suggests, 'la transposition de l'oral dans l'écrit aboutit à figer dans un cadre qui n'est pas le sien la parlure populaire, et à la 'condamner', clouée au pilori de la double norme écrite-graphique et orale-poétique'[4] (Barbéris 2009: 18). If, in 1930s French cinema, directors like Carné or Renoir among others would indulge – often for comedy purposes – in representing a stereotypically binary Parisian society, opposing the working class with its colourful *argot* and the middle class with its use of standard French, in today's gangster films slang can be heard in the language of the police, most of whom come from 'hybrid circles', as well as that of petty thieves. In the 1960s, Audiard's dialogues exaggerated the crypto-ludic effects of slang to cre-

---

2   The film begins with a profusion of images which disappeared as quickly as they appeared with the film-maker's desire to overwhelm the eye with a variety of sensations. As Carrière notes: 'Les effets de montage accéléré [...] ne furent longtemps que des recherches esthétiques' (Carrière 1996: 23) ('the effects of accelerated montage [...] were for a long time only aesthetic endeavours'). (Translations by the author.)

3   For a linguistic analysis of multilingualism in Hollywood movies related to diastractic and diaphasic parameters see Bleichenbacher 2008: 7–20.

4   'The transposition of spoken into written results in fixing popular French in a setting which is not its own, and in condemning it, is denigrated by both written-graphic and oral-poetic norms.'

ate a stylised, semi-invented language, associated with the criminal underworld[5], but in more recent French films like the *Ripoux* trilogy (1984, 1990, 2003), *A la petite semaine* (2003) or *36 Quai des orfèvres* (2004) one can see how the use of colloquial French and *argot* has spread to all social strata and is no longer restricted to a single social group. This use of *argot* does vary, however, according to the district and the suburb, and especially according to age.

Historically, French society has been moulded by a large influx of immigrants from Southern Europe and African countries and the picture we have of metropolitan French cinema in the 21st century has become that of a plurilingual cinema which has drawn its richness from a variety of accents. Contemporary French cinema, far from erasing accents, uses them for comedic purposes, for example Ticky Holgado's southern accent, Victoria Abril's Spanish accent, or the Jewish pied-noir accents of Roger Hanin, Jean-Pierre Bacri and Marthe Villallonga in *Le Grand Carnaval* (1983), or of Anconina and José Garcia in *La Verité si je mens* (1997, 2001). It is also the accent which provides the laughter for comedians from Popeck to Jamel and Gad Elmaleh, by way of Eli Kakou and Smain. More recently, the success of Dany Boon's *Bienvenue chez les ch'tis* (2008) testifies that the use of accents on the screen is still a major feature of French comedies. However, as the linguist Fernand Carton pointed out, the film often verges on the caricature rather than being representative of reality:

> 'Comme Molière quand il invente une parodie de picard pour faire rire [...] Rajouter des 'ch' partout, et des 'in' au petit bonheur, ça porte même un nom: on appelle ça 'faire de l'hyperpicard' '.[6]

The need to cling to an accent shows a visceral urge on the speaker's part to resist 'standardisation', 'parisianism' and 'mondialisation', Carton goes on.[7] The use of a patois is immediately associated with the lower class, but it has a particular flavour and is the language of the emotions, expressing feelings and revealing a sense of belonging to a cultural heritage that the French language can hardly express.

Francophone cinema is a plural, indeed multi-ethnic cinema. Since its appearance in the 1920s, French colonial cinema has been inspired by imagery inherited from literature and orientalist painting, which has made the North African landscape an exotic space of discovery and a locus for linguistic varieties. Today, Moroccan

---

5   Audiard's *Les Tontons flingueurs* (1963) is particularly significant with its accumulation of slang, its frequency of consonant clusters and schwa deletion: 'Mais y connaît pas Raoul ce mec. Y va avoir un réveil pénible. J'ai voulu être diplomate à cause de vous tous, éviter qu'le sang coule mais maint'nant c'est fini! Je vais l'travailler en férocité! L'faire marcher à coup d'latte, à ma pogne je veux l'voir! Et j'vous promets qui demandera pardon! Et au garde-à-vous!' [39:14–39:28]. 'But Raoul dunno this bloke. He's gonna have a difficult start. I have tried to be diplomatic because of you all, to avoid a blood flow, but now it's all over! I'm going to work on him ferociously. I'll have him under the cosh. I wanna see him under my thumb! I promise he'll say sorry! And I'll have him to walk under the beat of my drum!' (Our translation.)

6   'Like Molière, when he invents a parody of Picard to make us laugh [...] To add 'ch' everywhere and some 'in' randomly, this bears a name: one calls it 'speak hyperpicard'.' (Carton 2008)

7   Ibid.

cinema is in expansion with film directors such as Ismaël Ferrhouki, Souhel Ben
Barka or Saad Chraibi and the intermingling of French and Arabic language par-
takes in the building of a poetry and an aesthetics of sound and images reminiscent of
Iranian cinema. In the 1960s–1970s, after a hundred of years of neglect, Quebecois
Gilles Carle and Denys Arcand rehabilitated the Joual sociolect. Quebecois cinema
has experienced a resurgence of popularity with the recent success of *Les Invasions
barbares* (2003) and *C.R.A.Z.Y.* (2005), which was propelled to the top of the French
box office. It remains true that Quebecois films are often poorly distributed in France
and are not given the recognition they deserve. Indeed, Tristan Sicard (2006) suggests that 'le problème proviendrait de l'accent québécois dont les diphtongues, les
voyelles écrasées et les sonorités nasales dérangeraient plus d'un Français'[8]. Jeanne
Deslandes (2008) notes that France continues to enforce an embargo on the French
versions of some foreign films dubbed in Quebec, which would lead distributors in
Quebec to have them dubbed by French speakers of French origin. Black African
cinema, such as the cinema of the Senegalese Ousmane Sembène, is a cinema of diversity, influenced by its colonial culture, traditions and history. Since colonial cinema, in which it was heavily stigmatised, the African accent, as in Claire Denis's
Chocolat (1988), has been used to give a 'local colour' and to create African imagery. Africa is reminiscent of travel and dreams, and is no longer the land of danger,
terra incognita and *decorum* depicted in pre-war colonial films. Paulin's *L'Esclave
blanc* (1934) exemplified the traditional colonialist belief as a true hymn to 'la su-
périorité de l'homme blanc, et de ses bons droits à dominer les peoples d'Afrique'[9]
(Berg 2008). The film, set in Italian Somalia, starts with an introduction by explor-
er Henri de Monfreid. To give an African flavour, the film presents exotic animals,
scenes of hunting, local customs of gathering bananas and African dances. Through
her dialect, the native female African whose name does not appear in the cast list
brings African sonorities too. Plurilingualism here marks the dichotomy between
the coloniser and the colonised.

From Silent Cinema to Talkies: A Polyphony of Sounds

How far back can we date plurilingualism in French cinema? We might say first of
all that it has always existed. Silent films have never been mute, accompanied as
they were by music and intertitles to ensure comprehension of the plot of the story. Besides, characters in silent films also 'spoke', as they were often seen articulating words. Malraux's description of the aims of cinema would definitely bring
to mind silent cinema with its 'volonté de séduire et d'émouvoir, style et poésie de
théâtre, beauté des personnages, expression des visages. Au fond des siècles, un
masque lointain qui psalmodie, danse solennellement dans la lumière devant nous, le

---

8   'The problem stems from the Quebecois accent, in which the diphthongs, the squashed vowels and
     the nasal sounds would disturb no few French people.'
9   'To the superiority of the white man, and his right to dominate the African people.'

visage bouleversé des gros plans chuchote dans l'ombre qu'il emplit'[10] (Malraux 1951: 124). The characters are made beautiful in the close-ups and the facial expression part of the aesthetics of the film, but all seem to whisper. As Chion indicates, Garbo in silent movies had several voices, 'dreamed voices' (Chion 1999: 8) in the viewers' imagination, until her first talkies were released and they discovered that her 'voice was hoarse and [she] had a Swedish accent' (Chion 1999: 12). There was often a multilingual distribution for films in the silent era but the language of silent films was as Billard suggested pretty 'universal' (Billard 1995: 39). For films to circulate all over the world, one had simply to translate the intertitles, but even then the spectator who went to see a film would not always see it in the monolingual version but often both with the original intertitles and their translations. In Belgian cinema, there were certainly plurilingual intertitles in both Walloon and Flemish. For a French audience to understand a foreign film, it was necessary to present the original German intertitles subtitled in French, as in the films of Fritz Lang. In the days of silent French cinema, titles could even tend towards plurilingualism through the use of anglicisms. There are, of course, a number of French films made in the 1900s in which one sees diegetic objects and signs written in both English and French primarily for practical reasons: it would make it comprehensible for both a French and English audience. For example, in Méliès *Le Merveilleux éventail vivant* (1904) the box containing the fan bears a label written in both French and English ('L'éventail magique'/'the magical fan'). In *Le Roi du maquillage* (1904), the caricaturist finishes by drawing on the blackboard the words 'comic eccentric' in English, but a French person would have had no problem understanding it. Finally, in *Le Voyage à travers l'impossible* (1904) both words 'bagages' and 'luggages' are used on the top of the check-in desk and later the wagon bears the designation 'glacière' and 'ice tank'. The film was thus more easily exportable.

Titles of films could also make use of English lexical items in their French versions. The title of George Méliès' 1903 silent film *Le Cake walk infernal* for example refers to a popular dance from the turn of the century. The English 'clergyman' favoured over the French 'curé' ou 'prêtre' seems to endow the man of the church with a British identity in Dulac's title *La Coquille et le clergyman* (1928). The use of English words lends an air of specialisation and at times strangeness to documentaries and often seeks to demonstrate erudition. *La Bandera* (1935) with its title immediately transports the viewer to the Spanish foreign legion. Nor was it uncommon for intertitles to incorporate words from a foreign language. In this way, it was possible to situate the action in time or space and the use of English words lent local colour or a touch of mystery. In Jean Epstein's *Coeur fidèle* (1926), the words 'for ever' are written in chalk on the wall of the café and the phrase comes back several times printed as a watermarked intertitle in the celluloid. The epilogue closes on an

---

10   'Desire to seduce and move, style and poetry of theatre, beauty of characters, expression of faces.
     Down the centuries, a far off mask that chants psalms, dances solemnly in the light before us, the
     disrupted face of close-ups whispers in the shadow that it fills.'

image of the two lovers, still as if in a postcard, with the same words 'forever' superimposed until it is gradually revealed with a slash in the middle 'for/ever', reminiscent by way of assonance of the French 'faut rêver' ('one has to dream'). The slash
marks the separation rather than the union of both characters. Finally, in Germaine
Dulac's *L'Invitation au voyage* (1926), a cocktail menu is shown in the film simultaneously in four different languages (Hebrew, Cyrillic, Arabic and English) as a suc-
cession of superimposed intertitles, adding to the surreal atmosphere.

French film directors of the silent era would mostly avoid using foreign lexis in
their intertitles possibly for the sake of linguistic purity and because spectators were
asking for more French in cinemas (Billard 1995: 46). Silent scientific documentaries by Jean Painlevé, technical though they might be, remain accessible to a wide
audience and no English words have ever been used with French that would have tar-
nished the poetry of the narration.

The language of intertitles has given birth to a long and important conflict in
Quebec. Most of the films screened in Quebec and in Canada were American with
English intertitles. There were many 'bonimenteurs' (lecturers)[11] who carried out
their duties until the advent of talking films, translating subtitles. Around 1920, they
disappeared from big picture houses, and audiences begin to ask for intertitles in
French. Certain distributors would supply some, but the viewers would also see announcements on the screen specifying that a 'bonimenteur' would provide a commentary for the film, even if it had subtitles, which showed how much his narrative
presence and the tradition of storytelling were appreciated by the public. The major
contingents of immigrants in the 1920s–1930s were originally from Southern and
Eastern Europe. France, like Hollywood, has 'profited from foreign-language immigrants and other movie cultures' (Bleichenbacher 2007: 113). It is therefore hardly surprising to find a lot of Russian and Rumanian actors in the French cinema of
that period. Besides, a lot of actors popular in Germany such as Dita Parlo or Louise
Brooks would endeavour to extend their cinematographic careers by migrating tem-
porarily to France. The range of actors appearing on screen was of mixed European
nationality in the silent era, but things changed afterwards with the first talkies.

The advent of the talking era led to the demise of a dozen actors of silent movies
whose voice, stutter or pronounced accent on the screen became a real handicap.[12] The
Russian-born actors, stars of the silent movies, lost their prestigious images when cinema started speaking. With their Slavonic accents, actors such as Nathalie Lissenko,

---

11   In Africa, the tradition went on until the 1950s whereby a standing man would explain the actions
     on the screen with a stick. In Spain, the *explicador* that performed a similar role disappeared as
     early as the 1920s (Carrière 1996: 13–14).

12   The American comedy *Singin' in the rain* (1952) set in Hollywood in the 1920s shows the passage
     from silent movies to talkies and how the career of some actors like Lina Lamont, whose unap-
     pealing screeching voice and inability to sing in tune in a musical suffered a hard blow. One can
     imagine that the articulated and rather artificial diction of stage actress Sarah Bernhard declaiming
     Phèdre (made available online in 2008), who died in 1923, would also have had difficulties in
     adapting to the change of the talkies.

Nathalie Kovenko and Nicolas Rimsky quickly fell into oblivion (Barrot/Chirat 1994: 56–57). Certain accents would appeal to the viewers as they would see them match the body language and the appearance on screen, but some simply would not. The film *Prix de beauté* starring Louise Brooks was started in 1929 in a silent version, but during the shooting sound sequences were added dubbed in four different languages. Bilingual Anglo-Saxon artists and the British accent were popular in French productions but they were mainly restricted to secondary parts such as for Betty Stockfeld. The black American singer Josephine Baker did not encounter on screen the success she had met in the music-hall. The black pearl's swaying jungle and wild dances with her African costumes and American accent fascinated Paris and became the personification of the exotic, but her career in cinema was brief with only two major films *Zouzou* (1934) and *Princesse Tam Tam* (1935) in the 1930s.

The first dubbed films were created in 1931, and the talkies in their early days were really mere Babelism. In cinemas, one could see a film completely in French or completely in English or in a mixture of the two languages. Sometimes a silent movie was screened with musical parts and intertitles in a foreign language (Billard 1995: 39). A film like René Clair's *Sous les toits de Paris* (1930) was all in French but it was still in transition between the silent era and the talkies. This film, where for the first time one could hear the streets of Paris and the Parisian lower class, is a polyphony of sounds with its long silences and almost inaudible whispers, its singing interludes and dialogues.

Plurilingual Film Versions

Censorship was not yet ready to accept films intermingling different languages. Pabst's first talkie *Westfront 1918* (1930) was censored in its original version when it was first released in France. Soldiers were heard speaking in their own languages, French, German and English, and the film was finally replaced by a version which was all in French (Billard 1935: 40). With the distribution of English films across Europe and dubbing techniques still to be perfected, the problems of languages intensified and the first films coming from America often caused disappointment. They were mostly in English with, if any at all, only a few intertitles in French. For a Hollywood keen to exploit its films in Europe, this was the era of multiple versions. When the first talking films came along, they would be shot in several versions to make their distribution abroad easier. Between 1929 and 1935, before dubbing was optimised, films were made simultaneously in French, German, Spanish and Italian. Fritz Lang's *The Testament of Dr. Mabuse* (1933) was made first in German, then a shorter version was made in French in the same set, but with French actors. Only Rudolf Klein-Rogge playing Dr. Mabuse, one of Lang's iconic actors, appeared in both versions. He did not speak French, so the disembodied voice that spoke through the film was that of different actors. Carl Froelich's *La Vie est à nous* (1928) was shot in French but the actual shooting took place in Germany with music in the background in compliance with the original version. Paulin's *Pas besoin d'argent* (1933) was released in French one year after Carl Boese's version entitled *Man braucht kein Geld*. Pabst's *The Threepenny Opera* (1931) was shot simultaneously in German and French, the director swapping the actors with the French cast on the set. Bilingual actors like Maurice Chevalier and Colette Colbert would remain in both French and American versions of *La Grande mare* (1930). Charles Boyer, who was fluent in English, likewise played in both the French and American versions of *Caravane* (1934), recreating the French flavour of the original by means of his accent, but Annabella starred in only the French version and was replaced by Loretta Young in the same year for the Hollywood version. The shooting of films in two versions proved very costly and this solution to making films multilingual was quickly abandoned.

In the move from silent movies to talkies, cinema evolved into a polyphony of different genres: music-hall, operetta and accented cinema, which already asserted a fragmented and multicultural image of French cinema as well as the birth on the screen of distinctive regional and social identities. The stars of the music-hall with the likes of Milton, Fernandel, Mayol, Gabin and Raimu among many others, who became famous not only for their 'gift of the gab' but also for their 'facial expressions', and those of theatre such as Louis Jouvet and Elvire Popesco, were called upon to play in French movies. Speech appeared on the screen through the words sung by the cabaret artists and the comic actors. With the beginning of the talkies, it was not only gesture and expression which were important to the screen but actors' voices as well.

An Aesthetics of Sounds

At a time when film directors were still experimenting with processes of synchronisation and new sound techniques, the first talkies, in search of a new form of aesthetics, were imbued with a sense of visual poetry orchestrated by language, sounds and music. Just as the refraction of light on water produces a spectrum of colours with the rainbow, the fragmented speech merges into music. In Jean Vigo's *L'Atalante* (1934), the linguistic fragmentation of speech passes through various accents: Dita Parlo's German accent and Michel Simon's Vaud accent. In the transition from silent film to talking film, long silences and music highlight these differences. This is more than plurilingualism: it is more of a polyphony. Père Jules' words delivered by Michel Simon are often monosyllabic and nonsensical, as if the film was seeking a spiritual, ethereal language. For Vigo, it is a matter of finding the essence of purity. The voyage of the barge and that of its residents is essentially ontological.

Originally, Genesis shows how man in turning away from the divine Word (*Logos*) falls into Babelism. With the Fall, a single indivisible tongue became plural 'tongues'. The quest for God's quintessential Word in the linguistic multiplicity and fragmentation is a common theme of literature. The language of Lewis Carroll's poem *Jabberwocky* is a symbol of fragmentation too and a bit like a shattered mosaic which must be reconstructed. It does not belong to common language: the tessitura of the text is obscure and polysemic. Words fuse to open onto a world of imagination. The linguistic jumble brings to mind the primordial chaos of Genesis before the manifestation of God's creating Word emerged out of nothingness. The Word is the genesis of life and the genesis of language that succeeds to the original sound of the formlessness or silence. T.S. Eliot's *The Wasteland* is also a polyphony of voices and an invitation to a spiritual voyage with lines of foreign languages interweaving Latin, Greek, English and Italian. In Joyce's polyglot *Finnegans Wake*, one can find elements of different languages too, as well as many musical references, and plunges into the genesis of language looking for the essence of the Word behind polyphony.

At its release, critics qualified *L'Atalante* as an implausible narrative jumble where the half-angel, half-fiend bargeman is often 'reduced to a barely comprehensible babble', or 'a poetic nonsense' (Temple 2005: 132). The charismatic father-figure of Père Jules functions in the film as a catharsis or a *deus ex machina* which will restore equilibrium and harmony on the barge. He is a link between land and sea, between the real and the surreal, and a linguistic tie between Jean and Juliette. With his almost inaudible whispers he is also a bridge between silent movies and talkies.[13] Better than speech, he expresses himself by singing, the music of his accordion and the scratches of his phonograph.[14] Music is the cohesive element: it is really part of this polyphony at the beginning of talkies and takes the place of language in a desire to hold on to the dream-like quality of the film and to the image of the loved one. As the barge floats its way along the canal, Juliette, as evanescent as Eurydice, the mythological goddess, is the object of desire towards whom both music and Père Jules' surreal language aspire. For Gilles Deleuze, the water imagery is a common feature of 1930s French films and the language spoken is 'different from the language of the earth' (Deleuze 1983: 114). In this liquid world, everything is fluid, and Father Jules' elusive language flows, just like the fleeting images which this film presents. Jean's fall into the canal is in fact a movement ascending to the watermark-like image of Juliette, represented as dancing, smiling and perfectly white, up to the point of escape or liquefaction. It can also be interpreted as a *regressum ad originem*, the water symbol bringing to mind the amniotic fluid surrounding the foetus in the womb. In this world of imagination, only music prevails. For Jean, the exit from the water is a return to earth, and a shift from music to the monosyllabic language of Father Jules ('Eh quoi, il s'est jeté, hein où ça? T'es sûr que tu l'as vu se jeter à l'eau'[15] [01:09:15–01:09:17]).

Plurilingualism developed in the first talkies through a variety of accents not only regional but foreign. The use of a foreign language in a French film can have connotations of the exotic as well as the eerie or the unknown, but the foreigner be-

---

13 Père Jules in this respect brings to mind Harpo Marx. Harpo whistled and honked his horn but never uttered a single word even in his appearances on TV. He was the silent Marx brother, a missing link between silent cinema and talkies. The mime artist Marceau likewise created the silent character 'Pip', most certainly inspired by Charlie Chaplin and inherited from the silent years of cinema.

14 For the importance of Maurice Jaubert's music in *L'Atalante*, refer to URL: http://pedagogie.ac-toulouse.fr/musique/cinema/Atalante2.htm (28 February 2010).

15 'Well, did he throw himself in? Are you sure you saw him throw himself into the water?'

trayed by his/her accent is often the outcast. B. Conein and F. Gadet note that accent
'produit immédiatement un effet d'étrangeté'[16] (Conein/Gadet 1998: 108). 'Accent'
is a particularly fluid and rather subjective term (as Gadet notes, it is always the
other that has an accent). Instead of erasing accents, they were over-represented in
the 1930s. Cinema between the wars used exaggerated effects of regional varieties,
such as the Marseille accent or the Parisian vernacular. Marcel Pagnol's films such
as the trilogy *Marius* (1931), *Fanny* (1932), *César* (1936) and Maurice Tourneur's
Justin de Marseille (1934) popularised southern folklore and the Provençal accent.
Not only did they highlight 'regional colour' by basing their cinematic imagination
on the city of Marseilles, but they also rehabilitated the identity of characters from
the most underprivileged classes. Identity, as Naficy remarks, is not 'a fixed essence
but a process of becoming' (Naficy 2001: 6). Accents may be more or less standard-
ised, but the more marked they are, the more marginalised, and the sense of threatened and challenged identity is in constant evolution and always in the making. The
contrast between Marius' Marseilles accent and the Lyonnais accent of Monsieur
Brun highlights the linguistic plurality. We find a similar contrast in *Le Schpountz*
(1938), a story of a man from Marseilles who goes to Paris to become a star of the big
screen and finds himself in Parisian high society. The cinema of the 1930s relishes in
the lower-class Parisian accent and the presence of supporting roles such as Pauline
Carton and Carette became essential ingredients of the films of that period. In *La
Rosière des Halles* (1935), Paulette Dubost, who has come from her home in rural
France, is an object of curiosity for the Parisian bourgeoisie. For Pierre Larquey, the
writer lacking in inspiration, the young country girl with her strong accent becomes
an object of study and material for his next book. The accent in the 1930s is often
used for comic effect (creating both misunderstandings and incongruous situations),
and through its strangeness can bring about illusion. Bela Lugosi's Hungarian accent
played a large part in his vampire character, and similarly the marked accents of the
vamps in French cinema are a sign of ambivalence: they are both enigmatic and cap-
tivating, forewarning a danger to come. The lady of French cinema, such as Antinéa
in Pabst's *L'Atlantide* (1932), attracts the object of her desire like a praying mantis.
The French film actress of Polish origin Stacia Napierkowska was replaced for the
part of Queen Antinéa by Brigitte Helm, the star of *Metropolis* (1927), in Pabst's
version. She played versions in English, German and French with an articulated diction, in the latter tinged with a slight German accent.

Plurilingualism in 1930s Cinema

Actresses of foreign origins gave a plurilingual flavour to pre-war cinema, but their
popularity enjoyed varying fortunes. Rumanian-born Elvire Popesco charmed with
her inimitable accent, but Austrian Nora Grégor's transition from stage to cinema
was not as successful. Her part in Renoir's *La Règle du jeu* as Christine would re-

---

16   'Immediately produces an effect of strangeness.'

main her major screen appearance. Jany Holt, also of Rumanian origin, with a hint of an accent, was chosen to play the Russian prostitute Nastia in Renoir's *Les Bas fonds* (1936). The labyrinth of Algier's Casbah where French gangster Pépé is hidden in Duvivier's *Pépé le Moko* (1937) is a social microcosm with its prostitutes, petty thieves and traitors. With no significant accent, but made swarthy to look more Algerian, Dalio plays the part of the traitor. When one year later, he plays the part of the producer Marcel Adam in Jouvet's adaptation on stage of *Le Corsaire*, he takes on, for purely comic purposes, the caricatural Jewish accent imitated from his father, a 'dialect composed of German, French, Yiddish, and Russian' (Meyer-Plantureux 2005: 110), that provokes the audience's laughter.

One of the characteristic accents that marked French cinema of the 1930s was that of Erich Von Stroheim. In 1939, in the turmoil of the Second World War, the release of Delannoy's fourth film *Macao, l'enfer du jeu*, which cast the Jewish Von Stroheim with his Austrian accent, was finally banned in German-occupied territories and it was not until 1942 that a new version came out with Pierre Renoir replacing Von Stroheim in all his scenes. The original version still exists and the acting of the German-accented hero bears no resemblance to Pierre Renoir's performance. Previously, in 1937, Jean Renoir had exploited the issue of plurilingualism in *La Grande illusion*. The film takes place in a multilingual environment where German officers mingle with French, German and Russian prisoners and bits of different languages as well as extracts of popular songs[17] are heard throughout. As McLaughlin notices, language difference and degrees of formality or informality within the camps establish codes between the speakers that create distance, tension and lack of understanding or, on the contrary, a sense of solidarity:

> *La Grande Illusion's* prisoner-of-war camps are a veritable Tower of Babel, where a multitude of codes are too often mutually unintelligible. A great deal of the film's tension arises from the presence of monoglots in such a setting, where one's language is an instant label, and the rare capacity to use more than one language is equally empowering and dangerous. (McLaughlin 2008: 3)

The aristocratic French officer Bœldieu's use of a formal register of French when interacting with middle class Maréchal creates social distance, while the use of French by the German officer Rauffenstein (Von Stroheim) in one of their first encounters with the two French officers abolishes any social boundaries. In the banquet scene, Bœldieu shifts to English. Both Rauffenstein and Bœldieu share the same upper-class background and their common proficiency in English will become a *lingua franca* that establishes a form of solidarity between the two. In this miniature Europe, the Jewish officer Rosenthal's fluency in German (played by Marcel Dalio) enables him to understand the language of the enemy and situates him as a go-between and mediator not only linguistically, but also socially and culturally. At many points in the film, music brings 'some promise of communion' (Triggs 1988), but when

---

17   Such as 'Tipperary', 'Die Heimat', 'La Marseillaise' (Triggs 1988).

Bœldieu, planning an escape, plays the tune of 'Un petit navire' on his flute, it fails to provide a happy ending. Rauffenstein tries to reason with him in English, the only language the two of them share, before finally shooting him:

> Rauffenstein: Bœldieu, have you really gone insane?
> Bœldieu: I'm perfectly sane.
> Rauffenstein: Bœldieu, you understand that if you do not obey at once and come down, I shall have to shoot... I dread to do that. I beg you... man to man, come back.
> Bœldieu: It's damn nice of you, Rauffenstein, but it's impossible.[18] [01:18:48 – 01:19:18]

Immediately after, Rauffenstein, left on his own and a prisoner of his own class, is heard muttering in English 'that is why' before shifting to his native German and giving orders to his army to pursue the runaways. English, which has at first suppressed the dichotomy between the jailer and his prisoners, is finally replaced by the enemy's language which is echoed in the mouth of the German officer with the harsh words: 'So deshalb. Scheinwerfer in Aktion, Suchkolonnen und Hunde raus, der Gendarmerie, Militär, Zivilbehörden telefonieren, rapportieren Sie mir jede Viertelstunde'[19] [01:19:52–01:20:09].

A French audience might not have noticed the different accents at that time but when both characters speak English there are very noticeable stylistic contrasts. Whereas Fresnay speaks British English, Stroheim speaks with more of an American accent[20], and not with what you might expect, a posh English accent (in the 1920s–1930s, German aristocracy would certainly never have learnt American English). One hears it especially in the first few seconds of the scene, 'gone', 'insane', 'understand', 'shoot', 'man to man' – all his vowels are American. When he speaks German, he appears for an upper-class audience with a strong Austrian Viennese accent which is very nasal at times like in the pronunciation of the word 'Aktion' [ak'tsi̯oːn].

Chion notices that women are absent from *La Grande illusion* until the last episode of the film (Chion 1999: 62). A female singer's voice is heard from a gramophone at the beginning singing *Frou-frou*, but the woman remains an unattainable object of desire until Maréchal's final encounter with the farm woman played by German actress Dita Parlo. Elsa's accented voice is a final counterpoint to Erich Von Stroheim's. She speaks softly, and her intonation is melodious, highlighted by the gentle tune of the gramophone. Maréchal manages to communicate with her in broken German ('Lotte hat blaue Augen'[21]) [97:21–98:28]. In the comfort of her barn, Elsa's young daughter Lotte brings peace and innocence to the scene. In spite of the language impediment and social class and gender differences, the Christmas Eve scene is a symbol of communion and harmony. If plurilingualism throughout of the

---

18   Quoted by Triggs 1988.
19   'So that's why. Switch on the floodlights, send out search troops and dogs, telephone the gendarmerie, the military, and civilian authorities, report back to me every quarter of an hour.'
20   Von Stroheim started his career in Hollywood in the 1910s.
21   'Lotte has blue eyes.'

film emphasises differences and tension, the polyphony of voices is finally seen as a symbol of concord.

As French cinema moved from silent to talkies, it gradually learnt to deal with sound. Ill at ease with the intrusion of sound onto the screen, it developed around a diversity of voices. The cinema first learnt to speak by singing, then it discovered a variety of accents. Still at an experimental stage, film directors used sound to convey the emotional and the spiritual. Later, French talkies grew out of multiplicity, whether it was an accent typical of a social class, such as Titi's Parisian accent with its cheeky humour in the comedies of the 1930s, or accents of regional France, such as Provençal, to which were added the intonations of foreign actors. The melding of lexis, syntax and accent between the different voices which was already incipient in silent cinema became increasingly plurilingual, with language becoming the medium for the assertion of a vital sense of individual and collective identity.

Filmography

ALLÉGRET, M. (1939), *Le Corsaire.*

ALLÉGRET, M. (1934), *Zouzou.*

ARCADY, A. (1983), *Le Grand carnaval.*

ARCAND, D. (2003), *Les Invasions barbares* aka *The Barbarian Invasions.*

BOON, D. (2008), *Bienvenue chez les ch'tis* aka *Welcome to the Sticks.*

CHAREF, M. (1984), *Le Thé au harem d'Archimède* aka *Tea in the Harem.*

CLAIR, R. (1930), *Sous les toits de Paris* aka *Under the Roofs of Paris.*

DELANNOY, J. (1942), *Macao, l'enfer du jeu* aka *Gambling Hell.*

DULAC, G. (1926), *L'Invitation au voyage* aka *Invitation to a Journey.*

DULAC, G. (1928), *La Coquille et le clergyman* aka *The Seashell and the Clergyman.*

DUVIVIER, J. (1937), *Pépé le Moko.*

EPSTEIN, J. (1926), *Coeur fidèle* aka *The Faithful Heart.*

FROELICH, C. (1928), *La Vie est à nous* aka *Life is Ours.*

GILOU, T. (1997, 2001), *La Vérité si je mens* aka *Would I Lie to You?*

GRÉVILLE, E.T. (1935), *Princesse Tam Tam* aka *Princess Tam Tam.*

HENLEY, H. (1930), *La Grande mare.*

KARMANN, S. (2003), *A la petite semaine* aka *Nickel and Dime.*

LIMUR, J. de (1935), *La Rosière des Halles* aka *La Rosière des Halles.*

KASSOVITZ, M. (1990), *La Haine* aka *The Hate.*

KECHICHE, A. (2005), *L'Esquive* aka *Games of Love and Chance.*

KECHICHE, A. (2007), *La Graine et le mulet* aka *Couscous.*

LANG, F. (1927), *Metropolis* aka *Metropolis.*

LANG, F. (1933), *The Testament of Dr. Mabuse.*

MARCHAL, O. (2004), *36* aka *36 Quai des orfèvres.*

MÉLIÈS, G. (1903), *Le Cake walk infernal* aka *The Cake Walk Infernal.*

MÉLIÈS, G. (1904), *Le Voyage à travers l'impossible* aka *An Impossible Voyage.*

MÉLIÈS, G. (1904), *Le Merveilleux éventail vivant* aka *The Wonderful Living Fan.*

PABST, G. W. (1930), *Westfront* aka *Comrades of 1918.*

PABST, G.W. (1931), *L'Opéra de quatre sous* aka *The Threepenny Opera*.

PABST, G.W. (1932), *L'Atlantide* aka *The Lost Atlantis*.

PAGNOL, M. (1931), *Marius*.

PAGNOL, M. (1938), *Le Schpountz* aka *Heartbeat*.

PAULIN, J.-P. (1934), *L'Esclave blanc* aka *The White Slave*.

RENOIR, J. (1936), *Les Bas fonds* aka *Underworld*.

RENOIR, J. (1937), *La Grande illusion* aka *The Grand Illusion*.

RENOIR, J. (1939), *La Règle du jeu* aka *The Rules of the Game*.

TOURNEUR, M. (1934), *Justin de Marseille*.

VALLÉE, J.-M. (2005), *C.R.A.Z.Y.* aka *Crazy*.

VIGO, J. (1934), *L'Atalante*.

ZIDI. C. (1984, 1990, 2003), *Les Ripoux* aka *The Cop*.

References

BAKHTIN, M. (1970), *Problèmes de la poétique de Dostoïevski*, Lausanne: Ed. de L'Age de l'Homme.

BAKHTIN, M. (1978), *Esthétique et théorie du roman,* Paris: Gallimard.

BARBÉRIS, J.-M. (2009), 'Identité urbanisée, discours sur l'espace', in: *Cahiers de sociolinguistiques*, 13, 49–71.

BARROT, O. & R. CHIRAT (1994), *'Gueules d'atmosphères': Les acteurs du cinéma français 1929–1959*, Paris: Gallimard.

BERG, B. (2008), '*L'Esclave blanc* de Jean-Paul Paulin (1934)', URL:
http://www.lesdocs.com/fiches/dossier %20de %20presse/esclaveblanc.dossier %20 de %20presse.html (June 2009).

BERNHARD, S. (2008), 'Extrait sonore de *Phèdre*', URL: http://www.udenap.org/extraits_sonores/voix_disparues/bernhardt_sarah_phedre.mp3 (June 2010).

BILLARD, P. (1995), *L'Age classique du cinéma français*, Paris: Flammarion.

BLEICHENBACHER, L. (2007), 'This is Meaningless – It's in Russian'/Multilingual Characters in Mainstream Movies', in: Balz, E. & L. Michacak, *Cultures in Contact*, Tübingen: Narr, 111–127.

BLEICHENBACHER, L. (2008), *Multilingualism in the Movies: Hollywood Characters and their Language Choices*, Schweizer Anglistische Arbeiten, Vol. 135, Tübingen: Francke.

CARTON, F. (Consultation 2008), 'Te comprinds ch'picard?', in: *Libé-Lille*, URL: http://www.libelille.fr/saberan/2008/04/te-comprinds-ch.html (June 2010).

CARRIÈRE, J.-C. (1996), *Le Film qu'on ne voit pas*, Paris: Plon.

CHION, M. (1999), *The Voice of Cinema*, New York: Columbia U.P.

CONEIN, B. & F. GADET (1998), 'Le 'français populaire' de jeunes de la banlieue parisienne, entre permanence et innovation', in: Androutsopoulos, K. & A. Schotz (dirs.), *Jugendsprache, Langue des jeunes, Youth Language*, Frankfurt/Main: Lang, 106–123.

DESLANDES, J. (2008), 'L'embargo français VDF: Doublage cinématographique et télévisuel en version française', in: URL: http://cinema-quebecois.net/edition3/e_jd_1.html (June 2009).

DELEUZE, G. (1983), *Cinéma 1. L'image-mouvement*, Paris: Minuit.

DULAC, G. (1926), *L'Invitation au voyage,* URL: http://suspendu.free.fr/site/index.php?option=com_content&task=view&id=16&Itemid=40 (June 2010).

DULAC, G. (1928), *La Coquille et le clergyman*, URL: http://www.ubu.com/film/dulac_coquille.html (June 2010).

LACASSE, G. (2000), *Le Bonimenteur de vues animées: Le Cinéma 'muet' entre tradition et modernité*, Québec/Paris: Méridiens-Klincksieck/Nota Bene.

MALRAUX, A. (1951), *Les Voix du silence*, Paris: La Galerie de la Pléïade.

McLAUGHLIN, N. (2008), 'Code-use and Identity in *La Grande illusion* and *Xala*', in: Abecassis, M. (ed.) (2008), *Pratiques langagières dans le cinéma francophone*, in: *Glottopol,* 12, URL: http://www.univ-rouen.fr/dyalang/glottopol/numero_12.htm (28 May 2010), 123–134.

MEYER-PLANTUREUX, C., (ed.) (2005), *Les Enfants de Shylock ou l'antisémitisme sur scène*, Paris: Editions Complexe.

NAFICY, H. (2001), *An Accented Cinema: Exilic and Diasporic Filmmaking*, Princeton: Princeton U.P.

SICARD, T. (2006), 'Le cinéma québécois en France', URL: http://www.lemagazine.info/spip.php?article374 (June 2010).

TEMPLE, M. (2006), *Jean Vigo*, Manchester: Manchester U.P.

TRIGGS, J.A. (1988), 'The Legacy of Babel: Language in Jean Renoir's *Grand Illusion*', URL: http://www.leoyan.com/global-language.com/triggs/Renoir.html (June 2010).

The Other You.
Translating the Hispanic for the Spanish Screen

John D. Sanderson

The overwhelming modality of interlinguistic mediation in the reception of foreign screen fiction in the Spanish polysystem has always been dubbing. Whether this policy was established with the beginning of the sound era for political or economical reasons is debatable, but it is a fact that in 1941, two years after Franco's military takeover, his dictatorial regime banned the use of any foreign language on film as a means to protect the national language and identity (Gubern 1975: 34), with an aim that Chaume defines very accurately: 'Doblar una película era convertirla en un producto nacional'[1] (Chaume 2004: 50). The erasure of the original soundtrack, normally in English because of the nationality of the most prolific film-producing countries, and its replacement with dialogues in Spanish made it easier for the national audience to adopt the point of view of the predominant screen culture which, after all, was using their same language. Regarding the protection of the national identity, however, this policy would seem contradictory, since the average cinemagoer would eventually become more familiar with American film syntax, stars and, in some cases, even social customs than with local ones, since dubbing had the effect of reducing the sense of their reception as foreign.

An obvious problem would arise when the Spanish language and/or culture appeared in these foreign films since, if any national features were presented as alien or antagonistic for the overall perspective of the prevalent culture which had produced the film, the assumed process of identification of the audience could be hindered. As well as that, any interlinguistic dialogue would be technically rendered incoherent if, as a result of the dubbing process, everybody spoke the same language in the new target context. Therefore, in order to achieve a receptive reaction from the audience comparable to the one hypothetically produced in the source culture, some degree of linguistic manipulation was required that would inevitably also bear a cultural dimension because of the various social factors involved in the translation strategies applied in different periods.

---

1   'To dub a film was to turn it into a national product.'

The aim of this paper is to analyse how the Spanish polysystem has modified for the national reception the linguistic content of Anglo-American film and television productions which portrayed Hispanic characters, with examples from three distinct periods: Franco's dictatorship, the restoration of democracy, and the twenty-first century. In these examples migration is a major issue, concerning either the characters or the actors playing the parts, since it has shaped the presence of what is considered 'Hispanic', for the most predominant English-speaking film industry, always in an economical, social and even moral position of inferiority. This analysis will allow us to discern how the new target context reacts to different issues related to this portrayal, and how it either modifies the archetype for local consumption or transfers the generalised derogatory perspective to other communities.

Barefoot on Foreign Dirt: The Making of a Hispanic Hollywood Archetype
In every narrative, the point of view established by the story-teller assumes that a series of features adscribed to the character we are expected to identify with will be deemed acceptable as opposed to others considered differentiated and/or antagonistic. On film, the image will also incorporate a number of visual semes which can be at least as relevant as the dialogues or the development of the plot. As Ken Dancyger and Jeff Rush point out: 'This identification is useful because it quickly simplifies the relationship between the audience and the story. The audience enters the story through the character with whom it can identify' (Dancyger/Rush 2007: 177).

As a consequence of the global predominance of the Hollywood industry, the canonic structure of its screen syntax has become standard, overcoming in many countries, such as Spain, their own national modes of representation. Therefore, narrative development can be economised by the use of visual elements that will be easily decoded internationally thanks to immediate recognition. Even though Hollywood is logically trying to sell its productions abroad, and therefore is in contact with the outside world beyond its North American borders, the presence of foreigners in its cinema is the result of a local perception based, above all, on their historically massive migration to the United States. The canonised point of view is still that of the white Anglo-Saxon, and all other ethnic or cultural representations have been traditionally adscribed to subservient characters, which can also be very helpful narratively according to Berg (2002: 17), with 'recognition, differentiation and devaluation being key functions of the cinematic stereotype'. Therefore, a physiognomical differentiation and a non-standard accent would easily convey a wide variety of semes adscribed to a generalised origin.

The 'Hispanic' archetype is one of the most widespread options of 'otherness' in the Hollywood industry. For obvious reasons of proximity, from the very beginning of film Mexicans overwhelmingly represented the archetype, which included mainly negative features deriving from the historical confrontation for the annexation of California in the nineteenth century, with illegal immigration eventually becoming the key issue in the twentieth century in order to fixate the condition of inferiority adscribed to their cinematic representation. This portrayal generated official complaints from Mexico as early as the 1920s, which eventually led to a two-fold strategy from Hollywood: on the one hand, the archetype would not be presented so continuously linked to a specific country of origin; on the other, Mexican actors would be employed to play these parts in order to overcome this sense of antagonism with the national pride of having one of their own in the cast of a North American film. As Vasey remarks:

> Hollywood's most overt concession to foreign sensibilities was its employment and promotion of clearly recognizable international stars. Foreign audiences often responded particularly warmly to their own compatriots when they appeared in the full international context of the Hollywood industry, so when Hollywood producers 'poached' acting talent from other national industries, it not only weakened their competitors, but also recruited the affections and loyalties of foreign populations. (Vasey 1992: 624–625)

In spite of Franco's international political isolation, in the mid-twentieth century it was Spain's turn to experience this particular brand of distinguished migration. Sara Montiel was a major Spanish film star when she arrived in the United States via Mexico, where she had played the lead in a dozen films during the early 1950s until she was given her Hollywood breakthrough with *Vera Cruz* (Robert Aldrich, 1954). Her experience was short-lived, since she only made two other films before returning to Spain, *Serenade* (Anthony Mann, 1956) and *Run of the Arrow* (Samuel Fuller, 1957), but her reputation was already made in her home country, mainly due to her first film, in which she starred next to Hollywood icons Gary Cooper and Burt Lancaster playing the part of Nina, a Mexican peasant. She was, however, only second female lead to Denise Darcel, a French actress playing the part of wicked Countess Marie Duvarre, who planned to steal the Mexican gold and take it to her country of origin.

As far as language is concerned, the dubbing process for the Spanish screen did not pose a translation problem, since it was Hollywood's policy, not totally different from Franco's, that foreign characters would all speak in English with a thick accent, even to people of their own nationality. So in *Vera Cruz* French and Mexican characters communicated in perfect English with just the occasional '*chérie*', '*mademoiselle*', '*señor*' and '*gracias*' thrown in for authenticity, which was all easily dubbed into Spanish. As for the plot, Berry points out that 'Spanishness is often Hollywood's ethnically acceptable alibi for hot-blooded sexuality' (Berry 2004: 190), so, accordingly, Nina's first scene [14:40] involves her kissing a total stranger, Ben Traine (Gary Cooper), in the mouth while stealing his wallet, immediately giving away some determining features of her personality. Later on in the film, once both characters have got to know each other, Ben, an honest, traditional Southerner, points out how distinctive she is: 'You are different. Most girls don't steal wallets' [56:00], and goes on to reflect on how her upbringing may have had an effect on her skills: 'They say that a thief in Mexico today can disappear like a puff of smoke' [56:42], extending this feature of petty theft to her whole community. There is a redeeming factor in her, though, that her moral guide, Ben, will identify: her loyalty to her fellow citizens. As a consequence, he will help them get their gold back from the Gallic conspirators.

Countess Marie Duvarre also had to fit into a specific and differentiated French archetype. She is also sexually active, but far more calculating, convoluted, glamorous (she has a huge wardrobe Nina steals a dress from) and, on the whole, threatening than the Hispanic female. The Countess does not trust anyone, but is eventually attracted to Joe Erin (Burt Lancaster) once he reveals that he is willing to betray his long-life companion Ben in order to team up with her for the gold. His attitude would contradict many assumed archetypical concepts of the source culture if it were not for the Countess' soothing confirmation that: 'Joseph, you are born American, but at heart you are French' [01:09:35]. *Vera Cruz* was faithfully transferred to the Spanish polysystem via dubbing, including the Mexican and French stereotyping, without any alterations, and Sara Montiel was received back in Spain with open arms.[2]

Vera Cruz was released exactly the same year as *The Barefoot Contessa* (Joseph L. Mankiewicz, 1954), a film that involved an even more unusual example of migration, that of American actress Ava Gardner, who had decided to settle down in Spain after the positive impression she got while shooting *Pandora and the Flying Dutchman* (Albert Lewin, 1951) in the Costa Brava. In Mankiewicz's film it was the first time she would play a Spanish character[3], María Vargas, a dancer who is allured by an American producer to migrate from Madrid in order to become a film star in Hollywood, tangentially connecting with the plight of the real-life Spanish actress mentioned above. But, in contrast with *Vera Cruz*, the Spanish characters in *The Barefoot Contessa* do speak their own language, even though not one of the actors playing the parts had that nationality since, in order to avoid the strict control of Francoist censorship, the Madrid scenes were all shot in Cinecittà, the film studios in Rome. So when Ava Gardner and the Italian actors uttered lines in Spanish and generated an interlinguistic situation with the North Americans visiting Madrid, translation adjustments would eventually be required in Spain so as to render a coherent dialogue.

Ava Gardner's first scene in the film quickly establishes some easily recognisable stereotypical features assigned to her character. Multi-millionaire film producer Kirk Edwards (Warren Stevens), sitting at a table in a Madrid club with his public-relations manager Oscar Muldoon (Edmond O'Brien) and director and script-writer Harry Dawes (Humphrey Bogart), tells the latter to go into the dancer's dressing-room once her show has finished to ask her to join them for a drink. In doing so, he sees her bare feet behind a curtain extremely close to a pair of male shoes that, once the curtain is drawn, are revealed to belong to a musician of her band. She complains about Harry's intrusion in Spanish, and when he explains that he does not understand, she speaks in English. He replies:

---

2   In her other two Hollywood productions, she also played the part of a Mexican in *Serenade*, whereas in *The Run of the Arrow* she was a native American Indian.

3   She played another two Spanish parts after that: The Duchess of Alba in *The Naked Maja* (Henry Koster, 1958), and Soledad, a gold-hearted prostitute loyal to the II Republic in *The Angel Wore Red* (Nunnally Johnson, 1960). Neither of these films was released in Spain.

Harry: Your English is very good. Where did you learn it?
María (to the Spaniard): ¡No te quedes ahí plantado como un idiota! ¡Compórtate
como si fueras de mi familia! (To Harry) This man, he is my cousin.
Harry: This man, he is your cousin. [14:04]

Archetypical semes are instantly delivered: she is sexually active and she cheats,
not stealing anything here, but lying. And there is another issue characteristically
associated to 'Hispanic', or in more general terms to 'Latin', that is simultaneously
installed and transgressed here: the concept of close-knit family group. Traditional upbringing in these countries would result in families with many children whose
members, generation after generation, care for and support one another making up a
small community. The fact that María makes use of this assumption in order to jus-
tify her physical closeness to this Spanish male puts the issue into question. As is revealed by her dialogue in Spanish, 'Don't stand there like an idiot! Behave as if you
were a member of my family!', she is exploiting a positive feature universally associated with her culture to cover up her sexual availability.

María will eventually reveal herself as a good-natured character, not very different from the process carried out with Nina in *Vera Cruz*. But there was a big
difference concerning the Spanish polysystem: even though Ava Gardner is North
American, not Spanish, her character is Spanish, not Mexican, so no transgression
of morality or family values could be accepted by the Francoist regime in the portrayal, however positive otherwise, of a national character. The following modifications were considered necessary in the dubbing process:

Harry: Veo que tenían razón. Es usted demasiado impulsiva.
María: ¡Qué haces ahí plantado como un idiota! ¡Pórtate al menos con educación!
Este hombre es primo mío.
Harry: Este hombre es primo suyo.[4]

In order to render the interlinguistic communication coherent in the target culture,
Harry's reference to her English language skills is replaced by a remark about her attitude, 'hot-headed', which suitably fits into the context. What is remarkable is that
the original lines in Spanish have been modified, when technically there was no
need to, in an attempt to upturn the North American archetypical presentation and
transform María into a more virtuous character by expecting the Spanish audience
to believe that he is really her cousin, and that her concern is only due to the fact
that, as a member of her family, he is not behaving politely enough.

As the scene develops, María does agree to go with Harry to the table where
the other two Americans are waiting once she has told her alleged cousin to leave
her dressing room (he climbs out of the window!). Then Oscar, the public relations
manager, tries to persuade her to emigrate to Hollywood to become an actress, and

---

4   Harry: I can see that they were right. You are too hot-headed.
     María: What are you doing standing there like an idiot! At least behave with better manners! This
     man is my cousin.
     Harry: This man is your cousin.

rounds off his attempt by touching a sensitive issue which he, as well, typically associates to her culture:

> Oscar: There's no reason why, after a time, we can send for your mother. After all, a girl likes to have her mother with her, right?
> María: I would not like to have my mother with me.
> Kirk: Why not?
> María: Because I do not like my mother.
> Kirk: I am sure you don't mean that. Every mother should be loved.
> María: If they deserve it.
> Oscar: We can work all that out later too. [19:30]

The transgressive issue is still maintained, and even increased, in this verbal exchange, since María intensifies her disrespect for her family by publicly displaying her dislike for her own mother. It would be relevant to point out, however, that it is an assumed positive feature of the Hispanic archetype which is being questioned, not a negative one. And, on top of that, it is the North American characters who are actually portrayed here as standard-bearers of family values, shocked as they are at María's reaction. The process of stereotyping would then include the enhancement of the perceptive 'I' of the film by feeding it off with any remaining positive features of the differentiated archetypes. But this imposing strategy would find an even more imposing response from the Francoist censorship in order to protect what they considered one of the pillars of Spanish society:

> Oscar: No habrá inconveniente, pasado el tiempo, en que se lleve a su madre. Es natural que quiera tener a su madre con usted, ¿cierto?
> María: Tan cierto como imposible que pueda llevármela.
> Kirk: ¿Por qué?
> María: Ha muerto, ahora vivo con mi madrastra.
> Kirk: No veo inconveniente. Podrá traerse a su madrastra.
> María: No me interesa.
> Oscar: Ya discutirán ese asunto.[5]

Showing disrespect towards a blood relative would have been unthinkable for the official Spanish doctrine, far less towards one's own mother. The local censors seem to have thought that disposing of the mother and replacing her with a stepmother would make María's attitude more acceptable in this scene and those to come, since once she gets home she will have a huge row with her before leaving for Hollywood, and later on in the film her father murders her mother and she will have to come back to Spain to testify in court on his behalf. As a result, the source culture's willingness to disrepute this feature traditionally associated to the Hispanic archetype would find

---

5   Oscar: There's no reason why, after a time, we can send for your mother. After all, a girl likes to have her mother with her, right?
     María: As right as it is impossible that I can take her with me.
     Kirk: Why?
     María: She died. Now I live with my stepmother.
     Kirk: There's no reason why you can't bring your stepmother.
     María: I'm not interested.
     Oscar: You can work all that out later.

in Spain the censoring manipulation of the verbal content (her mother becomes her stepmother) in order to readjust the plot according to their moral standards.

For North American audiences it was not necessarily relevant to find any distinctions among Hispanic characters, as Rodríguez points out in her complaint about 'the dominant way they have been viewed by U.S. motion picture audiences, as Latins, Latinos, Hispanics or just 'Spanish', with occasional distinctions made by national origin' (Rodríguez 2008: viii). But a nuance that could help to identify Spaniards was a reference to the Civil War (1936–39), with which Franco's troops overthrew the legitimate government of the II Spanish Republic. Several Hollywood productions had approached the subject presenting the ordeal of English and American individuals who had joined the International Brigades in order to defend the Republican government against the fascist *coup d'etat*, with the cinematic perspective being that of the Anglo-Saxon hero within an exotic background. Coincidentally, the two stars of *The Barefoot Contessa* had already played parts which involved references to the Spanish Civil War.

In one of the most popular films in the history of Hollywood, *Casablanca* (Michael Curtiz, 1942), Humphrey Bogart is Rick Blaine, who, before opening his famous café, has already had a lifelong political involvement in defending 'good causes', as we hear from Captain Louis Renault (Claude Rains), in charge of security in this Moroccan city still under the control of the French Government:

> Renault: I suspect that, under that cynical shell, you're at heart a sentimentalist. Oh, laugh if you will, but I happen to be familiar with your record. Let me point out just two items. In 1935 you ran guns to Ethiopia. In 1936 you fought in Spain on the Loyalist side.
> Rick: And got well paid for it on both occasions.
> Renault: The winning side would have paid you much better. [19:10]

The Hollywood canonic narrative knows very well how to supply the characteristics that would allow audiences worldwide to identify with Rick and assume his perspective. Sentimentality, generosity and honesty were features adscribed to the North American archetype that the average Spanish spectator could also assimilate instantly, except for the fact that, as Agost points out in her analysis of the dubbing of this segment, 'la dictadura franquista no podía tolerar que la lucha en contra suya se definiera como 'una causa justa'[6] (Agost 2001: 18). Therefore, Captain Renault's flattering remarks had to be slightly modified: 'En 1935 introdujo armas en Etiopía. En 1938 luchó como pudo contra la anexión de Austria.'[7] The fact that there was no image related to the originally unacceptable political reference made it easier for the censors to modify the verbal content without any semiotic disruption.

---

6   'The Francoist dictatorship could not tolerate that fighting against it could be defined as 'a just cause'.'

7   'In 1935 you ran guns to Ethiopia. In 1938 you fought as hard as you could against the annexation of Austria.'

Two years before *The Barefoot Contessa*, Ava Gardner had starred in a free cinematic adaptation of a short story written by a good friend of hers, Ernest Hemingway: *The Snows of Kilimanjaro* (Henry King, 1952). Here the main character, writer Harry Street (Gregory Peck), travels all over the world looking for inspiration, and one of his intense experiences is in Spain during the war, where he has taken Cynthia Green (Ava Gardner) with him. In a narrative flashback, Harry (clearly Hemingway's alter-ego, since he himself had been reporting on the war from Spain at the time) is seen in a long battle scene [01:11:50] fighting for the loyalist side in a vast Spanish landscape when he comes across Cynthia, who lies dying after her Red Cross ambulance has been hit by a fascist bomb. In this case, the whole six-and-a-half-minute climatic scene was cut off for the film's release in Spain. The positive portrayal of the Spanish Republicans and the fact that the film's hero was providing an essential support to them in an obvious Spanish spatial context seems to have left the censors with no other choice.

Maltby remarks that 'Hollywood has always produced movies for international audiences as well as for its domestic market. In doing so, it has often Americanised the national histories of other countries, while the American product seems to be part of an international mass culture' (Maltby 2003: 30). The Spanish Civil War was yet another background used to praise the heroism of the North American individual, and it also contributed to specify the historical and geographical location of the setting. It would therefore come as no surprise that a reference to the war was also made in *The Barefoot Contessa*. When Harry is giving María advice in Madrid about how to handle her hypothetical film career if she finally decides to leave her home country, she recalls her traumatic childhood: 'And when the bombs came, in the Civil War, I used to bury myself in the dirt of the ruins to be safe. I would lie there, safe in the dirt' [29:53].

The Civil War would automatically connect her to the archetype 'Hispanic from Spain' as a historical detail that would differentiate her within the generalised term, though neither liberating her from other characteristics adscribed to it, nor from the rage of the Spanish censors who would again erase the cultural reference: 'En mi casa eran pobres, la vida era muy dura. Yo acostumbraba a mirar los escaparates de las zapaterías. Así huía de los gritos de mi madrastra.'[8]

'Civil War' is replaced by 'we were poor' but, even more remarkably, the recurrent reference to the alleged stepmother gives the impression that the parallel plot had to be permanently re-enforced so as to make it believable: her screams must have seemed a suitably resounding replacement for the fascist bombs.

At this stage of the film, the spectators of the source context could empathise with María once she has shown her vulnerable side, and would be ready to forgive previous inadequate attitudes, always from the perspective of the main char-

---

8   'At home we were poor. Life was very hard. I used to look at the shoe-shop windows. That's how I got away from my step-mother's screams.'

acter they have identified with, who will now acquire yet another role, coinciding with Shaw's remark: 'Even when the Hispanic characters have been represented as 'good', their screen personas are often naive, and in need of Euro-American heroes to save them' (Shaw 2007: 342). Harry Dawes, as, before him, Ben Traine with Mexicans, Harry Street with Spanish loyalists, and Rick Blaine also with Spanish loyalists, will provide that essential support needed by these 'naive' people to overcome difficulties. Harry is straightforward, honest, and even sarcastic (most parts played by Bogart were), all universally positive features that would make him a character automatically embraced as a subject to identify with by the Spanish polysystem, except for yet another minor detail that the Francoist censorship felt compelled to modify. In the open-hearted dialogue between Harry and María mentioned above, he gives a detail about his love life that became something completely different in the dubbed version:

> Harry: I'm afraid I've had three wives. I've been around with actresses, female writers, singers, painters, and even a female agent.
> Harry: Mi caso es distinto, no tengo un céntimo, pero soy buen amigo de actrices, pitonisas, cantantes y hasta tuve un representante femenino.[9] [28:00]

To identify with the narrative point of view of the source text, the fact that he had had three wives could not be assumed in a country where divorce was and would remain banned for another thirty-five years. On the other hand, analysing the censoring choices of the last two segments it would seem that, in poverty-stricken Spain, having no money was a useful feature to contribute to a favourable portrayal of the main characters one was expected to relate to under Spanish standards.

Spain was not the only country to have a stereotype imposed on in *The Barefoot Contessa*: the scope of characters was widened to include a South American tycoon of a non-specified nationality, Alberto Bravano, and an Italian noble, Count Vincenzo Torlato-Favrini.[10] Bravano's first appearance is at a Hollywood party held in honour of María Vargas' success, where he straightforwardly asks her to escape with him to the French Côte d'Azur. We immediately learn that he is an arrogant crook because, in his ensuing confrontation with American producer Kirk Edwards, who refuses to let her go, he flaunts his corrupt condition, but is also fair enough to admit the Anglo-Saxon moral superiority over the rest of the world in economical and even hygienic issues:

> Kirk: What about your flea-bitten country? What taxes do you pay?
> Bravano: It is a well known fact that everywhere in the world, except for the British Empire and the United States of America, the income tax can be easily avoided by anyone with income. I pay none. [01:03:09]

---

9   'My case is different, I haven't got a cent, but I am a good friend of actresses, fortune-tellers, singers and I even had a female agent.'

10 Bravano was played by Marius Goring, a British actor of German origin whose foreign roles were generally Nazi officers who spoke English with an accent, here portraying a different national archetype. Count Torlato-Favrini was played by Italian actor Rossano Brazzi.

The 'flea-bitten country' could be anywhere in Central or South America, but not in Spain, so this derogatory comment would not inflame the local censors. However, the way the predominant cultural communicators ascertain once again their role as worldwide models of honesty and efficiency would imply that Franco had not led his own country to these heights, contradicting the also exhausting propaganda aimed at the Spanish people, so some changes had to be made:

> Kirk: ¿Eso es mejor que tener el país infectado de moscas? ¿Qué impuestos paga usted? Bravano: Es de dominio público que yo los eludo casi en su totalidad; también en eso, demuestro mi superioridad sobre usted. Únicamente los paga por timidez porque usted quisiera no pagarlos. Le da miedo de todo (sic).[11]

If the North American character would not like to pay taxes in the dubbed Spanish version, then either the Anglo-Saxon archetype model proved to be flawed according to the new context or perhaps tax avoidance was not so condemnable after all from the censors' point of view. In any case, as expected, 'hot-headed' María is not submitting to Kirk Edwards' wishes, and is easily, perhaps too easily, persuaded by Bravano to go to France with him, a choice which is not sanctioned this time by Harry Dawes's approval. Their subsequent romance is expectably short-lived because he brings out other features related to the archetype he represents: he is quick-tempered and violent, demonstrated in his public outburst against María in a French hotel restaurant, where Count Torlato-Favrini intervenes, slaps his face, and invites her to drive with him to the Italian Riviera. She confirms the preconceptions we have of her by immediately accepting his proposal; at least in Italy she can continue her career as an actress, and her next film will be directed by her minder, Harry Dawes, who travels there to start shooting.

The noble Italian, a Latin who is not dishonest because he does not need to be, is romantic, generous and very tactful towards her, to the extent that he puzzlingly makes it clear that there will be no physical intimacy between them until they are married. This would hypothetically be yet another transgression of a cliché associated with a national archetype, since Italian males are supposed to be sexually incontinent. But the scriptwriter (Mankiewicz himself) had an ace up his sleeve: on their wedding night he confesses to her, in a very convoluted and not totally comprehensible way for the average spectator, that a wound in the Second World War left him impotent, with the consequence that his dynasty will come to an end. Then Latin virility would also be proven uncertain in the way this character is portrayed, though it might also prove some uneasiness about this issue on behalf of the source culture itself.

Spanish María will bring forward a defining characteristic of her class in another remarkable narrative twist. Shortly after her marriage she reveals to dumbfounded Harry that she has had an affair with a member of her husband's household staff and has become pregnant, it would seem, only for the sake of continuing the dynasty:

---

11   'It is a well known fact that I avoid almost all of them. In this I also prove my superiority over you. You only pay them out of shyness, because you would like not to pay them. You are afraid of everything.'

Harry: What about the father?
María: It is not his concern. The baby will be mine and my husband's.
Harry: Do you really believe that?
María: It will make Vincenzo happy. [01:57:20]

Harry Dawes, the 'I' of the spectator and a Hollywood scriptwriter, would seem to be far more familiar with Italian stereotyping than María, even though it is not that different from the Hispanic; jealousy and quick temper are issues to keep in mind when portraying Latins. A few minutes after she leaves Harry's apartment and goes back home to tell her husband, he realises how potentially dangerous this confession could be and rushes to their mansion, arriving just in time to hear two gun-shots off-screen and see Count Vicenzo carrying María's corpse outside to the patio: he has killed her and her lover, and will now call the police to confess.

As usual, if it did not affect Spanish identity, any foreign stereotyping was found acceptable by the standards of the Francoist censorship, so the Italian Count could be presented as an impotent, jealous murderer with no translation modifications required. But, institutionally, it was a well-known fact that no Spanish woman would ever have an affair outside her marriage, and even less become pregnant, so the whole plot twist was erased in the dubbed version:

Harry: ¿Qué pasa con tu marido?
María: Él sigue siendo el mismo. Yo ya sé que nunca va a cambiar.
Harry: ¿Entonces por qué no le dejas?
María: ¿Es que no comprendes que le quiero?[12]

Since in the new version there is neither lover nor pregnancy, her new claim that 'he is never going to change' could mean that she acknowledges that he will never give her a child, but she will still always love him. Then the fact that he murders her becomes incomprehensible, unless we are expected to believe that it is because of his frustration at his impotence that he kills her, as if this were a more reasonable cause. It is also remarkable that, in the censors' effort to protect the Spanish female character's reputation, they took the trouble of manipulating the sound effect track as well: in the dubbed version you can only hear one gunshot, not two, definitely killing off any remote suggestion that there had been a lover.

But that was not all. Once the film had been dubbed according to the Spanish moral standards, the advertising material sent over by the North American producers also proved to be unacceptable for local authorities, since it showed María being embraced from behind by a stranger, an image that would unsuitably represent a Spanish woman internationally. Not in Spain. The official iconography was also modified, as dialogue and sound effects before it: the male figure was removed from

---

12   Harry: What about your husband?
     María: He is still the same. I know that he is never going to change.
     Harry: Then why don't you leave him?
     María: Don't you understand that I love him?

the Spanish poster and, in the process, María's dress was re-tailored in order to prevent it from being so revealing.

As we have seen, the Hispanic archetype was represented according to the Hollywood master narrative with a recurrent combination of features that would facilitate the decoding of the audience to the extent that the first scene in which the representative character appeared would automatically set the standards. Negative characteristics such as sexual availability, untruthfulness, theft and 'hot blood' were automatically adscribed, with the intervention of the white male Anglo-Saxon as the only possibility for the Hispanic characters of redemption once he had verified their 'good nature'.

The Francoist censorship, on the other hand, would struggle to modify the verbal and even the visual content of the Hollywood film productions so as to upturn the negative Spanish archetyping and transform it into a virtuous representation according to their own moral standards, a concern which was not present when other communities were derogatorily portrayed, not even other nationalities included under the same generalising term of 'Hispanic'. As a concluding remark, it would probably be worthy of analysis from an advertising perspective if the hypothetically flattering slogan 'The World's Most Beautiful Animal' found in the source culture poster of *The Barefoot Contessa* could also be read as the lowest form of stereotyping: the animalisation of the foreigner. Ava Gardner played several ethnic parts during the 50s and 60s once she had left the United States never to go back, and this brand sentence stuck with her far beyond María Vargas. One wonders if a similar advertising strategy would have been applied if she had settled in Hollywood playing white Caucasian parts.

Faulty Archetypes: The European Spaniard and Derivations
Popular actors emigrating from and to Spain were a huge publicity stunt for a politically, economically and socially isolated Franco regime, an unusual event that had to be exploited because the norm was the massive immigration of unskilled Spanish labour to other European countries such as France, Germany, Switzerland and England. As for this last destination, Bravo-Moreno points out: 'The UK had an economic demand for cheap labour in the 1950s and 1960s, and this facilitated the entry of unskilled and semi-skilled workers from Spain with little regard for the work and economic conditions of the immigrants' (Bravo-Moreno 2006: 155), a reality very far away from the Hollywood stardust the dictatorship was foregrounding in its propagandistic media.

In Western Europe, the archetypical perception of the average Spaniard was based on issues such as the shortage of money, poor education and subservient attitude that were appreciated in the immigrants arriving in these richer countries. Concerning stereotypical screen representations, the most important European cultural communicator in this discipline, Great Britain, would eventually produce what still remains the iconographic referent of an unskilled Spanish migrant worker in Europe: Manuel, the

clumsy waiter working at a Brighton hotel in the television series *Fawlty Towers* (1975; 1979). If we take at face value Berg's summary of the Latino stereotype, '-simple-minded; -cannot master standard English; -and childishly regresses into emotionali-ty' (Berg 2004: 214), Manuel[13] would fit in perfectly, as he is extremely clumsy in his naivety, he is hopeless at understanding or learning the English language, and he over-reacts with bouts of joy or sadness at the consequences of his actions. As well as that, other characteristics blown out of proportion by the Hollywood industry also prevailed internationally two decades later.

Most Spanish migrant workers travelled abroad on their own and worked long hours in order to make money to support themselves and to send their savings to the families they had left back home. This situation is reflected in the third episode of the first season, *The Wedding Party*, when Manuel, a lone migrant, exaggeratedly express-es his gratitude to the owner of the hotel, Basil Fawlty, for having given him an um-brella as a birthday present and, on the whole, for what Manuel perceives as generosity towards him 'since coming here from Spain, leaving my five brothers and four sisters' [08:04]. The comic effect is produced by the obvious perception that Basil is not gener-ous at all with anybody, far less with Manuel. As Bartley points out, 'he views Manuel not as someone who may learn something from him but as a hindrance, someone who

---

13   Interestingly, this part was played by Andrew Sachs, another British actor of German origin whose
      accented English would prove very useful to portray different nationalities.

does not belong but is useful because he is cheap' (Bartley 2007: 7); Basil is exploiting him and being thanked for it. Later on in the episode, when Manuel comes back drunk to the hotel at night after celebrating his birthday on his own, he insists on his gratitude towards Basil 'since I came here from Spain, leaving my five mothers and four aunties' [16:00]. This effective comical reference to a perceived cliché related to the 'Spanish' might, however, also be suggesting yet again that those affected by this archetypical perception are using it dishonestly for their own advantage.

Basil is satirised as a British imperialist, conservative, xenophobic and prurient, and the audience is not expected to identify with him; in fact, it is his wife, Sybil, and the waitress, Polly, who are far more suitable representations of the point of view of the spectator. But when Basil degrades Manuel constantly, seeing himself so vastly superior, we understand him because the Spaniard's clumsiness is so extreme. In the very first episode, *A Touch of Class*, Basil felt in the need of justifying the erratic attitude of his worker in front of a customer, and uttered a facetious remark that became widely popular in Great Britain in order to imply incompetence and stupidity: 'We're teaching him. He is from Barcelona' [07:18].

When *Fawlty Towers*' rights were acquired in Spain after the end of the second season, Franco's strict censorhip had disappeared after his death, so a negative issue concerning Spanish identity would not be systematically modified any more. But the broadcasting of this series would technically pose an obvious translation problem if, once dubbed, they were all speaking the same language, since one of its most effective comical resources was the interlinguistic misunderstandings which often resulted in puns. A modification was therefore required in Manuel's nationality to render the dialogues coherent: he was an Italian waiter, Paolo, in the first episode of the series broadcasted on the second channel of Televisión Española on 3 February 1981. That day the Spanish audience heard Basil apologise to his customer saying: 'Le estamos enseñando. Es de Nápoles.'

Three years later, the Catalan channel TV3 started broadcasting regularly in its own language, and they also bought the rights for *Fawlty Towers*, whose first episode would be aired on 26 June 1986. Technically there was not a linguistic problem here because, after the dubbing process (also the norm for interlinguistic mediation in Catalonia and other Spanish autonomic communities with a language of their own), everybody would be speaking Catalan except Manuel. However, what was not so politically acceptable (even though it was linguistically possible) for Catalan television was that a character who came from Barcelona would not speak the local language, so a modification was required and, in the Catalan version, Basil's apology became: 'No és d'aquí. Es de Jalisco.'

Consequently, an analysis of the translation strategies implemented by Spanish and Catalan televisions for the dubbing of *Fawlty Towers* has to go beyond the linguistic content and tackle the cultural implications of the choices involved. In the same way as the Spanish character from Barcelona was being derided on British television, the dubbing process necessarily had to follow the same pattern, modifying the content accordingly to the nationality chosen in order to make the reception coherent, especially when culture specific items were involved. For instance, in the second episode of the first season, *The Builders*, Basil was away and had left Manuel in charge of reception, so when a delivery man arrived, chaos ensued:

> Delivery man: Where's the boss?
> Manuel: Boss is, er... Oh! I boss!
> Delivery man: No, no, where's the real boss?
> Manuel: ¿Qué?
> Delivery man: The... the Generalísimo.
> Manuel: In Madrid! [08:35]

This reference to Franco by means of his military rank would generate no ideological constraints in the 1980s in Spain (they were making enough fun of the deceased dictator within the country itself), but, having changed Manuel's nationality, translation adjustments had to be made. Catalan television used the same term, since it was also common in Mexico to determine the highest rank in the army. Manuel's answer, replacing 'In Madrid!' with '¡Está muerto!'[14] could, however, seem inadequate, since it is not applied in Mexico to any specific individual in the same way as it is to Franco in Spain. Spanish television made a different choice altogether:

> Delivery man: ¿Dónde está el capo?
> Paolo: En Palermo.

The British reference to the Spanish fascist regime could have been conveyed with an equivalent allusion to the Italian fascist regime, the only difference being that Franco was still alive when this episode was broadcast in Great Britain, whereas Mussolini had died in 1945. However, replacing it with a reference to the Mafia would bring forward another brand of national archetype, the linking of Italy with the organised-crime syndicate, a delicate issue for a country which has also raised complaints for the way they are portrayed by the Hollywood industry. This cultural translation choice could prove, then, that victims of universal stereotyping are also capable of inflicting it upon others. In any case, Spanish television cancelled *Fawlty Towers* after broadcasting only two episodes, and no official reasons were given for the cancellation. Many years later this dubbing has been recovered for the DVD edition.

There was definitely no consideration for the Spanish character in the original British context, with derision piling up episode after episode. The second season only got more intense as far as negative stereotyping was concerned. In *The Psychiatrist*, for instance, Manuel dropped a tray after being hit by Basil, and he again justified himself in front of the hotel guests: '[Basil]: I'm afraid that Spanish ape... sorry... person... bungled it again. Dago bird brain! God knows how they ever got an Armada together!' [22:04]. The animalisation of the Spanish character drags him to a new low in this series. Basil also includes a term taken from derogatory slang which originated in the United States to refer to Hispanic immigrants (it derives from the Spanish forename

---

14 'He is dead!'

Diego), and there is also a very convenient historical reference to the Spanish Armada, since they were defeated by the English army in the sixteenth century. Spanish and Catalan televisions necessarily had to make some adjustments:

> Basil: Pero a ese mono italiano, perdón, botones se le ha caído la bandeja. Inútiles. No me extraña que cayera tan pronto el Imperio Romano.[15]
> Basil: El mico aquest, la persona, aquest foraster és un desastre! Cervell de mosca! No sé por qué venen a treballar aquí![16]

The Spanish translation replaces the reference to the Spanish Armada for the easily recognisable Roman Empire, and at the same time produces a comically effective etymological figure with 'fall', suitably establishing a connection between the visual incident with the tray and the historical event, though, as Sanderson remarks, many academics still 'question whether translation is an appropriate term to be used when we are describing how a culture specific item has been erased from the TT or a foreign language is replaced by another'[17] (Sanderson 2009: 132). The Catalan version also erases but does not replace the historical reference, and it does not relate the animalisation to the nationality by name either, but the rejection of migrants, absent in the original and made up for the dubbed Catalan version with 'I don't know why they come to work here!', was and still is a very sensitive issue in the region with the highest migrant population in Spain.

It could be argued that bigoted Basil berates other nationalities throughout the two seasons of the series. Probably the most famous line in the history of television, 'Don't mention the war!', was uttered by Basil in the final episode of the first season, *The Germans*, to express his concern that the utterly hated but economically convenient tourists of this nationality might feel insulted in any way during their stay at the hotel. Even English-speaking tourists, Americans and Australians, were also victims of Basil's improper conduct. The main difference, however, is that all these national characters are presented as clever and well-educated, very much unlike Manuel.

Morgan points out about the British labour market in the 50s and 60s that: 'There was a visible European labour hierarchy, in which French and Germans were more likely to be highly skilled and in the non-manual occupations. In contrast, workers from the Southern tier of EU countries (Spain, Portugal, Italy, Greece) are over-represented in manual employment' (Morgan 2008: 142). This hierarchy was definitely maintained in the 70s as far as screen stereotyping is concerned. Manuel belonged to a different league altogether, of which we can also find other representatives in the series. For instance, in the fifth episode of the first season, *Gourmet Night,* Basil has employed Kurt, a Greek cook who feels sexually attracted to Manuel. As the latter rejects his advances, it provokes such an emotional crisis in the Greek character

---

15   'But that Italian monkey, sorry, bellboy has let his tray fall. Useless. I'm not surprised the fall of the Roman Empire came so soon.'
16   'This monkey, person, this foreigner is a disaster! They have the brains of a fly! I don't know why they come to work here.'
17   In her work on the translation of *Fawlty Towers*, she insists that 'any reference to Manuel's origins should be adapted' (Agost 2004: 75).

that it has an effect on the quality of the meals being served. Basil cannot understand what the source of the conflict is until Polly, a waitress, explains it to him. His reaction could be expected:

> Basil: I knew it. I should never have hired a Frenchman.
> Polly: He's Greek, Mr. Fawlty.
> Basil: Greek?
> Polly: Of course.
> Basil: Well, that's even worse. I mean, they invented it. [15:08]

Basil not only shows that he cannot tell and does not care about the difference between nationalities, but also that, once they have been clarified, he can automatically come up with an archetype for every one of them, in this case, considering homosexuality a morally unacceptable and, therefore, foreign custom. He also seems to believe that all these features are interchangeable when applied to low class nationalities, and even though his prurient nature is opposed to this unruly behaviour, he is capable of making an exception if it will benefit his business. When he violently shakes Manuel blaming him for the crisis, and the latter justifies himself by explaining in his broken English that 'he want kiss me!' [16:25], Basil replies: 'Oh, what's one little kiss…'. Hispanics are considered traditionally very proud of their manhood, so Manuel feels frightfully enraged that it is put into question, whereas Basil would consider that in the bottom scales foreigners are all the same. The Italian and the Mexican characters reacted accordingly to the Greek cook's advances on Spanish and Catalan televisions.

The analysis of the stereotyping of Manuel, the Spanish waiter, in this British television series has allowed us to find some recurrent elements already mentioned when reviewing the Hispanic archetype according to Hollywood, such as the disruption of any positive features that could be adscribed to the character, historical references that foreground the intervention of the source culture, or animalisation and other derogatory strategies which, on the whole, emphasise a position of inferiority which, in *Fawlty Towers*, is basically founded on incompetence. The interesting issue here is to verify how the Spanish polysystem, systematically a target of negative stereotyping from the leading Anglo-Saxon cultural communicators, also has the ability to transfer the oppressive features imposed upon it to other nationalities following the same pattern in the translation process. The character's physical appearance and behaviour would have implied for the new cultural context a specific form of verbal expression that had to be matched by the translations, turning the Spanish waiter into an Italian or a Mexican, nationalities which have been traditionally negatively stereotyped as well. So, by assigning these features to the representatives of the communities portrayed in their dubbed versions, Spanish and Catalan televisions would be perpetuating the patronising system of the dominant culture.

Puss in Boots: Hispanic Intertextuality

In the twenty-first century, Spain has become a destination for unskilled foreign migration, whereas Spaniards who emigrate are now far more skilled and sophisticated, such as the very publicised actors Antonio Banderas, Penélope Cruz, Javier Bardem and Paz Vega, who have managed to penetrate the Hollywood establishment with a certain degree of success. Interestingly enough, before these four actors began their North American professional experience, they had all previously starred in films directed by Pedro Almodóvar, whose work now epitomises modern Spanish identity internationally, lending therefore a sense of archetypical authenticity in their transfer to Hollywood.

The first of these actors to migrate was Antonio Banderas. As Perriam remarks:

> With his move to Los Angeles in 1991 and the shooting of *The Mambo Kings* (Arnold Glimcher), a shift into English-speaking roles, and his assumption into the hyperbolic imaginary of US show business, Antonio Banderas began for a time to be the most famous of twentieth-century Spanish actors. Simultaneously he became no longer Spanish but 'Hispanic'. (Perriam 2003: 45)

Banderas has never played a Spanish part in Hollywood, mainly Mexican or South American. The most popular one, at least as far as box-office is concerned, is his contemporary portrayal of the Mexican Zorro[18] in *The Mask of Zorro* and *The Legend of Zorro* (Martin Campbell, 1998, 2005) which has generated an interesting case of Hispanic intertextuality related to a character in the *Shrek* cartoon saga, Puss in Boots, who comically evokes him, and is actually dubbed by Banderas himself in both the original and the Spanish version. This cat is clearly an alien in the Far, Far Away country of *Shrek*, presented as a non-standard English speaker because of his accent and cultural references. His first scene is in *Shrek 2* (Andrew Adamson, Kelly Asbury & Conrad Vernon, 2004) when, as a mercenary killer employed by Princess Fiona's parents to dispose of Shrek (they do not consider him a suitable fiancée for their daughter), he fails to fulfil his commitment, being caught *in fraganti* by the ogre's closest friend, Donkey. When the latter discusses with Shrek what to do with the flunky murderer, some familiar issues arise:

> Donkey: Take the sword and neuter him. Give him the Bob Barker treatment.
> Puss in Boots: Oh, no! ¡Por favor! Please! I implore you! It was nothing personal, señor. I was doing it only for my family. My mother, she is sick. And my father lives off the garbage! The King offered me much in gold and I have a litter of brothers... [33:35]

As other Hispanic characters before him, Puss in Boots deviously manipulates this positive cliché linked to his culture for his own benefit, perhaps finally proving, once and for all, that it is not grounded on solid foundations. At the same time, one should also refer to 'The Bob Barker treatment', which would tactfully imply in a film for children that Donkey is suggesting the castration of the cat. As seen above, Hispan-

---

18   Original creation of American writer Johnston McCulley, who located his adventures in nineteenth century California before the American-Mexican war.

ic males overreact when their manhood feels threatened, so their hypothetical virility could also be presented as just another myth. A final remark can be made on the
occasional inclusion of 'por favor' and 'señor', which gives a Spanish aroma, and the
uneasy syntax of 'offered me much in gold', which confirms the perception of him
as a foreigner from his very first scene, even though we can still understand everything he says in English.

The Spanish polysystem does not require a change of nationality here since there
are no interlinguistic misunderstandings: the characters generally communicate in
English with each other and, as a result, they all speak Spanish in the dubbed version.
Interestingly, however, in Spain Puss in Boots has been turned into an Andalusian, a
regional identity traditionally associated with migration within the country and beyond, and linguistically differing from the standard national language in phonemic
and prosodic features. For instance, the first of the very few utterances in Spanish included in the original version is his complaint because Shrek is leaving him behind:
'¡Eh, tú! ¡Pedazo de carne con patas! ¿Cómo te atreves a hacerme esto?'[19] [53:58]. In
the Spanish dubbed version, the first expletive, '¡Eh, tú!' has been turned into the easily recognisable Andalusian '¡Ozú!', a derivation of '¡Jesús!' which originates from a
lisp traditionally associated to the inhabitants of this region by which /s/ becomes /z/,
together with the apheresis and apocopes that archetypically imply the feature of laziness, according to which they would never make an effort to pronounce the full word.

Bravo-Moreno refers to Andalusian immigrants in her analysis of the migratory
movement in the second half of the twentieth century:

> In this period the active population of whole villages in Andalucía (the southern
> region of Spain) for example, left after the harvest to work in the vineyards and
> sugar-beet fields in France. The conditions were hard and the contracts uncertain.
> Others left to work as waiters and chambermaids in the seaside hotels of the Spanish
> Mediterranean coast. [...] The exodus had begun in the 1950s and by 1960 Andalucía
> had lost over half a million workers; by 1970 1,600,000 Andaluces were living out-
> side their native provinces; 712,000 in Barcelona alone. (Bravo-Moreno 2006: 149)

These facts should be enough basis to erase any nuance of laziness among its people,
but their condition as aliens of a lower economic scale in other regions of Spain has
traditionally made them a target of this archetyping, which also includes other characteristics such as their comic nature, their willingness to sing and dance flamenco at
any occasion, and their profound religiosity, externally manifested by devoted wor-
shippers who carry heavy statuesque images of bloody crucifixions in processions.

Antonio Banderas does come from Málaga, one of the eight Andalusian provinces, but he has hardly ever played a regional part during his acting career in Spain,
and obviously none in Hollywood. As a matter of fact, the phonemic features present in the Spanish dubbed version do not belong to the actor's natural accent, having
been created on purpose for the character. Therefore, this choice would suggest an
intention of presenting Puss in Boots as an alien in the dubbed-into-Spanish imagi-

---

19 'Hey, you! You chunk of meat with legs! How dare you do this to me!'

nary world of *Shrek*, but carrying with it important cultural implications, since the transference of the portrayal of Hispanic 'otherness' by the Hollywood master narrative to the Spanish screen would also reveal the target culture's own perception of stereotypical features associated with cultural identities within its own country: the perlocutionary act of exclusion in the source text is recreated in the target text by performing a local transformation. Interestingly, the dubbed version for Catalonia, the region which holds the highest number of Andalusian immigrants, did not apply this strategy: Puss in Boots remained a Mexican.

As for the modification of culture-specific items in order to adjust them to the new identity, one can observe that the nature of the references in a cartoon production of the twenty-first century are very different from others analysed above, perhaps a sign of the commodification of the times. In *Shrek the Third* (Chris Miller and Raman Hui, 2007) we can foreground, as an interesting example, a comment of Puss in Boots' plans once the main male characters have started sailing away from the Far, Far Away country in order to look for an heir to the throne. It lacks any historical reference, but includes an easily recognisable cocktail: 'Puss in Boots: What I am talking about is you, me, my cousin's boat, an ice cold pitcher of mojitos, and two weeks of nothing but… fishing' [23:20].

In their book *Unthinking Eurocentrism. Multiculturalism and the Media*, Ella Shohat and Robert Stam remark: 'Multicultural bellies, full of tacos, felafel, and chow mein, are sometimes accompanied by monocultural minds' (Shohat/Stam 1994: 21). None of these gastronomical terms were italicised as far back as 1994, which can give an idea of their universality. Puss in Boots' original utterance could also exemplify this claim, as does the Spanish dubbing option, which replaces the 'mojitos' for an equally universally recognisable 'jarra de zangría frezquita'[20], with the local Andalusian lisping incorporated. Exotic drinks marketed worldwide would prove to be more effective as far as instant cultural decoding is concerned than distant historical references.

As a brief final note, just a remark on an interesting use of a term associated to religion in the source text that fits in suitably with the original Mexican character and is extensible to all other nationalities piled together under the term 'Hispanic'. Once they have found Artie, the unwilling heir to the throne of Far, Far Away, Puss in Boots tries to persuade him to sail back home with them, reassuring him that he will be protected by bodyguards, 'all of them willing at a moment's notice to lay down their lives out of devotion to you' [38:09]. In the Spanish dubbed version, the lexical field of 'devotion' is enhanced: 'Hombrez fielez dizpueztos a entregá la última gota de zangre por devozión a ti.'[21] The inclusion of blood, again with the archetypical lisping, clearly portrays Puss in Boots as an Andalusian who neither speaks the standard language nor has the same standard priorities as the other Spanish-speaking characters in the dubbed version of *Shrek the Third*.

---

20   'Jug of cold sangría.'
21   'Men ready to give the last drop of their blood for devotion to you.'

To sum up, the first conclusion we can reach is that the predominant Anglo-American audiovisual industry, as global cultural communicators, imposes an ethnocentrism based on its master narrative point of view, initially as an effective story-telling device but with other prominent socio-economical factors also involved, on a generalisation of differentiated and/or antagonistic cultural archetypes whose main features are presented in a position of inferiority. Migration towards the United States of America and Great Britain has only contributed to this patronising portrayal, and Spaniards as a specific nationality, or more generally included under the term of Hispanics, have been targeted with a series of features in order to fit into a stereotype that has been stabilised by means of repetition, as has happened with other national or ethnic groups.

Throughout this paper we have witnessed how the canonic universalising screen narrative has portrayed Hispanic characters stigmatised as liars, cheats, thieves or sexually incontinent, among other features, who always needed the moral guidance of the Anglo-Saxon *alter-ego* that bears the point of view of the spectator in order to redeem them for some individualised virtue, since the Hispanic as a representative of a community could not be shown as superior in any issue; if any positive cliché had survived the ferocious screen archetyping, such as tighter family bonds or virility, it had to be exposed as mere myth, and therefore false. This obsessive stereotyping attitude, however, could also reveal some degree of frustration on behalf of the master narrative transmitters.

When these audiovisual texts have reached Spain, they have been manipulated for different reasons, mainly linguistic, but also ideological, and always with choices that have unavoidably generated further cultural implications. The dubbing process, as established interlinguistic mediation system in the whole of the country, has sometimes found it necessary to either re-nationalise the Spanish characters or, at least, to adapt their lines in order to render the dialogue coherent and allow the viewing experience to be perlocutionarily equivalent to that in the source context. In a more distant period, the Francoist censorship would manipulate these films so that they adopted the propagandistic doctrine of the fascist regime concerning the idealised portrayal of Spanish men and women, very different from the similarly biased archetype that Hollywood was spreading internationally.

What has been remarkable, in any case, is that the Spanish polysystem, generally a victim of stereotyping, proves how well it can transfer this imposition on other communities, international as well as national, in order to recreate the derogatory portrayal of the Hispanic archetype in the source text using, in the examples analysed above, Italians, Mexicans and Andalusians as surrogate targets. The new cultural context, therefore, shows its own prejudice on other stereotyped groups, even sharing some negative characteristics imposed upon them by the Anglo-Saxon master communicators. A successful archetype definitely relies on the easiness with which it subsists in the collective subconscious, and many of the features presented in a distant past still seem to be living on well into the twenty-first century.

Filmography

ADAMSON, A./ASBURY, K. & C. VERNON (2004), *Shrek 2*, USA.

ALDRICH, R. (1954), *Vera Cruz*, USA.

CAMPBELL, M. (1998), *The Mask of Zorro*, USA/Germany.

CAMPBELL, M. (2005), *The Legend of Zorro*, USA.

CURTIZ, M. (1942), *Casablanca*, USA.

DAVIES, J. H. (1975), *Fawlty Towers* (Season 1), UK.

FULLER, S. (1957), *Run of the Arrow*, USA.

GLIMCHER, A. (1991), *The Mambo Kings*, France/USA.

JOHNSON, N. (1960), *The Angel Wore Red*, Italy/USA.

KING, H. (1952), *The Snows of Kilimanjaro*, USA.

KOSTER, H. (1958), *The Naked Maja*, Italy/USA/France.

LEWIN, A. (1951), *Pandora and the Flying Dutchman*, UK.

MANKIEWICZ, J. L. (1954), *The Barefoot Contessa*, USA/Italy.

MANN, A. (1956), *Serenade*, USA.

MILLER, Ch. & R. HUI (2007), *Shrek the Third*, USA.

SPIERS, B. (1979), *Fawlty Towers* (Season 2), UK.

References

AGOST, R. (2001), 'Aspectos generales de la traducción para el doblaje', in: Sanderson, J. D. (ed.), ¡*Doble o nada*! Actas de las I y II Jornadas de doblaje y subtitulación, Alicante: Universidad de Alicante.

AGOST, R. (2004), 'Translation in bilingual contexts. Different norms in dubbing translation', in: Orero, P. (ed.), *Topics in Audiovisual Translation*, Amsterdam/Philadelphia: John Benjamins, 63–82.

BARTLEY, M. (2007), ' 'Little Englander'–Fawlty Towers, a textual analysis of nationalistic ideology', in: *Networking Knowledge: Journal of the MeCCSA*. vol. 1:2, 1–13.

BERRY, S. (2004), 'Hollywood exoticism', in: Fischer, L. & M. Landy (eds.), *Stars: The Film Reader*, London: Routledge, 181–98.

BERG, Ch. R. (2002), *Latino Images in Film: Stereotypes, Subversion, & Resistance*, Austin/Texas: Texas U.P.

BERG, Ch. R. (2004), 'A crash course on Hollywood Latino imagery', in: Schatz, T. (ed.), *Hollywood: Cultural Dimensions: Ideology, Identity and Cultural Industry Studies*, London: Routledge, 211–224.

BRAVO-MORENO, A. (2006), *Migration, Gender and National Identity: Spanish Migrant Women in London*, Bern: Lang.

CHAUME, F. (2004), *Cine y traducción*, Madrid: Cátedra.

DANCYGER, K. & J. RUSH (2007), *Alternative Scriptwriting: Successfully Breaking the Rules*, London: Focal Press.

GUBERN, R. & D. FONT (1975), *Un cine para el cadalso. 40 años de censura cinematográfica en España*, Barcelona: Euros.

MALTBY, R. (2003), *Hollywood Cinema*, Oxford: Blackwell.

MORGAN, T. (2008), 'Spaniards in the UK – A successful female post-industrial migration', in: Ryan, L. & W. Webster (eds.), *Gendering Migration: Masculinity, Femininity and Ethnicity in Post-war Britain*, Aldershot/Hampshire: Ashgate, 137–152.

PERRIAM, Ch. (2003), *Stars and Masculinities in Spanish Cinema: From Banderas to Bardem*, Oxford: Oxford U.P.

RODRÍGUEZ, C. (2008), *Heroes, Lovers and Others: The Story of Latinos in Hollywood*, Oxford: Oxford U.P.

SANDERSON, J. D. (2009), 'Strategies for the dubbing of puns with one visual semantic layer', in: Díaz-Cintas, J. (ed.), *New Trends in Audiovisual Translation*, Bristol: Multilingual Matters, 123–132.

SHAW, D. (2007), "You are alright, but…': Individual and collective representations of Mexicans, Latinos, Anglo-Americans and African-Americans in Steven Soderbergh's *Traffic*', in: Codell, J. F. (ed.), *Genre, Gender, Race, and World Cinema*, Oxford: Blackwell, 342–357.

SHOHAT, E. & R. STAM (1994), *Unthinking Eurocentrism. Multiculturalism and the Media*, London: Routledge.

VASEY, R. (1992), 'Foreign parts: Hollywood's global distribution and the representation of ethnicity', in: *American Quarterly* 44:4, 617–642.

III. Polyglot Narratives of Migrant Communities in France

Back to the Future?
Language Use in Films
by Second-Generation North Africans in France

Alec G. Hargreaves/Leslie Kealhofer

Compared with states such as Spain and Italy, which until the 1980s were known as countries of emigration rather than of immigration, France is relatively unusual in that mass immigration from outside Europe, most notably French North Africa, pre-dates the end of empire and grew rapidly following the independence of Algeria in 1962. By the 1970s, settled minorities of North African origin, including members of a new generation born in France, were becoming visible in many French cities. They were initially seen relatively little on cinema screens, except in low budget productions by majority ethnic French directors or film-makers whose formative years had been spent in North Africa, but in the 1980s young directors from among the second generation of North Africans in France attracted considerable attention as exponents of what became known as 'Beur' cinema.[1] This label exemplified the complex cultural dynamics which shaped their work, within which the languages and cultures of migrants occupied a secondary position compared with the national language of the country of settlement. The first wave of these films, starting with Mehdi Charef's *Le Thé au harem d'Archimède* (1985), focuses on the experiences of second-generation North Africans growing up in France. As we will highlight in the first part of our analysis, the language use of the first-generation characters – in Arabic or heavily accented French – serves to underscore the extent to which the second-generation protagonists are rooted in the dominant language and cultural

---

1   See the special issues of *Cinématographe*, no. 112, July 1985: 'Cinéma beur' and of *CinémAction*, no. 56, July 1990: 'Cinémas métis: de Hollywood aux films beurs'. The word 'Beur' was a neologism coined in the 1970s by second-generation North Africans tired of the negative connotations that often attached to the word 'Arabe' in popular discourse in France. Using a form of French backslang known as *verlan*, they inverted and partially truncated the syllables of 'Arabe' to form the self-valorising designation 'Beur', meaning second-generation North African. This re-designation of self began with an ethnic marker from outside France but reworked it through a form of slang that was part of the French language, a language that second-generation North Africans generally spoke far better than the mother tongues of their migrant parents, i.e. Arabic or Tamazight (Berber).

norms of France.[2] We will see in the second part of our analysis the ways in which the focus of a significant number of subsequent films by second-generation directors shifts to the experiences of first-generation North Africans – the generation of the directors' (and many of the actors') parents, as evidenced by Yamina Benguigui's three-part documentary *Mémoires d'immigrés* (1997), Bourlem Guerdjou's *Vivre au paradis* (1998), Benguigui's *Inch'Allah dimanche* (2001), and Rachid Bouchareb's *Indigènes* (2006). We will endeavour to show how variations in the use of the French and Arabic languages in these films serve to elucidate the particular struggles that members of the first generation faced upon their arrival in France and in the years that followed. In these films, the directors shift the cinematographic spotlight onto the generation of their parents, and in doing so bring new perspectives to bear on the Arabic language. In the final part of our analysis, we will show how the use of language in both the early and subsequent films also reflects gendered differences, highlighting the very different experiences and challenges lived by first-generation men and women respectively.

Language, Identity, and Cultural Ties

For the protagonists in early films directed by second-generation North Africans such as Mehdi Charef, Rachid Bouchareb and Malik Chibane, the question of language was scarcely an issue. The young men at the centre of these films – it was not until later that young women gained significant attention – felt in an almost literal sense at home in the French language and demonstrated their confidence in the use of it by peppering their speech with slang and neologisms. If this sometimes made their speech difficult for majority ethnic viewers to fully comprehend, the effect was not so much to exoticise (or mark as foreign) this new generation but rather to position them as a sub-culture or sub-class within French society. It is true, however, that this sub-class was – and is – heavily marginalised and that it often lacks the cultural capital inherited by more affluent parts of French society. We are reminded of this, for example, in the sequence which gives Charef's *Le Thé au harem d'Archimède* its title [01:14:51–01:16:04]. In this scene, a high school student of North African origin, Balou, is asked to write on the blackboard in French the name of Archimedes' principle, 'le théorème d'Archimède'. Instead, he writes the near-homophone 'le thé au harem d'Archimède' (tea in the harem of Archimedes). It is not completely clear if this is a mistake or a deliberate word-play on the part of the student. The most likely explanation is that it is a mistake – one that reflects his ignorance of the mathematical formula and its Greek origins – but not, it should be noted, ignorance of the French language. Moreover, even if Balou is not wholly in control of the cross-cultural currents at work in this scene, it is clear that the writer-director, Charef, is very much in control, even using the title of the movie to play with the expectations

---

2   Although a significant proportion of first-generation Maghrebis in France speak Tamazight (often referred to as Berber) rather than Arabic, in the films discussed here there is little, if any, use of Tamazight.

of the viewer in a very deliberate fashion. Instead of an alluringly exoticised Other of the kind conjured up by notions of sipping tea in a harem, Charef presents us from the opening scene onwards with almost the exact opposite: a dead-end world of social disadvantage located on the lowest rungs of French society in distressed urban spaces known as the *banlieues*. Furthermore, we are repeatedly shown that the foreign origins of Madjid, the main character of North African origin, are of only secondary importance compared with the social disadvantages which place him on par with his buddy and co-protagonist Pat, a working class youth of French origin with whom he shares in a life of unemployment, poor housing and petty crime.[3] Pat and Madjid also share the same colloquial French, heavily peppered with street slang.

In contrast with their son, who despite his social marginalisation appears perfectly at ease in the French language, Madjid's parents appear verbally disadvantaged. His father's communication is limited to gestures and non-verbal sounds following an industrial accident which has left him permanently disabled. His mother, Malika, speaks heavily accented French and when overcome by emotion often switches into Arabic – a language that Madjid understands but does not speak. Despite the fact that Madjid's linguistic and cultural ties are clearly stronger with France, Malika considers her son to be Algerian and thinks that a trip to Algeria to do his military service there will straighten him out: 'Madjid, mon fils, je suis épuisée. Je vais demander au Consulat de t'emmener au bled. Faire ton service militaire. Tu connaîtras ton pays. Tu apprendras ta langue et tu deviendras un homme… c'est la seule solution'[4] [01:17:53–01:18:26]. The idea that Madjid would need to learn about 'his' country, Algeria, and learn (presumably to speak and perhaps to write) Arabic, 'his' language, in practice underscores the distance separating him from Malika's roots. Playing on this distance, Madjid deliberately tries to provoke his mother at one point by telling her, in French, that he does not understand her when she speaks in Arabic.

While Malika clearly considers herself to be Algerian first and foremost, this is not to say that she establishes no ties of her own to France. She in fact develops important relationships with her majority ethnic female neighbours, with whom she speaks French. As is the case for Madjid and Pat, it is their socially disadvantaged class that first brings Malika and these women together. In two notable scenes, Malika even steps in to help these women, first physically rescuing her neighbour, Madame Leveque, from domestic violence at the hands of her drunken husband, and later convincing her friend Josette not to commit suicide as she is preparing to jump off her balcony.

Le Thé au harem d'Archimède may be seen as in many ways as a template for numerous subsequent films depicting the North-African minority in France, commonly located in the *banlieues* (suburbs) and often featuring characters from other eth-

---

3   Unlike Pat, however, Madjid is also the victim of racial discrimination, for example at the local job agency, which further reduces his chances of finding a job or professional training that interests him.

4   'Madjid, my son, I'm exhausted. I'm going to ask the Consulate to send you home to do your military service. You'll get to know your country. You'll learn your language and you'll become a man… it's the only solution.'

nic backgrounds alongside those of North-African origin, suggesting that what they share as members of a quasi-underclass on the margins of French society is more important than any cultural or ethnic divisions. By the mid-1990s, this template had become so familiar that majority ethnic directors began using it, most famously in Mathieu Kassovitz's *La Haine* (1995), which pits a *Black-Blanc-Beur* (Black, White and 'Beur') trio of young male protagonists in head-on confrontations with members of the French police, seen as representatives of an exclusionary and repressive social order. The critical and box office success of Kassovitz's film helped to change the dominant paradigm in which cinematic representations of minority ethnic groups were articulated. It became less common to speak of 'Beur' cinema and increasingly common to speak of 'banlieue' cinema (Jousse 1995; Videau 1995). Yet almost simultaneously, many 'Beur' film-makers were turning their attention in different directions, partly out of fear that the *banlieues* might become a cinematic and not just a social dead-end and partly out of concern to address issues which they felt had been unduly neglected. Among the latter were the experiences of generations of North Africans who had preceded them as migrants in France, and before that as colonial subjects on the other side of the Mediterranean. As we will see, this shift of focus towards earlier generations was accompanied by a new audibility of Arabic.

Shifting the Spotlight to the First Generation

The cinematographic shift in focus from the second generation to the first generation of North Africans in France was ushered in most obviously by a critical and commercial success, Yamina Benguigui's three-part documentary series, *Mémoires d'immigrés* (1997), which gained wide audiences first on French television, then in movie theatres and in video cassette and DVD formats. The title of the documentary series ('Migrant Memories') and the decision to devote the first two of the three parts – titled 'Les Pères' ('Fathers') and 'Les Mères' ('Mothers') – to migrants, with the final part representing their children, reflected this shift in the centre of gravity. Whereas, in *Le Thé au harem d'Archimède*, the seemingly exotic language practices of migrants serve to underscore the cultural Frenchness of their children, in *Mémoires d'immigrés* the attentiveness of the younger generation (implicitly represented by Benguigui) towards the experiences of their parents encourages the viewer to look beyond language differences and listen to the substance of what is being recounted rather than the manner of its telling. Furthermore, Benguigui edited out her own voice in all of the interviews in order to ensure that the viewer concentrates solely on the migrants' experiences and voices. According to Sylvie Durmelat, Benguigui 'chose to erase signs of her presence, both on the screen and on the sound track, in order to privilege what her interviewees have to say. This, in conjunction with the absence of a guiding voice-over commentary and the relative paucity of insert titles, reinforces the impact of the speakers' voices' (Durmelat 2000: 180).

A similar process of shifting the focus to the migrant experience is at work in Bourlem Guerdjou's feature film *Vivre au paradis* (1998), which was released at almost the same time as *Mémoires d'immigrés*. *Vivre au paradis* recounts the story of Lakhdar, an Algerian immigrant worker, whose wife Nora and their children come to join him in France during the Algerian war of independence. The fact that the film focuses almost exclusively on the experiences of first-generation protagonists is all the more striking when the film version of *Vivre au paradis* is compared with the book on which the movie is based, an autobiographical narrative published by Brahim Benaïcha in 1992.[5] Benaïcha's text, like many previous narratives by second-generation North Africans, is firmly focused on the experiences of young people of immigrant origin growing up in France, with migrant parents occupying only secondary roles. The film adaptation, directed by another second-generation Algerian, Guerdjou, radically shifts the focal point away from his own generation to that of the parents (Hargreaves 2000: 347).

Moreover, the native tongue of the older generation – Arabic – is given a prominence in the movie that has no counterpart in Benaïcha's text. For example, the film opens with a group of migrant workers, among them Lakhdar, awakening in the hut which they share in a shantytown on the outskirts of Paris. The sporadic dialogue between the men in this scene takes place in Arabic, subtitled in French. If this, together with their grim surroundings, is liable to mark them as alien in the eyes of majority ethnic viewers, it also gives them a certain dignity because they are not placed in the position of speaking in an imperfectly acquired language to interlocutors occupying positions of strength in the majority ethnic culture. At the same time, it also sets up the viewer for a shock when a caption reveals that this shantytown is actually in France, and scarcely a stone's throw from Paris: '1960, Nanterre, à 3 kms de Paris'[6] [03:18–03:24].

The Arabic language functions differently in another film that focuses on a group of colonial subjects: Rachid Bouchareb's *Indigènes* (2006), which recounts the story of four North-African colonial soldiers, Abdelkader, Messaoud, Saïd, and Yassir (played by four second-generation Maghrebis) fighting for France during the Second World War. The commitment of artists of Maghrebi origin to the revalorisation of Arabic is apparent not only on-screen but also in the fact that one of the four leading actors, Samy Naceri, who had lost almost all competence in the language, had to relearn it in order to play the part of Yassir (Allociné, n.d.). Unlike the other films that we have examined, which are set almost entirely in France, the first scenes of *Indigènes* take place in North Africa.[7] In the opening sequence, using Arabic subtitled in French, a village leader rallies the men of his village to join the war effort in support of the French: 'Il faut libérer la France de l'occupation allemande. Allez!

5   Brahim Benaïcha (1992), *Vivre au paradis: d'une oasis à un bidonville*. Paris: Desclée de Brouwer.
6   '1960, Nanterre, 3 kilometres from Paris.'
7   Another film which we will examine below, *Inch'Allah dimanche* (2001), begins in North Africa, just as the protagonist, Zouina, is about to board the boat leaving for France with her children and mother-in-law.

Venez avec moi! Il faut laver le drapeau français avec notre sang'[8] [02:37–02:45]. This scene sets the stage for key themes examined in the course of the film: the role of colonial soldiers in the French army, on the one hand, and questions of justice and injustice, on the other.

Code-switching functions in *Indigènes* as a means of highlighting the particular injustices inherent in both the colonial army and the colonial system in general. We see this, for example, when a high-ranking French official delivers a speech to the troops before they leave Italy for France: 'Le rêve... se matérialise enfin. Vos blessures, vos souffrances, tant de peine... bientôt nous verrons la France, la mère patrie. Nous rentrons chez nous!'[9] [30:12–30:32]. This officer's uplifting discourse glosses over the injustices that this scene – and the film in a larger sense – ultimately bring to the fore: the colonial subjects fighting for the 'mère patrie' are at the same time shown to be being systematically discriminated against by it. As a result, grandiloquence in French becomes implicitly associated with injustice.

When the colonial troops first arrive in France, their experiences – and their exchanges in the French language – initially appear very positive in nature. They receive a hero's welcome in Marseilles, where Messaoud falls in love with a French woman, Irène, and even decides that he wants to make a life for himself in France, which appears to offer personal equality of a kind that is denied to colonial subjects in Algeria. The crossing of ethnic boundaries that is taboo in Algeria – 'Dans mon pays, on ne va pas avec les femmes françaises'[10] [37:34–37:38], Messaoud tells Irène – appears initially to be possible in France. In the end, however, the love affair between Messaoud and Irène is destined to fail because of discrimination that is endemic in the institutional structures of France, which are shown to be the source of (rather than an antidote to) colonial injustice in North Africa. After his unit moves on from Marseilles, Messaoud's letters are intercepted and blocked by French army censors, so that Irène does not receive them and wrongly concludes that her love for Messaoud is not reciprocated. The army thus directly intervenes in order to prevent Messaoud, a colonial subject, from using the French language to pursue a personal relationship with the French citizen with whom he has fallen in love. In this way, the institutional manipulation of French becomes emblematic of the duplicitous nature of the colonial system as a whole, promising equality while constantly denying it.

Among the main characters, it is Abdelkader who believes most ardently in the discourse of assimilation, by which he too will be shown finally to have been duped. We first encounter him studying in an army class, convinced that an education in French will enable him to rise through the ranks in line with France's long-standing promise of liberty, equality and fraternity. In practice, he witnesses and person-

---

8   'We must liberate France from German occupation. Let's go! Come with me! We must wash the French flag with our blood.'
9   'The dream... is finally coming true. Your wounds, your suffering, so many difficulties... soon we will see France, the motherland. We're going home!'
10   'In my country, we don't go out with French women.'

ally experiences a constant stream of injustices, including an admission that, contrary to official rhetoric, colonial subjects will never be granted army promotions on an equal footing with French citizens. Half way through the film, Nazi airplanes drop leaflets over a forest in Eastern France in which Abdelkader's unit, poorly equipped for the harsh weather conditions, is stationed. The leaflets – written in Arabic and addressed to the 'soldat musulman' ('Muslim soldier') – call upon France's colonial soldiers to desert, arguing that they are being exploited and sacrificed by the French army, which by this stage in the film we know to be true. The pamphlets, read out to his comrades by Abdelkader, the only one among them able to read Arabic, declare 'L'Allemagne te donnera ta liberté. L'heure de l'indépendance a sonné pour l'Afrique'[11] [57:50–57:57]. The German position vis-à-vis French colonial North Africa is of course anything but altruistic in nature, but the key point in this scene is the emergence of the question of independence which, significantly, is formulated in Arabic. While seemingly tempted by the prospect of independence as an alternative route to emancipation, Abdelkader persuades his comrades to continue fighting for the liberation of France, arguing that their courage will force the French to make good their promises. All except Abdelkader will perish in battle. Sixty years later, in the final scenes of the movie, he will be shown to have remained the victim of colonial injustices that have persisted even beyond the formal end of French rule overseas. By now Abdelkader is an aging immigrant worker living in a rundown hostel in France separated from his family in Algeria because this is the only way he can draw his army pension at the full rate. A final caption informs the audience that since independence former colonial soldiers living in North Africa and other territories formerly ruled by France have received pensions worth only a fraction of those paid to the French citizens at whose side they fought.[12]

French, Arabic, and Representing Gendered Experiences

In the first part of this chapter, we suggested that the use of language in early 'Beur' films such as Le Thé au harem d'Archimède underscores the fact that 'Beur' youths such as Madjid are culturally and linguistically tied to France, whereas their parents' cultural roots are still firmly grounded in their home country. We then examined the way in which subsequent films directed by members of the second generation shifted the focus of their films to the experiences of first-generation Maghrebis in France. As we will see in the final part of our analysis, the interplay of the French and Arabic languages in certain films also highlights the experiences of first-generation North Africans along specifically gendered lines. That is to say that the French and Arabic languages very often do not function in the same way in the films with regard to the experiences of first-generation men and women, respectively. We see this

---

11   'Germany will give you your liberty. The hour of independence has sounded for Africa.'
12   The only way for former colonial subjects to receive army pensions at the full rate was by residing in France, which in most cases was impossible. The injustices of this system were finally addressed by President Chirac after he viewed Indigènes in 2006 (Hargreaves 2007: 204).

clearly, for example, in Benguigui's documentary *Mémoires d'immigrés*, which consists primarily of interviews with migrants and children of migrants, together with – especially in the first part, dealing with those categorised as 'fathers' – a significant amount of archive footage. All of the migrants interviewed, male and female, speak in French, often heavily accented (and sometimes subtitled to facilitate comprehension), but at times some of the women – never the men – switch to Arabic (with subtitles in French). Because they are speaking to an unseen and unheard co-ethnic interviewer (Benguigui, the daughter of an Algerian migrant worker) in whose company they appear relaxed, the language in which they speak does not feature as a marker of ethnic distance in a way comparable to that seen in earlier films, such as *Le Thé au harem d'Archimède*. In many ways, especially in the case of the 'fathers', the language in which they choose to speak actually shows their own close connectedness to France. It is notable that all of the 'fathers' whose interviews are included in the documentary – as well as all of the migrant men that Benguigui chose to present through the use of archive footage – speak exclusively in French. In addition, a significant number of these men comment specifically on the fact that they wanted to learn to read and write the French language, for various reasons: for most, in order to communicate and defend themselves in the work place; for others, to contribute to rebuilding Algeria upon their (planned) return. The importance of learning French is reinforced by clips of archive footage inserted between different interviews conducted by Benguigui, in which several of the men are even being interviewed *during* French literacy classes. Benguigui's choice to include interviews in which the 'fathers' speak exclusively in French emphasises the ways in which the 'fathers' she interviews have become rooted in France, making it misleading to think of them simply or even primarily as migrant workers.[13] This is highlighted with particular clarity by the last of the men to be interviewed, Hamou Goumed, who explains that he has been connected to France throughout the various stages of his life: 'Ma vie s'est toujours passée avec les Français, comme le travail, comme l'armée, comme civil'[14] [39:05–39:19]. He even prefers to remain in France instead of permanently moving back to Algeria with his wife and children; and he states that when he does travel to Algeria for vacation, 'quand ça ne me plaît pas, je reviens ici'[15] [43:24–43:27].

In a similar way, the languages that the 'mothers' speak in the second part of the documentary do not serve as a means to underscore ethnic difference but instead serve to bring the viewer into the intimacy of the women's experiences. While many of the men are interviewed in a work-related setting – for example in an old factory – most of the women's interviews take place within the intimacy of their home or within proxim-

---

13   Sylvie Durmelat comments on the extraordinary amount of work that went into making and editing this documentary film, which included choosing footage from 350 interviews (Durmelat 2000: 171). It seems unlikely that *none* of the 'fathers' interviewed spoke at any point in Arabic while the cameras were rolling, yet in the footage selected by Benguigui for the movie, we hear them speak exclusively in French.

14   'My life has always been spent with the French, at work, in the army, and as a civilian.'

15   'when I don't like it, I come back here.'

ity to it. In addition, all but two women are filmed in pairs, a difference that significantly alters the dynamic of their interviews as compared to those with men, who are interviewed alone, and the 'children', who in the third section of the film are interviewed
in much larger groups. While the women filmed in pairs respond to Benguigui's questions – posed in French – at times they also speak to each other. Even more significant,
however, is that when they speak to each other, they speak in Arabic. During these
brief moments, they appear to forget about the camera or at least take a step back from
it. For non-Arabic speakers watching these private moments with the aid of subtitles,
the women's use of Arabic serves not to alienate the viewer but as a kind of guarantee
of the privileged access being enjoyed at these moments in the film.

In *Vivre au Paradis*, the French and Arabic languages reflect the different struggles and challenges faced by male and female Algerian immigrants, respectively, living in a shantytown in France in the early 1960s. Against the backdrop of the mount-
ing political conflict between French and Algerian nationalism, including the events of
17 October 1961 (House/MacMaster 2006), most of the film focuses on events among
the Algerian migrant population, and most centrally on tensions between the two protagonists, Lakhdar and Nora. These tensions evolve throughout the film, and the characters' use of language serves as a lens through which we can understand the changing
dynamics within the couple, on the one hand, and between the individual characters and the Algerian community, on the other. The use of Arabic in scenes between
Lakhdar and Nora endows them with a sense of intimacy that is seldom found in earlier representations of migrants by second-generation North Africans. At the same time,
however, the languages that they use in other contexts reflect a growing rift between
them. Lakhdar's use of the French language reflects in many ways his attempt to assimilate into French culture in order to improve his family's situation and move them
out of the shantytown. For example, he is confident that if he fulfils the necessary financial requirements and completes the necessary forms, he will secure an apartment
for his family. When he tells his Algerian friend, Rachid (with whom he speaks almost
entirely in French throughout the film), that he has put in an application for an apartment, Rachid scoffs at him: 'Une demande? Tu crois que ça suffit une demande? On
n'est rien nous ici'[16] [06:32–06:38]. Lakhdar, however, believes that the French system
is one in which the people who succeed are those willing to adapt to it: 'On n'est rien
parce qu'on ne veut pas changer. Moi je vais trouver un appartement'[17] [06:38–06:41].
As the film goes on, however, and Lakhdar's application is denied, his initial confidence turns into disappointment and frustration, which in turn motivates him to try to
scrape together enough money to acquire an apartment via means which have the effect of distancing him from his compatriots. In one memorable scene, he takes posses-
sion of a piece of land in the shantytown – a space used by another couple for storage
and to hang their laundry – and builds another shack there with the intention of sell-

---

16   'An application? You think that an application is all that's needed? We're nothing here.'
17   'We're nothing because we do not want to change. I'm going to find an apartment.'

ing it to an Algerian acquaintance. When this man is not able to pay in full, however, Lakhdar refuses to give him the shack until he completes the payment with his wife's jewels – jewels taken directly off her body during this scene. At several moments during the film, Lakhdar even tries to avoid paying dues to support the Algerian independence movement, since it takes away from the money needed to pay for the apartment.

The Arabic language, instead of betokening solidarity between Lakhdar and his compatriots, serves increasingly to mark his selfish reflexes. Lakhdar shows his true colours when he speaks in Arabic. His discourse in that language is at times quite malicious, which appears all the more shocking to the extent that it is directed against fellow Algerians. For example, when addressing the couple mentioned above, Lakhdar initially tells them, in French, of his intention to build a shack on the space of land that they had been using. When the other man says that it is not possible, Lakhdar slips impatiently into Arabic, snapping at his compatriot in harsh tones: 'Écoute. Enlève ces ordures ou je les fous sur ton toit!'[18] [01:03:29–01:03:33]. The man then also replies in Arabic, expressing his surprise at Lakhdar's tone of voice and behaviour: 'Tu me parles comme ça?'[19] [01:03:33–01:03:35]. The transition into Arabic, which remains Lakhdar's spontaneous language of expression, highlights the selfishness driving his attempts to put down roots in France. Rachid's condemnation of Lakhdar's behaviour and changing mentality is equally revealing, as he tells him in French: 'Tu n'as rien à foutre du pays. Tu parles comme un Français, Lakhdar'[20] [01:05:53–01:05:57], and then, as if to drive the point home, he adds, in Arabic this time: 'Un Français'[21] [01:06:04–01:06:05].

The Arabic language expresses something very different when used by the prominent female characters in the film, Nora and her friend Assiä. Here it is associated with nationalist discourse – underscoring the women's participation in the Algerian independence movement through the activities of the *Front de Libération Nationale* (FLN) – and more generally with their rootedness in the culture and traditions of their home country. It becomes a language of empowerment for these women, and especially for Nora, who at the beginning of the film is directed by her husband to stay in their shack, alone, while he is at work. Eventually, it is with the encouragement of Assiä that Nora ventures out into the shantytown to meet other women and later even participates in the liberation movement without her husband's knowledge or permission. Assiä's use of the Arabic language (subtitled in French) is revealing in many ways: first, she uses it to recruit Nora by informing her of the valuable contributions women make to the liberation movement: 'Chacune peut faire quelque chose. Certaines portent des tracts: les femmes, on les arrête moins. On est nombreuses à lutter. Plus on est nombreux, plus on est fort, et plus tôt on vaincra'[22] [50:00–50:20].

---

18 'Listen. Get rid of this trash or I'll throw it on your roof!'
19 'You speak to me like that?'
20 'You don't give a damn about our country. You talk like a Frenchman, Lakhdar.'
21 'A Frenchman.'
22 'Every woman can do something. Some carry pamphlets: because women get stopped less. There are many of us fighting. The more of us there are, the stronger we are, and the sooner we will win.'

Later, it is Assiä who rallies a large crowd of Algerians before their protest march to Paris. Nora also becomes increasingly vocal, criticising her husband's behaviour just as Rachid did: 'Lakhdar... tu as changé. Tu as oublié les coutumes et les traditions de nos ancêtres'[23] [01:13:17–01:13:24]. The Arabic language – which in the first scenes of the film is associated with a disadvantaged and almost entirely male immigrant population – is thus revalorised and empowered when employed in scenes involving Algerian nationalist discourse and the clandestine activities of the FLN. Significantly, these are also scenes in which the impetus for change is represented as coming, in a large part, from women's activities and discourse.

In the end, however, it is Nora's participation in the FLN that ultimately destroys Lakhdar's dream: the police destroy the shack that he built because Nora had hidden members of the FLN in it while Lakhdar was at work. When the family to whom Lakhdar had sold the shack then comes to him for a refund of their money, it is Nora who again speaks out against her husband, this time in front of other Algerians – and in Arabic: 'J'ai fait mon devoir. Et maintenant, tu dois rendre l'argent des autres'[24] [01:23:50–01:23:56]. Lakhdar's dreams are thus shattered, and he soon gambles away the rest of his savings in a vain attempt to win back the money he had lost. In the final scene of the film, Lakhdar dejectedly packs his suitcase and prepares to leave the shantytown – and his family – but Rachid eventually convinces him to stay. When he meets up again with Nora, he utters his last words of the film – this time in Arabic: 'Nous rentrons dans notre pays'[25] [01:32:07–01:32:08]. A final caption indicates that this was not the case in reality, however. Lakhdar can neither achieve his dream in France nor find satisfaction by returning to Algeria. Instead, the family will languish for a further eight years in the shantytown in France before being re-housed in a *cité de transit* (transit camp), still well short of the regular apartment they dream of.

Uses of the French and Arabic languages are particularly revealing along gendered lines in a further contribution to what has sometimes been called 'heritage cinema': Yamina Benguigui's *Inch'Allah dimanche* (2001).[26] Significantly, this is the first feature film to be centred on the experiences of a North-African migrant woman. Like Nora in *Vivre au paradis*, the protagonist, Zouina, comes to France with her children to join her immigrant husband. Zouina initially does not communicate in French but her relationship with the Arabic language is rendered problematic by the gendered nature of her treatment by her husband and mother-in-law, who frequently abuse her verbally and sometimes physically. Unlike Nora and her friend, Assiä, however, for whom the Arabic language is a language of empowerment and action, these scenes – in which Zouina is largely silent – tend to associate the Arabic lan-

23 'Lakhdar... you have changed. You have forgotten the customs and the traditions of our ancestors.'
24 'I did my duty. And now you must give these people their money back.'
25 'We're going back to our country.'
26 See also Gaëlle Planchenault's essay in this volume. On the concept of heritage cinema, see Higson (2003) and Durmelat (2000).

guage with patriarchal values that stifle her capacity for self-expression. This is reinforced visually in one scene in which Zouina's husband returns from work and
greets everyone in the family except for Zouina – who then is even reduced, by the
frame of the camera shot, to an arm that serves coffee. Gradually, Zouina does find
areas of personal freedom outside the home and simultaneously acquires a growing capacity to speak French. The French language becomes implicitly associated
with ideas of personal equality and fulfilment – things that Zouina finds in France
through her relationship with French women and the discovery of French culture. It
is thus fitting that when she finally speaks out against her husband for the first time
– in the very last scene of the film – she does so in French. As Carrie Tarr notes: 'In
her final stand against her husband, she asserts that in the future she will be the one
to take the children to school (the principal agent of integration), and she unexpect-
edly gains his assent' (Tarr 2005: 178). It is French, then, which becomes the language of empowerment for Zouina.

In conclusion, we have examined the ways in which language use in films directed by second-generation Maghrebis reveals a significant shift in focus between early 'Beur' films and later 'banlieue' or heritage films. As we have shown, language
use in the early films highlights the ways in which second-generation youth are rooted in French culture, as opposed to their parents, whose cultural ties are still firmly
connected to their country of origin. Later films directed by members of the second
generation reflect a concerted effort to bring to the fore the experiences of an earlier
generation: that of their parents, either as migrants in France or as colonial subjects
in North Africa. The use of the French and Arabic languages in these films sheds
light not only on common challenges faced by disempowered populations; it is also
a particularly revealing means of highlighting, often quite subtly, the different ways
in which these experiences affect men and women, respectively.

Filmography

BENGUIGUI, Y. (2001), *Inch'Allah dimanche*, France.

BENGUIGUI, Y. (1997), *Mémoires d'immigrés: l'héritage maghrébin*, France.

BOUCHAREB, R. (2006), *Indigènes*, Algeria/France/Morocco/Belgium.

CHAREF, M. (1985), *Le Thé au harem d'Archimède*, France.

GUERDJOU, B. (1998), *Vivre au paradis*, France/Belgium/Norway.

KASSOVITZ, M. (1995), *La Haine*, France.

References

ALLOCINÉ, n.d., 'Secrets de tournage', in: URL: http://www.allocine.fr/film/anecdote_gen_
cfilm=58934.html (29 February 2009).

BENAÏCHA, B. (1992), *Vivre au paradis: d'une oasis à un bidonville*, Paris: Desclée de
Brouwer.

HENNEBELLE, G. & R. SCHNEIDER (eds.) (1990), *Cinémas métis: de Hollywood aux films* beurs,
CinémAction, Special issue, no. 56, July.

DAZAT, O. (ed.) (1985), *Cinéma beur*, *Cinématographe*, no. 112, July.

Durmelat, S. (2000), 'Transmission and Mourning in *Mémoires d'immigrés: l'héritage maghrébin*: Yamina Benguigui as "Memory Entrepreneuse" ', in: Freedman, J. & C. Tarr (eds.), *Women, Immigration and Identities in France*, Berg: Oxford, 171–188.

Hargreaves, A. G. (2000), 'Resuscitating the Father: New Cinematic Representations of the Maghrebi Minority in France', in: *Sites: The Journal of 20th Century/Contemporary French Studies*, vol. 4, no. 2, 343–351.

Hargreaves, A. G. (2007), '*Indigènes*: A Sign of the Times', in: *Research in African Literatures*, vol. 38, no. 4, 204–216.

House, J. & N. MacMaster (2006), *Paris 1961: Algerians, State Terror and Memory*, Oxford: Oxford U.P.

Higson, A. (2003), *English Heritage, English Cinema*, Oxford: Oxford U.P.

Jousse, T. (1995), 'Le banlieue-film existe-t-il?', in: *Cahiers du cinéma*, no. 492, 37–39.

Tarr, C. (2005), *Reframing difference:* Beur *and* banlieue *filmmaking in France*, Manchester: Manchester U.P.

Videau, A. (1995), 'Cinéma: les banlieues sont de sortie', in: *Hommes et migrations*, no. 1192, 60–64.

Intergenerational Verbal Conflicts, Plurilingualism and *Banlieue* Cinema

Cristina Johnston

The French term 'banlieue' refers, literally, to the suburbs of major French cities. Over recent decades, it has come to evoke 'outlying urban areas [...] synonymous with poor quality housing projects, high unemployment, and heavy concentrations of minority ethnic groups' (Hargreaves 1999: 34). The *banlieue* film, by extension, is one in which, for the first wave at least, the action takes place in such suburban environments, focusing on issues of what could broadly be described as social exclusion or 'fracture sociale' to use Will Higbee's term (Higbee 2005: 123). Later *banlieue* films have begun to shift their action, for instance, from the suburbs to the provinces, but the focus remains on *banlieue* characters placed in these alien surroundings.[1] One crucial primary site and source of conflict which has emerged in the French *banlieue* film movement arises across onscreen generations, generally within a family context, either between children and parents, or between children and grandparents:

> Young Beurs[2] are pulled apart by two opposing forces: family obligations and Maghrebian traditions lie at one pole and at the other are the social institutions of France. These 'two spheres of reference are stacked together [...] but do not speak the same language and are often problematic'. (Orlando 2003: 406)[3]

This conflict is often marked verbally, especially in earlier *banlieue* films, by a framework of plurilingualism through characters' use of at least two languages, typically standard French (though also frequently non-standard forms of French) and dialectal Arabic, primarily of the countries of the Maghreb. While the latter is occasionally, though by no means always, subtitled into French, the reverse is never the case. Although the above quotation makes explicit reference to a socio-cultural and socio-linguistic situation faced by a younger generation of French *beurs*, they are not alone in their struggle between what Azouz Begag and Abdellatif Chaouite have termed 'double identity magnets' (Begag/Chaouite 1990: 47). Rather, through close analysis of the use of language in Thomas Gilou's *Raï*, released in 1995 as part of the

---

1   See, for instance *Le Ciel, les oiseaux et... ta mère* (Djamel Bensalah, 1999) or *Total Western* (Eric Rochant, 2000).
2   The term 'Beur' is a verlanised version of the French word 'Arabe' and has come to be used to describe youths of Maghrebi origin. While it has come to be used in common parlance, it is nevertheless not a universally accepted denomination (see, for instance, Begag 1997).
3   The notion of 'spheres of reference' used by Orlando is drawn from *Ecarts d'identité* (Begag/Chaouite 1990: 47).

first wave of *banlieue* films, we will examine the extent to which this notion can be said to fully encapsulate the struggle depicted onscreen, in order to demonstrate that these 'identity magnets' in fact have a transgenerational impact.

In many ways, the success of Mathieu Kassovitz's *La Haine* in 1995 overshadowed the release of Thomas Gilou's *Raï* a month later. As is the case in *La Haine*, but also in a forerunner to the 1995 *banlieue* films, Malik Chibane's *Hexagone* (1993), *Raï* presents its audience with a small group of central protagonists, rather than focusing on one single central character. In common with those other early *banlieue* works[4] the action in Gilou's work follows the relatively mundane day-to-day existences of its characters, as we watch them hang around their housing scheme, go to nightclubs, and lounge about in various apartments. As Erin Schroeder puts it, 'we spend much fairly inconsequential time with groups of youth' (Schroeder 2001: 148) and, as is also the case in *Hexagone*, tension onscreen in *Raï* is most frequently expressed in relation to drugs and women.

All of the members of the core group of central characters are of Maghrebi origin. Prominent among this group are two brothers: Djamel (Mustapha Benstiti), for whom a sexual betrayal by the woman he loves is the trigger for an outpouring of frusration and rage directed towards the police, and Nordine (Samy Nacéri), a drug addict who is ultimately shot by a policewoman who mistakenly believes him to be armed.[5] On its release, *Raï* received a degree of critical acclaim, albeit on a lesser scale than Kassovitz's slice of *banlieue* living. It won the Golden Leopard at the 1995 Locarno Film Festival, in Switzerland, and earned a Special Prize at the same festival for Nacéri's depiction of Nordine. Overall, however, *Raï* was considered a less significant work. Its box office figures were decidedly more modest than Kassovitz's film, attracting only 126,419 viewers across France (Tarr 2005: 216) in sharp contrast to the almost 2 million viewers who went to see *La Haine* (Higbee 2006: 1), and, until recently, it has been relatively overlooked in academic writing on *banlieue* film.[6] Like his fellow cineastes of the *banlieues* Malik Chibane and, to a lesser extent, Mathieu Kassovitz, Gilou strove for a degree of authenticity by involving *banlieue* inhabitants in the making of his film. Nevertheless, a degree of scorn was poured on the significance of its social comment due, at least in part, to Gilou's decision to cast Tabatha Cash (an ex-porn star) in the central female role. Jean-Michel Frodon, for instance, singles out other *banlieue* works of the 1995 *cuvée* as worthy of praise for their incisive social comment but argues that *Raï*, '[prend] [...] 'le social' comme décor, sinon comme prétexte folklorique pour y imposer ses mécanismes de fiction plutôt que de se mettre à l'écoute de ce qui se passe'[7] (Frodon 1995).

---

4   We could also cite here *État des lieux* (Jean-François Richet, 1995) or *Krim* (Ahmed Bouchaala, 1995).
5   The structure of this climax is reminiscent to the infamous ending of *La Haine* but also foreshadows the conclusion of *Wesh Wesh, qu'est-ce qui se passe?* (Rabah Ameur-Zaïmeche, 2001).
6   Two recent exceptions to this are Erin Schroeder's (2001) parallel analysis of *La Haine*, *Raï*, and the American film *Menace II Society* (Hughes & Hughes, 1993) and Tarr (2005: 75–78) in which she compares and contrasts *Raï*, *La Haine*, and *État des lieux*.
7   'Uses 'social' issues as a backdrop, if not as a pretext upon which to impose their fictional mechanisms, rather than in order to listen to what is happening there.' All translations, unless otherwise

Despite any failings *Raï* can be accused of having, we will argue here that it does, nevertheless, have something significant to tell audiences about the construction of complex identities in the *banlieues* of the turn-of-the-century French republic. We will focus, first, on the construction of a plurilingual framework through the parallel onscreen use of French and dialectal forms of Arabic, particularly between the two male central characters, Nordine and Djamel, and their mother. Attention will then shift to an analysis of what we will term, following Begag and Chaouite, 'verbal spheres of reference' (Begag/Chaouite 1990: 47), that is to say domains which are linguistically contained within the French language but with resonances that span cultures. We will agree, to an extent, with Carrie Tarr that, while bringing to the forefront the specific problems faced by 'second/third generation immigrants' of Maghrebi origin, *Raï* 'does so in a way which, however unintentionally, plays into racist stereotypes of an alien immigrant culture spawning an irresponsible, violent youth culture' (Tarr 2005: 78). However, we will also argue that an analysis of the intergenerational verbal conflicts in the film nevertheless maintains an important role to play in an understanding of the complexities of ethnic identities as they are challenged and renegotiated through the medium of *banlieue* film.

Ultimately, it will be argued that, while the notion of 'double aimantation identitaire'[8] (Begag/Chaouite 1990: 47) does encapsulate the dilemma of a search for self within a broader framework of conflicting and opposing identities, the limitations of the implicit binary (double identity magnet) fail to do justice to the complexities of the identities under construction. Rather, as we will see in *Raï*, and can see examples of in other *banlieue* films[9], Begag and Chaouite's 'spheres of reference' (Begag/Chaouite 1990: 47) encompass at once a 'homeland' (mythical or mythologised), a somewhat rigid contemporary French metropolitan republican framework, and the specificities of individual subjectivities emerging against an intrinsically multiethnic backdrop, schematically divided between 'traditional' home and 'modern' public space, but in fact demonstrating a far more pluralist reality than the republican model is yet ready to admit.

---

stipulated, are by the author.

8   'Double identity magnets.'

9   The decision to focus primarily on this single filmic text should not be read as an indication that the work is unique in exemplifying a preoccupation with this issue. We could, for instance, have examined the scenes between Félix and his Jewish grandmother in Kassovitz's 1993 work *Métisse* (while this may not fit the pattern of straightforward *banlieue* cinema, Félix is a white, working-class Jewish *banlieue* youth and through his character Kassovitz gives us a depiction of the lives of another distinct ethnic group living in the *banlieues*) or the paradox of the apparent lack of conflict between Toussaint and his mother in the living-room/dining-room sequences in *La Squale* (Fabrice Genestal, 2001), to cite but two other examples.

Arabic and French in *Raï*

What is particularly interesting in *Raï* is Gilou's decision to include scenes which involve either particular groups of characters or specific individuals onscreen conversing in (subtitled) Arabic while others, often belonging to a younger generation, reply in French. The scenes I will examine in detail here involve Djamel, his elder brother Nordine, and their mother. Whereas a good deal of the film (in common with many other *banlieue* works from 1995 and later) is shot in external locations, the scenes involving these three characters (or combinations thereof) take place indoors, either in their family home, or in other apartments in the *cité*. This in itself indicates an initial source of division and a sign that Gilou will present us with something other than a straightforward binary. Djamel and Nordine's verbal ties with a (mythical) 'homeland' come within the physical confines of the family home whereas direct encounters with representatives of the social, cultural and/or political values of republican France take place in public spaces. At one point, for instance, Nordine is arrested in a cinema [34:50–37:40]; when he is shot towards the end of the film [01:14:36], the police have been called to the estate because he has made his way onto the rooftop of a high-rise block from which he has been shooting cars and pedestrians on the pavements below; the shooting of Nordine takes place outside one of the blocks, in the most public of *banlieue* spaces.[10]

The first scene in which we are witness to a bilingual intergenerational exchange involves Djamel and his mother. Not only does this scene take place within the home – by no stretch of the imagination a privileged site of action in other *banlieue* films – it in fact takes place in the mother's bedroom, with her lying in bed, and Djamel sitting at her bedside. As the scene begins, we learn that Djamel has returned home to find his brother lying, in a drug-induced stupor, in the doorway of their flat. Djamel carries Nordine into his bedroom and then goes to speak to his mother [16:26–18:27]. Throughout the exchange, Djamel speaks French, while his mother replies in Algerian Arabic. Crucially, there is no indication that either has any problems of understanding. Given the apparent mutual intelligibility of the languages in which they choose to express themselves verbally, what are we, as viewers, to make of the bilingual nature of the scene? What is the significance of the fact that it is the Arabic which is subtitled into French, but not the French which is subtitled into Arabic? While this may seem a relatively obvious point to make, it is nevertheless worth noting that the translation policy of the film is not straightforward and does not always present Arabic in this way. Indeed, in some subsequent scenes in which insults are delivered in Arabic by *banlieue* youths to their peers, there is no accompanying subtitling or translation of their words. It would appear, then, that

---

10 A similar division is also evident in the scenes in *La Haine* which focus on questions of intergenerational conflict and which centre, there, on divisions between generations in the family of one of the trio of central characters, Vinz. While Vinz, Saïd, and Hubert are outside, in public locations, the main oppositional force they encounter is that symbolised by representatives of the republic, from the riot police in the *cité* to the police officers who arrest them in a Parisian street. However, in one of the few interior shots we see, we are given a brief glimpse of Vinz's relationship with his (large) family as his grandmother berates him for not attending synagogue.

even within the plurilingual context that is being depicted, Gilou is able to indicate that versions of the same language can have different social/cultural meanings. Furthermore, by subtitling only one character's words here, it immediately ensures that these words are doubly marked as other, first aurally to the non-Arabophone viewer, and secondly visually by their onscreen translation. In this way, Arabic is marked symbolically, not as a language spoken by portions of the French population, and understood by (at least some) French citizens with no apparent difficulty, but rather as a foreign language, thus, perhaps controversially, constructing standard French, and standard French alone, as the language of the republic[11]:

> La domination du français est incontestable: langue de l'école, langue des médias, langue revendiquant une place dans les milieux internationaux. Par ailleurs, l'arabe dialectal est dévalorisé au niveau des représentations dans les pays du Maghreb, mais aussi en France par ses locuteurs eux-mêmes.[12] (Caubet 2002: 120)

For some critics, the use of a language other than French in some metropolitan French households can lead individuals to 'déformer, reformer, jouer avec la langue officielle apprise à l'école' (Begag 1997: 33).[13] Begag goes so far as to suggest that 'lorsqu'on puise son langage parlé dans deux registres linguistiques différents, mais qu'on n'en maîtrise aucun suffisamment, des confusions apparaissent inéluctablement.'[14] Without lapsing into what Begag terms 'positivisation idéologique'[15], I would argue that, certainly here in *Raï* and, by implication, in at least some of the French households Gilou is attempting to represent, 'confusion' is not necessarily the end result. Instead, Gilou's use of a plurilingual[16] framework serves to direct the audience's thoughts and attention towards the complexities of the onscreen households and their anchoring in a series of interlocking national, cultural, and linguistic frameworks. Rather than analysing such sequences in simple linguistic terms, it is through the topics *addressed* in the dialogue that we come closer to an understanding of the symbolic nature of the division between the generations, and between the home and the republic towards which such plurilingualism allows Gilou to nod.

Djamel's mother, for example, is insistent that he take a talisman and place it in his brother's wallet [37:06 – 37:20] to protect him against evil, namely his ad-

---

11   As evidence of this, we might consider, for instance, the Immigration law of 26 November 2003 which states that places mastery of the French language (and no other languages spoken in the Hexagon) as one of the pre-conditions to naturalisation. Or, indeed, the Constitution of the Fifth Republic, Article 2 of which stipulates 'la langue de la République est le français' ('the language of the Republic is French').

12   'The domination of the French language is indisputable: the language of schools, language of the media, a language that stakes its claim in the international arena. Dialectal Arabic is also devalued within representations of the Maghreb countries, but also in France by those who speak it.'

13   'Deform, reform, and play with the official language learned at school.'

14   'If one's spoken language is drawn from two distinct linguistic registers, but one does not master either sufficiently, confusions will inevitably arise…'

15   'Ideological positivisation.'

16   My description of the situation here as plurilingual should be understood as a reference to the combination of standard French, specific varieties of Arabic and non-standard French on the part of interlocutors onscreen.

diction to drugs. The mother has been given the talisman by a *marabout*[17], and the talisman in question is a small, folded sheet of paper, written in Arabic, which Nordine is expected to keep in his wallet. Djamel sees Nordine's drug addiction as part of a social, but also a personal, problem, something his brother has to be cured of by being removed from the *banlieue* and given an opportunity to live outside a context in which drugs are relatively freely available.[18] His mother, however, remains faithful to the customs and traditions of another society and culture and believes that a curse has been put on her eldest son by someone who is jealous of her for having had the good fortune of having two sons. The contrast between sociocultural reality and tradition here is inescapable and is only heightened by Gilou's decision to divide the dialogue here between French discourse about the *banlieues* and the difficulties of coming off drugs within that context, and Arabic discourse about tradition, rivalries, curses, and healers. It is also interesting to note that, when Nordine is arrested later in the film, one of the arresting officers finds the talisman in his wallet and unfolds it [37:06–37:20], assuming that it will contain drugs, and is then bemused by its content, clearly lacking the cultural awareness which would allow him to recognise it for what it is.

On this basis, we can clearly understand why Carrie Tarr views the film as feeding into 'racist stereotypes of an alien immigrant community' (Tarr 2005: 78). However, this would be to ignore the underlying conflict which is being said to exist between the 'spheres of reference' impacting on the lives of *banlieue* youths and resulting precisely from their multiethnic origins: a 'homeland', now several generations removed, a republic which subtitles the experience of part of its population, *and* an emergent group of citizens which has yet to find its place, 'urban immigrant communities in France […] carving out their own identities and championing their […] right to be different' (Orlando 2003: 397).

There are two further important scenes involving the mother, both centring, once again, on questions of tradition and cultural experience thereof. In the first, Djamel's mother has learned of his relationship with Sahlia and, apparently of her own accord, pays a visit to Sahlia's mother to agree the terms of their relationship and to celebrate it [54:10–56:00]. This entire scene takes place indoors, in Sahlia's mother's living-room, with Sahlia present in the background, but with the two mothers' conversation being held in Arabic, subtitled throughout. The Arabic in this scene is consistently subtitled, with the exception of when Djamel's mother asks permission to 'pousser des youyous', in other words to issue the jubilant onomatopoeic *youyou* cry associated with celebration in some Arab cultures.

---

17   A traditional healer who, within some communities, is considered to have magical powers.
18   In many ways, Djamel's vision of a positive future seems to rely on a move beyond the frontiers of the suburb in which he lives, whether for himself, his girlfriend or his brother. Once again, this contributes to the multi-layering of the context with which Gilou is presenting his audience. Djamel is embedded in the suburb but strives for a future beyond it. Clearly, this can be interpreted as a reflection of the lack of opportunities within the *banlieues*, but it also demonstrates an ability to live across temporal contexts for *banlieue* inhabitants.

A number of strategies are being employed which serve to underline the delicate nature of the position of individuals of the generation of Djamel's mother within the (linguistic) framework of the republic. This entire scene is concerned with a possible binary conflict between modernity and tradition, represented by the problematic relationship between Djamel and Sahlia, on the one hand, and their respective mothers' apparent desire to view that relationship not in terms of its complexities but as a simple and straightforward route to marriage, on the other. Djamel and Sahlia speak to each other and their peers in French, and yet their mothers both speak Arabic within the home and maintain the traditions, at least symbolically, of the 'homeland', an Arabic which is understood by the children's generation but subtitled for the viewing public. This subtitling, however, still assumes a degree of cultural, if not linguistic, knowledge, on the part of that same viewing public, insofar as they are expected to understand Djamel's mother's request when she asked to be allowed to give the *youyou* cry, and to recognise its significance when it follows without subtitled explanation or translation. On the one hand, then, we have a marking of the Arabophone mothers as fundamentally other to a Francophone metropolitan French context, but, at the same time, we have an implicit recognition, through subtitling, of a degree of expected cultural awareness on the part of a metropolitan French viewing audience, in that they are expected to recognise and understand the cultural specificity and connotation of the *youyou* in the present circumstances.

'Ici, on marche en baskets …': Verbal Spheres of Reference

The second crucial scene comes towards the end of the film, after the shooting of Nordine, and again involves Djamel and Nordine's mother [01:14:29 – 01:15:29]. This time, however, she is part of a larger group of women of her generation, all speaking Algerian Arabic to each other and all trying to console her on the loss of her eldest son. Djamel arrives in the flat to find the women gathered there, crying and speaking loudly. His feelings of loss and guilt seem to be compounded by his feelings of cultural and linguistic isolation in this context, perhaps most clearly illustrating the ways in which *banlieue* characters can be said to be torn between diverse 'spheres of reference' (Begag/Chaouite 1990: 47). The processes of mourning his mother and her peers are engaged in here exclude Djamel, in gendered terms, but also linguistically and culturally. He feels obliged to leave the family home and to return to the public space which is now associated with the killing of his elder brother. All of this occurs in almost total silence for Djamel, but with the sounds of his mother and her peers as aural backdrop, a clear illustration of what Orlando has explained as follows:

> [T]he traditionalism which often goads the children of immigrant communities. Habitually this traditionalism is viewed by the Beurs' parents as the only way to hold onto memories of a homeland to which they will never return. For their children, reference to the 'homeland' is mythical, having become "deformed by a heritage that suffers from a de-valorization [of] its imagery" because it is so far removed from the Beurs' field of reference. (Orlando 2003: 405, quoting Azouz Begag and Abellatif Chaouite)

It is particularly worth considering these three scenes from *Raï* involving mothers and sons, in the context of another sequence, this time involving Djamel and Nordine and their absent father, which takes place on the rooftop shortly before Nordine is shot. Thus far, the viewer has seen Nordine as something of a lost cause who does little to endear himself either to the off-screen audience, or indeed his onscreen family. Here, however, we hear him talk, for the only time in the film, about his experience of life, and what, in his view, has led him to the position in which he now finds himself. It is interesting to note that Nordine makes explicit reference to the conflicts and divisions which exist between the mythical 'homeland' and the contemporary national republican frame of reference when he says, for instance, berating the absent father: 'Arrête de nous dire qu'en Algérie tu marchais pieds nus, ici on marche en baskets et on a le cœur gelé'[19] [01:12:18–01:12:31]. Until this point, it has been left to the viewer to extrapolate a conflict which might arise between the generation and aspirations of the youths' mother, on the one hand, and their own, on the other. Through this rooftop sequence, this conflict is made explicit with a direct contrast drawn between their reality in late twentieth-century France and the past life in Algeria about which the youths' father clearly told them.

And yet again, it is far from sufficient to consider this conflict in purely binary terms. It is not simply a case of Nordine saying that life in Algeria is no longer relevant to them, but that his parents' generation needs to understand that there has been a move to a new national and cultural context and that this move is now permanent and no longer the transient state they may once have thought it was. While these strands, too, underlie Nordine's words, a closer reading shows that they are more complex. He pleads with the absent father to stop talking to them about a reality they do not know and certainly do not experience, and he signals the fact that they are anchored in a very different world through reference to the symbolic difference in footwear (*pieds nus* as opposed to *les baskets*). However, Nordine's words do not construct a straightforward modernity versus tradition binary, since he rounds off his plea by adding, 'On a le cœur gelé.'[20] There is a physical reality to which he seeks to draw the absent father's attention, but there is also an underlying cultural or social reality which seems equally important and which signals that they are not yet happy with the position they find themselves in within the new republican framework.

Conclusion

Overall what we see here in *Raï* is a clear indication of the need for a renewal or renegotiation of identities, particularly in the contemporary *banlieues*, specifically around the poles of ethnic identity, but by no means restricted to a binary division between metropolitan French and immigrant other. Rather, Begag and Chaouite's 'spheres of reference' (Begag/Chaouite 1990: 47) encompass at once a 'homeland'

---

19   'Stop telling us that you walked barefoot in Algeria. Here we walk in trainers and our hearts are frozen.'
20   'Our hearts are frozen.'

(mythical or mythologised), a somewhat rigid contemporary French republican framework[21], *and* the specificities of individual subjectivities emerging against an intrinsically multiethnic backdrop. These 'spheres of reference' may be schematically divided between 'traditional' home and 'modern' public space, but in fact demonstrate a far more pluralist reality than the republican model is yet ready to admit. The hybridity which thus emerges can therefore be seen as leading towards a renegotiation of the French republican model to accept within its discursive (and, by extension, more broadly socio-cultural) limits, a 'French other' and the paradox inherent in this term. The figure of 'the other' is no longer placed beyond the confines of the national in linguistic, social, or any other terms, but rather is firmly embedded within the national, modifying and challenging from within, and underlining the existence of a far more pluralist and plurilingual reality.

Filmography

AMEUR-ZAÏMECHE, R. (2001), *Wesh Wesh, qu'est-ce qui se passe?*, France.

BENSALAH, D. (1999), *Le Ciel, les oiseaux et... ta mère!*, France.

BOUCHAALA, A. (1995), *Krim*, France/Canada/Switzerland.

CHIBANE, M. (1993), *Hexagone*, France.

GENESTAL, F. (2001), *La Squale*, France.

GILOU, T. (1995), *Raï*, France.

HUGHES A. & A. HUGHES (1993), *Menace II Society*, USA.

KASSOVITZ, M. (1993), *Métisse*, France/Belgium.

KASSOVITZ, M. (1995), *La Haine*, France.

RICHET, J.-F. (1995), *État des lieux*, France.

ROCHANT, E. (2000), *Total Western*, France.

References

BEGAG, A. (1997), 'Trafic de mots en banlieue: du 'nique ta mère' au 'plaît-il?', in: *Migrants-Formation*, 108, March, 30–37.

BEGAG A. & A. CHAOUITE (1990), *Écarts d'identité*, Paris: Seuil.

CAUBET, D. (2002), 'Métissages linguistiques ici (en France) et là-bas (au Maghreb)', in: *Ville-École-Intégration* 130, 117–132.

DEBRAY, R. (1989a), 'Êtes-vous démocrate ou républicain?', in: *Le Nouvel Observateur* (30 November–6 December), 49–55.

DEBRAY, R. (1989b), *Que vive la République*, Paris: Odile Jacob.

DEBRAY, R. (2003), *Ce Que Nous Voile Le Voile. La République et le sacré*, Paris: NRF/Gallimard.

FRODON, J.-M. (1995), 'Le Jeune Cinéma Français connaît un renouveau prometteur', in: *Le Monde* (29 June), URL: http://www.lemonde.fr (September 2009).

---

21 This traditional vision of the Republic and Republicanism could, for example, be seen in the writings of Régis Debray (see, for example, Debray 1989a; 1989b; 2003), to be contrasted with what some might term the realities of contemporary France which encompass a multiplicity of regional differences.

HARGREAVES, A. G. (1999), 'Boys in the Mud. Maghrebi Filmmakers in France', in: *Middle East Report*, Summer, 34–35.

HIGBEE, W. (2005), 'The Return of the Political, or Designer Visions of Exclusion? The Case for Mathieu Kassovitz's *Fracture Sociale* Trilogy', in: *Studies in French Cinema*, 5 (2), 123–135.

HIGBEE, W. (2006), *Mathieu Kassovitz*, Manchester: Manchester U. P.

ORLANDO, V. (2003), 'From Rap to Raï in the Mixing Bowl: *Beur* Hip-Hop Culture and *Banlieue* Cinema in Urban France', in: *Journal of Popular Culture*, 36 (3), 395–415.

SCHROEDER, E. (2001), 'A Multicultural Conversation: *La Haine, Raï,* and *Menace II Society*', in: *Camera Obscura* 46, 16 (1), 143–179.

TARR, C. (2005), *Reframing Difference. Beur and Banlieue Filmmaking in France*, Manchester/New York: Manchester U.P.

Displacement and Plurilingualism in *Inch'Allah Dimanche*: Appropriating the Other's Language in Order to Find One's Place

Gaëlle Planchenault

Introduction

Is home the place where one is born or the space that one has a feeling of belonging to? How is the experience of home affected by gender and migration? How does migration impact upon women's choice of language? These are among the issues often raised in exilic and diasporic cinema. I intend to show here that linguistic practices are key elements in the foundation of a feeling of 'home', in particular in the depiction of migrant women in films. According to bell hooks:

> Home is that place which enables and promotes varied and ever-changing perspectives, a place, where one discovers new ways of seeing reality, frontiers of difference. One confronts and accepts dispersal, fragmentation as part of a new world order that reveals more fully where we are, who we can become, an order that does not demand forgetting. (hooks 1996: 50)

If language plays a part in the attachment to a place, it would first appear that it has to do with the mother tongue or with the language which one speaks at home and that permits one to feel whole. However, linguistic identity can be varied and ever-changing. For people who live with several languages, the relation between language and home is complex. For immigrant women who hardly leave their home and speak mostly the minority language, the acquisition of the majority language is often seen as the key to the construction of a new identity. This is certainly the case in Yamina Benguigui's film *Inch'Allah Dimanche* (2001), a Franco-Algerian co-production whose story is set in the seventies during a period of immigration called *regroupement familial* ('family reunion'). If the facts that the French director was born in France and that nearly all of the film was shot in this country make questionable its affiliation to what is today called *transnational* cinema (Ezra/Rowden 2006), the themes depicted in *Inch'Allah Dimanche* make it without doubt an *accented* film (Naficy 2001). The *Migrant and Diasporic Cinema in Contemporary Europe*'s website defines *accented cinema* as 'an aesthetic response to the experience of displacement through exile, migration or diaspora'.[1] *Inch'Allah Dimanche* depicts Zouina's

---

1   See URL: http://www.migrantcinema.net/glossary/term/accented_cinema/ (25 July 2010).

ordeal to reconstruct a home with a husband who has become estranged from her, in a new society where the language, culture and codes of behaviour are very different from the place of her birth, and at a time when racial integration was virtually non-existent. At first she feels alienated and the sense of isolation and vulnerability that immigrant families experience upon their arrival is depicted by her muteness (is she silenced or does she keep silent willingly?) and apparent numbness to the external world. But as she masters the foreign language and starts articulating her self, she finds herself empowered and freer than she has ever been. In this article, I will argue that it is through the appropriation of the second language that Zouina finds her place in the foreign country. For this purpose I will first study the links between home, gender and language(s). I will then propose a linguistic analysis of *Inch'Allah Dimanche*'s dialogues and study the forms of code-switching between the majority language (French) and the minority language (Algerian Arabic), focusing primarily on the lines of the female protagonist. This linguistic analysis will permit to reflect on the fact that deterritorialisation or interstitial perspective must not lead us to believe that accented film-makers are detached from nation-based political issues.

Plurilingualism in Exile

For centuries in Western societies the ideal concept of home was related to unity: one family under one roof sharing one goal and one language. This notion has been contested recently by postmodernist cultural studies (Jones 2007). Scholars had indeed to allow for the effect of colonialism and migration on identity. The ideal of a home cannot be linked to a unique house nor to a space of birth, less still to a single language. Considering the rise of exogamous families or second generation immigrants speaking the majority language in their home and code-switching between two or more languages (i.e. young *beurs* speaking Arabic and French to their parents and siblings), plurilingualism has come to be seen as a norm. In a globalised era it seems that it is more common – or it is widely seen as more common – for people to spend at least a part of their life in a foreign country. Therefore the sense of belonging to a place is no longer a common reality, but has thereby acquired the quaint charm of a feeling that belongs to the past. Emotional attachment to a lifetime space is not a defining criterion to the concept of home anymore as with the multiplicity of human movements and the increasing complexity of living in the modern world, the feeling of belonging to a unique place can be difficult to achieve. In the film that will be analysed, the female character Zouina does not show any mourning for the displacement from her birth land (apart from one of the earlier scene shortly after her arrival in the new home when she takes a picture out of her bag and cries out her mother's name [00:12]). The representations of the concept of home found in novels and films are constantly changing and displacement is nowadays a major theme in literature and cinema.

However, feelings of being displaced are not only geographical: one could feel displaced (i.e. out of place) in his/her own home as it is the case for Zouina in her new 'home' in France. Homi Bhabha introduced the concept of the *unhomely* which he explains in these terms: 'To be unhomed is not to be homeless, nor can the "un-homely" be easily accommodated in that familiar division of social life into pri-vate and public spheres' (Bhabha 1994: 9). This division between private and pub-lic spheres is especially true when considering the relation between women and the home. For N. Edwards and C. Hogarth, '[w]omen have long been associated with the "home" and hearth while men have been assigned space, place and authority beyond it' (Edwards/Hogarth 2008: 7). This association of woman/home and man/public space was considered as being a key to happiness and social equilibrium. They also declare that' "Home" [...] was once the place that best represented calm and secu-rity from a potentially hostile outside world' (Edwards/Hogarth 2008: 2). It will be shown later how feelings of safety in the home can be related to the intimacy of the languages spoken in the private sphere. However, it has also been argued that the no-tion of security within the home is all relative as one cannot omit the subservience to which women have been subjected within it or ignore the fact that it is also a place where domestic violence and psychological, verbal or physical abuse can take place (Duncan 1996: 132). For Bhabha:

> By making visible the forgetting of the 'unhomely' moment in civil society, femi-nism specifies the patriarchal, gendered nature of civil society and disturbs the sym-metry of private and public which is now shadowed, or uncannily doubled, by the difference of genders which does not neatly map on to the private and the public, but becomes disturbingly supplementary to them. This results in redrawing the domestic space as the space of the normalizing, pastoralizing, and individuating techniques of modern power and police: the personal-is-the political; the world-in-the-home. (Bhabha 1994: 10–11)

Gaining independence of movement in the public sphere and breaking with the stereo-typing of the safety of a home could be a key to freedom, particularly for the wom-en trapped in an 'unhomely' situation. Among them, for those who are bilingual, the language spoken in the outside world is related to liberation from a patriarchal order.

Private/Public Spheres and Language(s): The Second Language as a Key to Freedom

The relationship between home and language(s) is a complex one. However, it has often been over-simplified, as Trinh Minh-ha argues:

> Home and language tend to be taken for granted; like Mother or Woman, they are often naturalized and homogenised. The source becomes then an illusory, secure and fixed place, invoked as a natural state of things, untainted by any process or outside influence [...] or else, as an indisputable point of reference on whose authority one can unfailingly rely. (Minh-ha 1994: 14)

This process of simplification can also be seen clearly with respect to bilinguals. According to Anna Wierzbicka, '[a] point which seems to me particularly impor-tant is that experience of bilingual people should not be construed as merely their experience of speaking two languages but rather as their experience of living with other people through two different languages' (Wierzbicka 2004: 98). A key point that I propose is the emotional relationship that bilinguals have developed with the different languages according to the use of these languages in private/public spheres. For late bilinguals (for whom the second language was learnt after the age of 5), it was long thought that the mother tongue was the preferred language to express emotions whereas using L2 permitted/caused emotional distance (for example, bilingual speakers have attested that taboo and swear words provoked less anxiety when uttered in a second language – see Dewaele 2004). Recent research on bilingualism and emotions[2] has showed the complexity of the phenomenon. Five years ago, Aneta Pavlenko and Jean-Marc Dewaele set up a web-based questionnaire which aimed at discovering whether bilinguals felt they were different people according to the language they were speaking. The success of the survey (1039 persons from around the world filled out the questionnaire) and the publications that followed (Dewaele/Pavlenko 2004; Pavlenko 2005) are a clear reflection of the awareness of bilinguals on such issue in an increasingly multicultural world. For bilingual authors writing in a foreign language such as Nancy Huston and Eva Hoffman, their relation to the second language is at the crux of their work. On the one hand, writing in a second language does permit a distance that the intimacy with the mother tongue prevents. For Nancy Huston (talking about French): 'Elle était, par rapport à ma langue maternelle, moins chargée d'affect et donc moins dangereuse. Elle était froide, et je l'abordais froidement. Elle m'était égale. C'était une substance lisse et homogène, autant dire neutre'[3] (Huston 1999: 63). On the other hand, one cannot associate second language and emotional distance this easily. In her article on bilingualism and emotions in the texts of Nancy Huston, Celeste Kinginger argues:

> In the case of Nancy Huston, what we find is a personal investment in emotional distance and detachment, enabled by the second language. There is relatively little distress or discomfort in the reduced capacity for emotional self-expression in the adopted language, but active pursuit of the capacity for self-control and refined sensibility enabled by it. (Kinginger 2004: 160)

Moreover, the two languages are not neatly separated from one another. For the American writer of Polish origin, Eva Hoffman: 'When I speak Polish now, it is infiltrated, permeated, and inflected by the English in my head. Each language modifies the other, crossbreeds with it, fertilises it. Each language makes the other relative' (Hoffman 1989: 273). As for the way bilinguals deal with their emotions in the two languages, Anna Wierzbicka argues that: 'For bilingual people, living with two languages can mean indeed living in two different emotional worlds and also traveling back and forth between those two worlds' (Wierzbicka 2004: 102). It is also true to say that the conflict between the two languages is obviously greater for those expressing themselves in the language of a coloniser (Dion et al. 2006; Gauvin 1997,

---

2   For more details see Pavlenko 2005, 2006; Pavlenko/Dewaele 2004; Dewaele 2007; Wierzbicka 2008.

3   'It was, in relation to my mother tongue, less charged with emotion and therefore less dangerous. It was cold, and I approached it coldly. I did not mind it. It was a smooth and homogeneous substance, in other words neutral.' (Translations by the author.)

2007). What about languages spoken in the private sphere vs. those spoken in the public sphere? For bell hooks, talking in the vernacular means using 'the intimate sounds and gestures I usually reserve for family and loved ones' (hooks 1996: 49). I will show that it is not the case in *Inch'Allah Dimanche* as Zouina starts speaking only in French to her children from very early on.

Plurilingualism in *Inch'Allah Dimanche*

The director of *Inch'Allah Dimanche,* Yamina Benguigui, was born in 1957 in France of Algerian parents. Many of her movies and documentaries have been dedicated to themes such as memory and immigration from Maghreb countries as is the case with the 1997 documentary *Mémoires d'immigrés: l'héritage maghrébin (Immigrants' memories)* that made her famous. She says in an interview: 'La douleur de l'exil, je l'ai reçue en héritage, c'est dans les gènes.'[4] She sees herself as a director 'with a cause' and says that what links all her films is 'l'enracinement' (i.e. the putting down of one's roots). Moreover her commitment to the depiction of mainly female characters and themes such as patriarchal oppression, domestic violence, and arranged marriages shows a feminist affiliation. *Inch'Allah Dimanche* (2001), her first long feature film, is set in the seventies in a period of immigration that has been called *regroupement familial* ('family reunion') – a name which actually designates the law passed in 1975 by Chirac's government that permitted women to join the male member of the family who had migrated to France in the fifties and sixties to work in the French industry. The film opens with a scene that shows Zouina departing from her native Algeria, torn between her mother, whom she leaves behind, and the new life ahead of her. She is rejoining her husband who has been working in the North of France for ten years and is accompanied by her mother-in-law, a cruel woman who bullies her. Adjusting to life in France is hard: her mother-in-law treats her like a slave and the neighbours are not welcoming. Naficy says: 'Loneliness is an inevitable outcome of transnationality, and it finds its way into the desolate structures of feeling and lonely diegetic characters' (Naficy 2001: 55). However, after half an hour into the film, Zouina finds her place and makes a few friends – a young divorcee, a widow and a bus driver – all French. Despite the oppression that she experiences every day in her home, she manages to create windows of liberty for herself through books and French radio programmes such as the legendary *Jeu des 1000 francs* and Ménie Grégoire's talk show. One day she discovers that another Algerian family lives in the same village. She decides that she has to meet the wife and leaves the house, even though for a woman going out on her own is *haraam* – forbidden.

---

4   'the pain of exile, I received it as an inheritance; it's in my genes'. See URL: http://www.art-et-essai.org/actions_promotion/soutiens_2001/inch_allah_dimanche.htm (25 July 2010).

Two languages are spoken throughout the movie with equal importance: French and Arabic. However, the characters have different linguistic practices. These can be divided into four categories:

- characters who speak Algerian Arabic only
- characters who speak French only
- characters who speak mostly Algerian Arabic with occasional code-switching in French
- characters who speak Algerian Arabic and French but code-switch rarely.

There are hardly any characters in the first category since even the mother-in-law uses a few French words when she speaks Arabic. It is important to bear in mind that French has been used widely since the colonisation of Algeria by France (i.e. in the administration or in business), and that many people, especially the older generation, use French words without always realising it in the form of borrowings. In the second category of characters, one obviously finds the French characters with whom Zouina interacts: Nicole, Madame Manant, the bus driver, the grocers, the neighbours, etc. In the third category come Zouina's husband and his colleague who have been living in France for more than ten years and interact with French people on a daily basis. The following excerpts are a few examples of code-switching in French noted in a dialogue from the beginning of the movie when the husband and his colleague speak in Arabic about the family reunion: 'Je suis très content'; 'J'ai pas confiance'; 'C'est tout'; 'la prochaine fois'; 'Bon courage, hein?'[5] [00:07–00:09]. A few minutes after this scene, Zouina's husband lectures his children in Arabic about the fact that they have to be serious at school and should not wander when coming back in the evening, using the following words in French: 'l'école' ('school'); 'les cartables' ('satchels'); 'les manteaux' ('coats'); 'les chaussures' ('shoes'); 'la route' ('the road'); 'l'usine' ('the factory'); 'interdit' ('forbidden'); 'danger' ('danger'); 'dangereux' ('dangerous'); 'Allez, c'est fini' ('Come on, that's it') [00:15–00:17].[6] Finally, in the fourth category, we can find Zouina and her children. They speak in Arabic or French and code-switch rarely between the two languages. I will argue later that this linguistic behaviour could be regarded as the most conventional ideal of integration. I will analyse several excerpts from the film, primarily focusing on the ones where Zouina interacts and I will see how her use of the two languages (Algerian Arabic and French) evolves throughout her spiritual journey. There are three periods in this journey that can be summarised as follows: Zouina's silences; Zouina's voice; conflicting voices.

---

5 'I'm very happy'; 'I don't trust them'; 'That's all'; 'Next time'; 'Keep it up'.
6 I would like to insist on the fact that these instances of code-switching are fairly realistic and linguistically motivated, in contrast to the majority of current films (Bleichenbacher 2008: 191–213).

Zouina's Silences

Zouina is not a very talkative character. In spite of the fact that she appears in most of the scenes in the film, she speaks very little. On the 40 scenes counted in which she appears, she speaks in only half of them. In the twenty remaining scenes, she is either on her own or silenced by her husband and/or mother-in-law, particularly at the beginning of the film. It is worth noting that in the first 25 minutes she hardly says anything and utters in total less than 10 words in three scenes, starting with the first two words in the opening scene where she cries 'Mother' in Arabic twice [00:03], emphasising the loss of her real mother as well as the loss of the motherland. In the following scene, the spectator can hear her think when she meets her husband after an absence of probably more than a year: 'I forgot he had a moustache' [00:05] (the words are uttered in Arabic but a subtitled translation is provided). However, she does not say it out loud as her lips are not moving. In the second of her speaking scenes, she is alone in a bedroom and cries again: 'Mother, my dear mother' in Arabic [00:12]. Finally, in the third scene and 20 minutes into the film, she gives her name to Nicole, the young divorcee who leaves next door [00:20]. The audience could understandably believe that she is somewhat dim-witted and it comes as a surprise when she finally has a full conversation with her children in the garden of their house, in French, in the tenth scene in which she appears [00:26–00:28]. From this point onward, Zouina's linguistic principle in the private sphere is to speak in French with her three children and to keep silent with her husband and/or her mother-in-law. Moreover it is interesting to note that her French is relatively accent-free and closer to Standard French than her husband's or Malika's.

The linguistic practices that she adopts outside, in the public space (first in the garden and then when she flees from her home after 40 minutes into the film [00:41–00:46]), are more complex and correspond to the part where Zouina finds a voice. However, this does not mean that she will never be silenced in the public sphere as some of her interaction with the neighbours and the grocers shows. For example, the couple of times when she gives her name provoke patronising comments from her interlocutors: 'Hum, ça sent le sud'[7] says Nicole; 'Dites à Monsieur Zouino'[8] says the grocer's wife who thinks that adding a final 'o' to a foreigner's first name suffices to form the masculine name of the husband [00:55].

Before moving onto the second stage in Zouina's development, it is worth noting that there is a bridge between private and public spheres that takes the physical form of a window and a door through which Zouina observes a bus that passes her street everyday and the bus driver who smiles tentatively to her. This daily encounter with the seductive and amiable young man reminds Zouina that she is a beautiful and desirable woman, and embodies her growing need to free herself and to reach

---

7   'It smells of the south.'
8   'Tell Mr. Zouino.'

out to the community. I will show that at the end of the movie, the liberation is accomplished when Zouina finally takes the bus and talks to the bus driver.

Zouina's Voice

Zouina gradually finds her voice through interaction with three female characters: Nicole, Mme Manant and Malika. Interestingly, the first two characters are men-less women – one a divorcee and one a widow. Even Malika is shown without her husband (who is presumably at work) and it is worth noting that the constant mentioning of Zouina's husband by the latest will be the spark to the argument that will nip their friendship in the bud. Does this show that there is no true freedom or happiness for a wife?

Moreover, each of these female characters embodies an aspect of the modern history of women and of the relationship of France with Algeria (Carpenter Latiri 2003):

- Nicole: women's liberation and the discovery of sexual freedom (also seen in the well-known radio programme hosted by Ménie Grégoire)
- Mme Manant: the too recent and painful past of France and Algeria (symbolically buried by Zouina with Mme Manant's dog [00:49–00:51])
- Malika: the pain of the exile lived as an imprisonment, the resignation of suffering and the refusal to open oneself to the new country's cultural practices.

The French programmes that Zouina listens to on the radio are at the crux of the personal evolution of her character and the liberation from the yoke of the husband and the mother-in-law. The first is the famous *Jeu des 1000 francs*. Presented by Lucien Jeunesse on France Inter for more than thirty years, it was a national institution. Then there is the radio programme hosted by Ménie Grégoire. The journalist and writer was particularly famous in France for her involvement in the defence of women's rights, a campaign that she led especially through the programme she animated from 1967 to 1981 on RTL. In this programme, she received calls from people who wanted to talk about personal problems, especially emotional and sexual issues. Ménie Grégoire was one of the first radio presenters to talk openly about subjects that were then considered taboos, such as homosexuality, and to give advice in a free and natural manner.

As well as these scenes, signs of Zouina's liberation are given in the linguistic practices of two scenes very close to one another nearly an hour into the film. In the first of these two scenes, responding to her mother-in-law who is accusing her of being lazy, she retorts in French, provoking a reaction from the old woman ('You have forgotten Arabic! You speak French now?' [00:48]), which emphasises that her use of French is perceived as an act of rebellion. Then soon after when her husband explains to her in Arabic the tasks that she is to do and allows her for the first time to leave the house to do a couple of errands, she interrupts him to say in French: 'Où est le magasin?'[9] [00:50]. He seems surprised by her boldness but does not react. At this point it seems that Zouina has found her own voice and is able to express herself and to put forward her rights to independence and freedom of speech. However, the path to liberation through linguistic appropriation is not a smooth one: there are conflicting voices in the world surrounding Zouina as well as in her personal linguistic practices.

Conflicting Voices

After one hour of the film, it seems that Zouina is finding her voice and is on her way towards liberating herself. However, in the last half hour, she comes into conflict with the women who are key to her liberation, especially Nicole and Malika. The first conflict with Nicole comes when the young and beautiful divorcee talks to Zouina about sexual liberation and the association of divorcees that she has created and invites Zouina to join them. Zouina refuses explaining that it would be 'péché'[10] [01:16]. Nicole is dumbfounded by the retort. Before the second conflict, in the six following scenes which slowly build up to the climax of the film, Zouina is silent – silenced by her husband who is more and more violent to her. In one scene he beats her harshly after finding a book that Nicole has lent her and which, being illiterate himself, he considers as a provocation: 'You read now?' [01:20]. He tears the book to pieces. With the book, it seems that Zouina's attempts to gain freedom are also being shred to smithereens.

The second conflict is with Malika. At the beginning of the scene, just after meeting for the first time, Zouina and Malika speak in Arabic but after a couple of sentences Zouina switches to French (it seems that it would have been impossible for her to speak about these new experiences in Arabic) and becomes animated while describing the radio programmes that she has been listening to and getting onto the subject of sexual liberation. To this flow of verbal independence, Malika explodes in Arabic: 'The woman is crazy'. She goes further: 'Sexuality is shameful' [01:26] and finally expulses Zouina from her home [01:28]. Zouina and Malika spoke the same languages but they did not understand each other. After the collapse of all possible friendship with her fellow country-woman, Zouina is shattered. But this break-up is a trigger for her as on an impulse she decides to board the same bus that she has passively seen passing her by for days. In a lyrical scene, the young and seductive bus driver, delighted to have Zouina with him, asks the passengers, to their dismay, to leave the bus. He takes Zouina and her children for a ride and beams at her with satisfaction [01:32]. They hardly talk as what they would like to say to each other is beyond words. However, it is obvious to the audience that Zouina seems really happy for the first time in the movie. When the bus driver leaves her in front of her door, the whole family and the neighbours are waiting for her. As usual, the mother-in-law

---

9   'Where is the store?'
10   'a sin'

abuses her but this time Zouina's husband interrupts his mother in French: 'Laisse-la tranquille, dégage'[11] [01:33], which signals a turn in their relationship. The old woman is shocked: 'Look at what France has done to me!' she says in Arabic. At the end, Zouina faces the camera and beams with satisfaction when she says: 'Demain c'est moi je les emmène à l'école'[12] [01:34] (French school is considered to have a major role in migrants' integration). Her liberation is complete.

Conclusion

I tried to show that in *Inch'Allah Dimanche* the female protagonist's appropriation of the second language participates in the construction of her identity and in the development of a feeling of home. It is through the progressive articulation of her self in French that Zouina liberates herself of the yoke of the traditional male order and opens up opportunities in the new country. In the film, Arabic is used to embody roots and traditions with women confined in the past such as Malika and the mother-in-law. French, on the other hand, opens up a world of freedom and modernity through the media and interaction with liberated women. At the same time, one could resent the fact that Zouina finds happiness through French and one could feel that this depicts a conservative vision of bilingualism and immigration. At this point, it is important to stress that we are not dealing with realistic linguistic phenomenon but with subjective representations of immigration and plurilingualism. As Yamina Benguigui was born and brought up in France, and putting aside the hereditary legacy that she mentions[13], it is clear that she has never experienced the events that she describes. One can argue that there is a part of stylisation in her depiction of migrants and their language and that her film seems to present a rather conservative view of the immigrants who in order to 'fit in' must master the majority language. It seems that in order to provoke empathy from a French audience, Benguigui was willing to compromise her discourse and twist it into something much more dema-gogical. Another explanation of this truncated perspective could be the one proposed by Sylvie Durmelat in her review of Benguigui's *Mémoire d'immigrés*:

> Cependant, on peut aussi voir là une question de distance de classe en train d'émerger, d'une part entre des élites issues de l'immigration qui ont la légitimité que leur octroie la société d'accueil en quête de représentants et, d'autre part, ceux qui subissent de plein fouet les conséquences de la crise économique [...].[14] (Durmelat 2008: 274)

It is true that it is rare in contemporary movies to have several languages co-existing in this way without one language taking over the other one. *Inch'Allah Dimanche*, despite its flaws, brings an interesting perspective on what it is to live with several

---

11   'Leave her alone! Go away!'
12   'Tomorrow I'll be the one taking them to school.'
13   Or that according to Carrie Tarr (2005: 174), the story was 'loosely inspired by her mother'.
14   'However, one could also see here the matter of an emerging social gap, on the one hand, between elites from the immigration who have gained a legitimacy from the host society which is looking for models, and on the other hand, those who are suffering from the consequences of the economical crisis [...].'

languages. However, I believe that the audience should be made aware of the ideological implications of linguistic choices in the public and private spheres. Indeed, it is high time for films to address the fact that linguistic preferences expressed at home are complex and linked to personal and community speech representations to minority and majority languages.

References

BHABHA, H. K. (1994), *The Location of Culture*, London: Routledge.

CARPENTER LATIRI, D. (2003), 'Représentations de la femme migrante dans *Inch' Allah Dimanche*', in: *The Web Journal of French Media Studies*, 6, URL: http://wjfms.ncl.ac.uk/LatiriWJ.htm (17 July 2010).

DEWAELE, J.-M. (2004), 'The emotional force of swearwords and taboo words in the speech of multilinguals', in: Special issue of *Journal of Multilingual and Multicultural Development* 25, 2–3, 204–222.

BLEICHENBACHER, L. (2008), *Multilingualism in the Movies*, Tübingen: Francke.

DEWAELE, J. M. (2007), 'Becoming bi- or multi-lingual later in life', in: Auer, P. & L. Wei (eds.), *Handbook of Multilingualism and Multilingual Communication*, Berlin/New York: Mouton de Gruyter, 101–130.

DION, R./LUSEBRINK, H.-J. & J. RIESZ (eds.) (2006), *Ecrire en langue étrangère. Interférences de langues et de cultures dans le monde francophone,* Québec: Nota Bene, Cahiers du CRELiQ.

DUNCAN, N. (1996), 'Renegotiating gender and sexuality in public and private places', in: Duncan, N. (ed.), *BodySpace: Destabilizing Geographies of Gender and Sexuality*, London/New York: Routledge, 127–145.

DURMELAT, S. (2008), *Fictions de l'intégration: Du mot beur à la politique de la mémoire,* Paris: L'Harmattan.

EDWARDS, N. & C. HOGARTH (2008), *Gender and Displacement: "Home" in Contemporary Francophone Women's Autobiography*, Newcastle: Cambridge Scholars Publishing.

EZRA, E. & T. ROWDEN (2006), *Transnational Cinema: The Film Reader*, London/New York: Routledge.

GAUVIN, L. (1997), *L'Écrivain francophone à la croisée des langues*, Paris: Karthala.

GAUVIN, L. (2007), *Écrire pour qui?: L'écrivain francophone et ses publics*, Paris: Karthala.

HOFFMAN, E. (1990), *Lost in Translation: A Life in a New Language*, New York: Penguin.

HOOKS, b. (1996), 'Choosing the Margin as a Space of Radical Openness', in: Garry, A. & M. Pearsall (eds.), *Women, Knowledge, and Reality: Explorations in Feminist Philosophy*, New York: Routledge, 48–55.

HUSTON, N. (1999), *Nord perdu,* Paris: Babel.

JONES, E. H. (2007), *Spaces of Belonging: Home, Culture and Identity in Twentieth Century French Autobiography*, Amsterdam: Rodopi.

KINGINGER, C. (2004), 'Bilingualism and Emotion in the Autobiographical Works of Nancy Huston', in: *Journal of Multilingual and Multicultural Development*, 25, 2–3, 159–178.

MINH-HA, T. T. (1994), 'Other than myself/my other self', in: Robertson, G./Mash, M./Tickner, M./Bird, J./ Curtis, B. & T. Putnam (eds.), *Travellers' Tales: Narratives of Home and Displacement*, London/New York: Routledge, 9–28.

NAFICY, H. (2001), *An Accented Cinema: Exilic and Diasporic Filmmaking*, Princeton, NJ: Princeton U.P.

PAVLENKO, A. (2005), *Emotions and Multilingualism*, Cambridge: Cambridge U.P.

PAVLENKO, A. (2006), *Bilingual Minds: Emotional Experience, Expression and Representation*, Clevedon, GBR: Multilingual Matters.

PAVLENKO, A. & J. M. DEWAELE (eds.) (2004), *Languages and Emotions: A Crosslinguistic Perspective*, Special double issue, *Journal of Multilingual and Multicultural Development, 25*, 2/3.

TARR, C. (2005), *Reframing Difference:* Beur *and* banlieue *Filmmaking in France*, Manchester/New York: Manchester U.P.

WIERZBICKA, A. (2004), 'Preface: Bilingual Lives, Bilingual Experience', in: *Journal of Multilingual and Multicultural Development, 25*, 2–3, 94–104.

Language and Cultural Contact:
Vive la mariée... et la libération du Kurdistan

Salih Akin

Introduction

Although the emergence of Kurdish Cinema is recent, an evident qualitative and quantitative increase in Kurdish films can already be observed. A number of Kurdish film festivals organised in different continents as well as the prizes attributed to Kurdish directors show a genuine activism in this field. Best known as a 'diasporic or exilic cinema' (Naficy 2001; Arslan 2009: 337), as it has been founded abroad, Kurdish cinema focuses on the issues expressed by all minorities, such as persecution, repression, exile, poverty, war, banishment, etc. Perhaps surprisingly, however, the conflicts and internal tensions of the Kurdish diaspora have rarely been treated. *Vive la mariée... et la libération du Kurdistan*[1] (shot in France by Kurdish filmmaker Hiner Salem in 1997) which is the first film dealing with such issues, seems to be a field of research on the contact of languages and cultures from a sociolinguistic point of view. The questions that I deal with in this article are twofold. On the one hand, I will analyse the cinematic representations of the language contact between French and Kurdish. The film, written mainly in French, alternates between several Kurdish dialects. This multilingualism is accentuated by the conflictual relationship of the Kurds from Turkey with Turkish language. On the other hand, I will investigate the way Kurdish refugees perceive the French language and culture and also how these perceptions are represented. I will initially summarise the emergence of the Kurdish cinema, with its main film-makers and recurrent issues.

The Emergence of Kurdish Cinema

We can date the emergence of Kurdish cinema to the 1990s. Although in the past many films, like *Zarê*, made in 1926 in Armenia, had already dealt with Kurdish themes, it was only in/not until the 1990s that we witnessed such an increase in the value of the Kurdish films, conceived and produced by Kurdish directors, that

---

1   *Long Live the Bride... and a Free Kurdistan.*

the expression 'Kurdish cinema' could install itself on the landscape of international cinematography. The reason for such a late inception compared to other cinemas
is basically related to the sociopolitical situation of the Kurds, living in four states
where, except for Iraq, they do not enjoy real recognition. What is more, the linguistic and cultural repression prevailing in the Kurdish territories has hindered any
possible artistic creation. Like many Kurdish militants and activists, numerous in-
tellectuals, authors, journalists and singers fled the country in the 1970s and 1980s,
forming a diaspora of more than one million individuals in Europe. Initially, a number of them had no intention of being film directors, yet the cinema turned out to be,
among others, a tool, maybe even the most efficient one, to express and represent the
sociopolitical situation of the Kurds.

Kurdish Cinema: 'An Accented Cinema'?

The absence of a sociopolitical status and of a certain recognition of the Kurds led to
the consequences that has deprived the Kurdish cinema of the constitutive elements
of a cinema industry. Equally negative are the hostile politics of the states in which
the Kurds live. As a matter of fact, these states have negative attitudes towards all
the attempts intending to introduce and promote Kurdish language, culture, history
and traditions. In this respect, apart from a limited number of Kurdish directors like
Bahman Ghobadi and Kazim Oz who could shoot films in their countries (Iran and
Turkey), it is only in exile and in their host countries that the Kurdish directors could
enjoy the freedom and also the material and human resources to shoot films. Some
directors like Y. Guney were even obliged to direct the shooting of their films from
inside their jail. For instance, the film *Yol* (*Permission*, Palme d'Or, Cannes 1982)
was shot in Turkey while Guney was in prison. The film was edited in Switzerland
when Guney himself went to exile in France.

Hence, Kurdish cinema has emerged as a cinema of diaspora and exile. In terms
of its characteristics and its themes and production modes that we will discuss below, Kurdish cinema can be considered as an accented cinema following the formu-
lation of Naficy (2001). Defining the form of 'accented cinema' as cinema essentially
situated in exile and diaspora, Naficy considers it to be 'an increasingly significant
cinematic formation in terms of its output, which reaches into the thousands, its variety of forms and diversity of cultures, which are staggering, and its social impact,
which extends far beyond exilic and diasporic communities to include the general
public as well' (Naficy 2001: 4).

The Kurdish Film-makers

Kurdish directors can be regarded as belonging to the second of Naficy's groups of
exiled and diasporic film-makers (the first being those who went into exile between
the late 1950s and mid-1970s largely as a result of decolonisation and the expansion
of the USSR, the second having emerged in the 1980s and 1990s as a result of the
failure of nationalism, socialism, and communism; the ruptures caused by the emer-

gence of postindustrial global economies, the rise of militant forms of Islam, the return of religious and ethnic wars, and the fragmentation of nation-states) (Naficy 2001: 10–11). As the Kurdish migration towards the west started to accelerate starting from the 1980s, Kurdish directors seem to bear the characteristics of the second group. Following the Islamic Revolution in Iran in 1979, the military coup of September 1980 in Turkey, the long and fierce Iraq-Iran conflict and the extermination campaign (Anfal) waged by the Iraqi regime against the Kurds, successive waves of political Kurdish refugees arrived in western European countries and to a lesser extend in North America. The launching of a campaign for the evacuation and destruction of Kurdish villages in Turkey starting from 1992, intensified with the assassination of Kurdish elites by the death squadrons of paramilitary Turkish forces, amplified the Kurdish migration to Europe. The Kurdish question was thus internationalised both in terms of its reach and in terms of public awareness and opinion. Among the Kurdish directors who went to exile during this period we can name Yilmaz Guney (France), Nizamettin Aric (Germany), Hiner Salem (Italy and France), Yuksel Yavuz, Yilmaz Aslan (Germany), Jay Jonroy (USA) and Ahmed Zîrek (France). The movement initiated in the diaspora for the creation of an independent Kurdish cinema was reinforced in the Kurdish territories by a limited yet progressive recognition of Kurdish identity by states like Turkey and Iraq. Thanks to these evolving conditions, film-makers like Bahman Ghobadi in Iran and Kazim Oz in Turkey were able to shoot films relating to the Kurdish reality. These film-makers are examples of those who are considered by Naficy as operating in internal exile in opposition to those forced to an external exile (Naficy 2001: 11). According to Naficy, the artistic and moral authority of the directors operating in internal exile is more important than that of directors driven away from their country:

> Many filmmakers who could escape internal exile refuse to do so in order to fight the good fight at home – a fight that often defines not only their film style but also their identity as oppositional figures of some stature. By working under an internal regime of exile, they choose their 'style of struggle' and their potential social transformation […]. When they speak from this site at home, they have an impact even if, and often because, they are punished for it. (Naficy 2001: 11)

It is because of political and legal troubles related to his filmmaking in Turkey that Guney was forced into exile in France. Similarly, Bahman Ghobadi continues to suffer reprisals in Iran's Islamic regime which does not appreciate the art of cinema, especially when it is used to throw light on the Kurdish reality.

The Themes Anchored in the Kurdish Reality

Like all oppressed nations investigating and recreating themselves in cinema, the Kurds have also transformed cinema into a tool for emancipation and self-expression. As a tool of representation for the denunciation of poor living conditions, the underdevelopment of Kurdish regions and repressive state politics, the cinema has been instrumentalised for multiple functions by Kurdish directors. Yilmaz Guney, the first symbol and a legendary figure of Kurdish cinema, deals in his films with the tragedies experienced by the Kurds. In the films he directed and played in as an actor (*Seyit*

Han and *Topragin Gelini*[2] 1968), he always took the role of persons facing injustice. In other films (*Aç kurtlar*[3] 1969, *Umut*[4] 1970, *Umutsuzlar*[5] 1971, *Acı*[6] 1971, *Ağıt*[7] 1971), he placed the oppressed person at the centre of his questioning.

These themes are also at the centre of the films directed by Iranian Kurdish director Bahman Ghobadi. In his first feature film *A Time for Drunken Horses* (1999), the first Kurdish film made in Iran and crowned by a *Caméra d'Or* in the 2000 Cannes Film Festival, he narrates the fate of five orphan brothers and sisters left to their own devices. With *The Turtles Can Fly* (2003), evoking the destiny of the children collecting mines to sell, the film-maker denounces the misery of these mutilated, injured kids bearing the suffering in both body and soul. In *Ax*[8] (1999), Kazim Oz, a Kurdish film-maker from Turkey, narrates the tragedy of an old Kurd who does not want to leave his land despite the destruction carried out by the Turkish military. Hiner Salem, in *Kilomètre Zero* (2005), the first film presented in the Cannes Film Festival as a production of Kurdistan, deals with the forcefully enrolled Kurdish soldiers during the Iraq-Iran war.

The displacement of the population, forced exile and life in the diaspora are also among the aspects treated by diasporic directors. In *Klamek bo Beko* (*A Cry for Beko*, 1992), Nizamettin Ariç traces the story of the forced and risky escape of the son of a Kurdish peasant, Beko, from the Turkish part of Kurdistan to Germany. Yuksel Yavuz, in *A Little Bit of Freedom* (2006), tells the story of a young Kurd taken in by his relatives in Hamburg after the death of his parents. In *Fratricide* (2005), Yilmaz Arslan works on the tensions between Kurdish and Turkish communities in Germany through the story of two Kurdish asylum seekers who come to be friends. As we see, Kurdish cinema seems to be firmly anchored in the Kurdish reality. It is even a powerful tool for the exteriorisation of this reality otherwise veiled by authoritarian regimes. For several years, these 'engagé' films shot by the diaspora have been able to find their place in movie theatres and make themselves known to critics. This growing success has led to the establishment of the *Kurdish School of Cinema*, founded in 2007 in Salaheddin University, in Iraqi Kurdistan. Various Kurdish films festivals organised in the major cities throughout the world[9] are witness to the vivacity of this emerging cinema.

---

2   *The Bride of the Earth.*
3   *The Hungry Wolves.*
4   *Hope.*
5   *The Hopeless.*
6   *Pain.*
7   *Elegy.*
8   *Soil.*
9   Cologne, London, Montreal, 2006; Hamburg, Melbourne, 2007; Paris, 2007, 2008, 2009; Frankfurt, 2009.

Vive la mariée... et la liberation du Kurdistan

The film *Vive la mariée... et la libération du Kurdistan* is one of those films produced in the diaspora, with the Kurdish community in Paris as its theme. Unlike the
other films that favour showing the consequences of the cultural and political repres-
sions waged against the Kurds, *Vive la mariée... et la libération du Kurdistan* takes
the spectators into the contradictions of a exile community. Its tragicomic approach
is further supported by a critic of some of the practices of resistance movements and
of certain Kurdish traditions. The film was shot in Paris in 1997 by the Kurdish film-
maker Hiner Saleem. The director, an Iraqi Kurd, left his country at 17, went into exile first to Italy and finally settled down in France. He has directed a number of films,
one of them being autobiographic entitled *Passeurs de rêves*[10] (2000). His other films
are *Vodka lemon* (2003), *Kilomètre zéro* (2004), *Dol ou la vallée des tambours*[11] (2006)
and *Les Toits de Paris*[12] (2007).

The screenplay of *Vive la mariée* is written by Hiner Saleem and it can give a realistic image of the practices of members of the diaspora. The director states:

> This situation reflects the Kurdish reality. The first generation of Kurdish refugees,
> not many, could not return to the country. Their families would take the responsibil-
> ity of finding them wives. This was done through the photos that the parents would
> send to their sons. When the son would agree, the girl would be 'sent' to him with a
> guarantee on her moral and corporal integrity. This type of marriage was ironically
> called a 'postal marriage'. Nowadays, the video camera has drastically modified this
> practice, we talk about the 'video marriage'. (Interview with the film-maker, Dossier
> Distributeur[13])

The film is set in the tenth district of Paris, where the Kurds, Turks, Indians and
Tibetans are concentrated. With a length of 1h 40, the film was produced by *Les
Films Du Rivage* with the technical advisory of Bertrand Tavernier and it won prizes in 1998 at both the Festival d'Angers and the Mannheim-Heidelberg International
Film Festival. The director mixes professional and unprofessional actors. Except for
six professional actors [Georges Corraface (Çeto), Marina Kobakhidzé (Mîna), Fatah
Soltani (Maşko), Şahla Aalam (Leyla), Tuncel Kurtiz (Uncle Ismet), Serge Avedikian (Azad), Stéphanie Lagarde (Christine), Bruno Lopez (Misto Vidéo)], the other actors, themselves political refugees, are members of the Paris-Kurdish community and
work in diverse domains like the catering, textile and construction industries. The director legitimises his preference for mixing professionals and unprofessionals by his
desire to 'work with people who have internalised a double culture, an uprooting'.[14]
That is why we find among the actors playing the Kurds an Armenian (Serge Avedikian), a Turk (Tuncel Kurtiz, the main actor in *The Herd*, 1978, by Yilmaz Güney),
a Greek (Georges Corraface), and a Georgian (Marina Kobakhidzé). This presence of

---

10 *Beyond Our Dreams*.
11 *Dolor the Valley of the Drums*.
12 *Under the Roofs of Paris*.
13 See URL: www.abc-lefrance.com/article.php3?id_article=1217 (1st February 2010). The extract is
    translated from French into English by the author.
14 See URL: www.abc-lefrance.com/article.php3?id_article=1217 (1st February 2010).

actors speaking different languages and from different cultures gives a multilingual and multicultural dimension to the film.

The film is a window on Kurdish society and its contradictions in the diaspora. Çeto, a Kurdish refugee in Paris, who has a friendly French girlfriend Christine, wants to get married to an authentic Kurdish girl. We first meet him selecting the most beautiful girls from a video catalogue from his homeland. The girl who arrives in Paris, however, is Mîna, not the girl he had chosen but her elder sister. The reason is that according to Kurdish traditions, older girls have to get married before their younger sisters. Çeto is shocked at the sight of this timid and plain girl. Other Kurds in the diaspora, active in unions struggling for Kurdistan's freedom, intervene to put pressure on Çeto, while Mîna, shy and locked up at first, blossoms in a union of Kurdish feminists. A number of other themes are treated through this marriage story seen from the viewpoint of a comedy of values: life in the diaspora, the conditions of Kurdish women who do not hesitate to confront prejudices and traditions, the reception of newcomers, the solidarity within the community, the resistance movement and its condemnable practices such as collecting 'revolution taxes', the celebrations, integration to the French society, and the way this society is seen by the Kurds.

The Filmic Representation of the Language Contact

Vive la mariée... et la libération du Kurdistan is clearly a 'polyglot film': 'The polyglot film [...] is naturalistic: languages are used in the way they would be used in reality. They define geographical or political borders, 'visualise' the different social, personal or cultural levels of the characters and enrich their aura in conjunction with the voice' (Wahl 2005: 2). There are several languages used very naturally in the film, of which the most used and thus the most in contact with each other are Kurdish and French. The French spoken in the film is standard French, though it also shows variations, with the Kurdish accent dominating the sequences where Kurdish characters are at stake. Other immigrant accents are also exhibited during the procedures at the prefecture. As for Kurdish, two of its four dialects are used in the film: the interaction between the main characters takes place mostly in the Kurmanji dialect which is spoken by the majority of the Kurds in Turkey and Syria and by some of the Kurds in Iraq and Iran. The Sorani dialect, spoken by the other Kurds in Iraq and Iran, is used principally in relation to Leyla, a Kurd from Iraq. Turkish is not used in the film directly, yet it haunts the interactions in the group, transferring the conflictual relationship of languages in the native country is to the host country.

Kurdish music and songs that frequently ornament the sequences of celebrations, engagement parties, and folkloric dances but also funerals, emphasise the polyglot dimension of the film. Şahla Aalam (Leyla) and Temo (grocer) are two well-known professional musicians in Kurdish community and they sing in the film in their respective dialect: Şahla Aalam in Sorani and Temo in Kurmanji. Finally, a French song, *Ignace*, illustrates the misadventures related to the name conversion of Fayaz which I will discuss below. It must be added that '[...] because they [polyglot films] are anti-illusionist in the sense that they do not try to hide the diversity of human life behind the mask of a universal language' (Wahl 2005: 2), all sequences in Kurdish are subtitled in French. Thus, language contact seems to be overly emphasised in the film. As will be seen, this language contact is regularly transformed into a reflection on the position of languages in the native country, in diaspora and in the identity construction processes of individuals.

Kurdish-French Language Contact

The theme of the film makes Kurdish and French the central pivot of verbal interactions. The shift from one language to the other does not only aim to facilitate the transmission of messages but also plays a certain role in showing the identity and the otherness of the characters. From that perspective, it acquires a semiological function, raised by Wahl: 'Language itself as a semiotic system is part of the message of the film and not only a vehicle of content' (Wahl 2005: 1). Showing the origin and identity of the characters by way of language is what we observe in the following sequence where Çeto, accompanied by his friends, makes his way to Invalides train station in Paris to pick up the fiancée whom he had chosen on the video:

> Mîna: Ez Mîna me.
> Çeto: Ben/c'est pas elle/c'est pas elle/Misto/c'est pas elle/dis-moi que ce n'est pas elle!
> Misto: Non.
> Azad: Alors?
> Çeto: Na/ka Berîvan can/ka Berîvan can?
> Leyla: Attends/tu n'as pas le droit de lui parler sur ce ton.
> Çeto: Je t'assure Leyla/ce n'est pas la fille de la video!
> Leyla (à Mîna): Ez zor xweşhal im hatim pêşvazî/zor bi xêr/pirr giran neke/hemû tişt zu dirûst dibî.[15] [13:20 – 14:45]

This sequence, which also constitutes the thematic node of the film, puts Kurdish and French into contact. The actors look for the right code in their linguistic stocks to be able to communicate according to the linguistic profile of their interlocutors. Mîna, who has just arrived in France, does not speak French yet, while all the other participants of the sequence are bilingual in Kurdish and French. The absence of lexical interference phenomena within the utterances is evidence that these characters have a good command of these two languages:

> Çeto: Ez lêviyê Berîvanê me/he/ez te nasnakim/bibêje!
> Mîna: Berîvan xwişka min a/a piçûk e.
> Çeto: C'est la sœur aînée/et ben/moi je ne veux pas.[16] [14:54 – 15:38]

---

15 Mîna: I am Mîna.
    Çeto: But/this is not her/this is not her/Misto/this is not her/tell me that this is not her!
    Misto: No, she's not.
    Azad: So what?
    Çeto: No/where is Berîvan can/where is Berîvan can?
    Leyla: Hold on/you don't have the right to talk to her this way.
    Çeto: I assure you Leyla/this is not the girl on the video!
    Leyla (to Mîna): I am glad to meet you/welcome/don't worry/everything will well be alright.
16 Çeto: I am waiting for Berîvan/I do not know you/tell me!
    Mîna: Berîvan is my younger sister.

Contact between Kurdish Dialects

The contact between Kurdish and French is emphasised by another contact, relating to an intralingual frame. Kurdish is a polydialectal language comprises of four principal dialects (Dimili, Gorani, Kurmanji, and Sorani) (Akin 2008: 145; Blau 2006: 323). In the film, the dialects in contact are Kurmanji and Sorani, the dialects spoken by the majority of the Kurds. The dialect choice seems to depend basically on the origin of the actors. The Kurdish actors originally from Syria and Turkey use Kurmanji while those originally from Iraq and Iran speak mainly Sorani. There is nothing surprising in this choice because it corresponds to the sociolinguistic profiles of the actors; however, we can question the choice of a dialect for non-Kurdish actors.

Çeto (Georges Corraface), Mîna (Marina Kobakhidzé), Uncle Ismet (Tuncel Kurtiz), and Azad (Serge Avedikian) all speak the Kurmanji dialect. Even if the film does not show explicitly the country of origin of the Kurds, extracultural knowledge explains why the non-Kurdish actors also speak Kurmanji. The film is based on the Kurdish community in Paris, which consists mostly of Kurds from Turkey who principally speak Kurmanji. Thanks to their demographic dominance, they are also the most active Kurds in political and associative domains. Thus, the theme of the film is inspired by their reality. That is why the operation of associative structures, the photos of the martyrs exhibited in the association and at demonstrations, the textile workshops and certain real facts brought up in the film (such as the Susurluk affair, whose name comes from a Turkish city where a traffic accident had revealed the collusion between the government and the Turkish mafia) (Raufer 2005), refer to the world of the Kurds in Turkey. This world is further confirmed by the sequence where Mîna describes her hometown, Farqîn, situated in Turkish Kurdistan, and compares it to Paris in a letter that she sent her parents.

Though the sequences are subtitled in French, in the sequences where two of the dialects are used there are no clues that allow French locutors to detect this contact. Nevertheless, a kurdophone can immediately detect this dialectal variation which, I think, is aimed particularly at Kurdish spectators. Thus, in a sequence where Leyla and Mîna, alone in Leyla's place, switch the two dialects:

Leyla: Tu dixwazî tiştek vexweyî?
Mîna: Erê/hinkek av dixwazim.
Leyla: Danişe/malik min gewre nîne/lê bo Parîsê baş e/zanî/lêre azad im/mêrek nîne li ser min.
Mîna: Te mêr/zarok nînin?
Leyla: Na/mêrkim hebû/balam têkçû/dizanî/min her tim îş kirdiwe/mêrên kurd naxwazin jin kar bike/dixwazin her danişe li mal.
Mîna: Çî kar dikî?
Leyla: Ez parêzer im/ez serpereştî komelekî jinanî Kurdistanî jî dikim.[17] [18:36–19:40]

Çeto: She's the elder sister/I want none of this.
17 Leyla: Would you like to drink something?
Mîna: Yes/I would like some water.
Leyla: Sit/my home is not big/but it is good for Paris/you know/I am free here/I have no husband.
Mîna: You have no husband/children?

Leyla, an Iraqi Kurd, speaks the Sorani dialect, while Mîna speaks Kurmanji. Even if the two dialects are the closest ones, the morphological features that distinguish them are a difference of case (nominative and oblique), and of gender in names and pronouns, and an agentive construction of past tenses of transitive verbs. Besides, declension and gender have disappeared in Sorani. In this dialect, reflexive suffixes, which do not exist in Kurmanji, have largely taken the position of case functions. In this sequence, the mutual intelligibility between these two locutors is presented as flawless. Hiner Saleem places the closest two dialects in the same sequence through this filmic representation of mutual intelligibility. Beyond the unity through linguistic diversity, his objective is to show the national unity of the Kurds by a filmic representation. This sequence, just like the others where the two dialects are in use hand in hand, is essentially aimed at the Kurds and their prejudice concerning the absence of unity among them.

The Contact of Kurdish – Turkish – French

This division accentuated by the state frontiers separating the Kurds is instilled into the heart of another sequence putting Kurdish, Turkish and French into contact, where the community members, gathered in their association, announce the forthcoming marriage of Çeto:

> Azad: Baş e/heval/wek hûn dizanin hevalê me Çeto dê jin bîne/baş e heval!
> Kurdish character 1: Excuse-moi camarade/je ne comprends pas/parler le kurde/est-ce que tu peux parler le turc?
> Kurdish character 2: Jamais de la vie!
> Kurdish character 3: C'est toujours la même chose/moi aussi je suis kurde/j'ai grandi à Istanbul/je ne parle pas le kurde!
> Fayaz: Et alors/toi tu ne parles pas le kurde/mais ici/tout le monde ne parle pas le turc/lui/il est kurde d'Iran/lui/kurde de Syrie/lui il est kurde/moi/kurde de l'enfer/ merde/et toi/tu ne veux pas que tout le monde apprenne la langue turque pour ta gueule!
> Misto: Non ça c'est vrai/Fayaz a raison.
> Fayaz: Et je te rappelle que je ne m'appelle pas Fayaz!
> Azad: Du calme/du calme/du calme/on garde nos prénoms kurdes et on parle français/comme ça tout le monde comprend.[18] [03:52–05:43]

Leyla: No/I had a husband/but he left/you know/I have always worked/Kurdish husbands do not want women to work/they want their wives always to stay home.
Mîna: What is your work?
Leyla: I am an advocate/I also lead an association of women from Kurdistan.
18 Azad: Ok/comrade/as you know/our comrade Çeto will marry/ok comrade!
Kurdish character 1: Excuse me comrade/I do not understand/speak Kurdish/can you speak Turkish?
Kurdish character 2: No way!
Kurdish character 3: It is always the same thing/I am a Kurd too/I've grown up in Istanbul/I don't speak Kurdish?
Fayaz: So what/you don't speak Kurdish/but here/they don't all speak Turkish/see/he's a Kurd from Iran/and/he's a Kurd from Syria/he is a Kurd/I/a Kurd from hell/shit/and you/you'd like everyone to learn Turkish just for your bloody benefit!
Misto: No/that's true/Fayaz is right.
Fayaz: I remind you my name is not Fayaz!

This sequence drives us into the heart of the ethnolinguistic conflict that characterises the Kurdish context. We observe that the phrase uttered by Azad in Kurdish is not understood by all, thus creating a linguistic insecurity. The demand that they speak in Turkish runs up against a fierce resistance by other members who see in it the culmination of a linguistic assimilation process. This sequence transposes the division among the Kurds to the diaspora context, yet, even more importantly, it shows how some of the Kurds have been alienated from their own language. Beyond the problems of mutual understanding, the director points here to what we could consider a 'linguistic tragedy': the locutors, what is more, even the committed militants, do not know their language and request the others communicate in the language of their political opponents. This is a major paradox that has characterised the principal Kurdish resistance movement in Turkey, the PKK (Workers' Party of Kurdistan), and that the director criticises rightfully. The dialectal variation that crosses through Kurdish and the usage of Turkish that imposes itself as a consequence of the assimilation process give way to French, the language of the host country, that intervenes as a factor of neutralisation for this conflict. As a matter of fact, further discussions end with a consensus of French as the language of communication, as Azad concludes: 'We keep our Kurdish names and we speak in French/this way everybody will understand' [05:35]. Some other sequences of the film are also studded with fierce reactions *vis-à-vis* Turkish. This is especially the case with a celebration sequence [01:08:00] during which the audience whistle for a Kurdish singer, Cano, upon the announcement of his name. The audience know him very well because in Kurdistan he had not had the courage to sing in Kurdish. Even if Turkish is not brought up directly, the sociopolitical practice refers directly to Turkey, the only country that had banned Kurdish music up until the beginning of the 1990s.

Filmic Representation of Language and Identity Mutation

Language contact is also a component of a process which is sometimes related to integration to the host society and sometimes to identity construction processes of individuals. Two sequences of the film point directly at the linguistic trajectory that many newly arrived immigrants in Europe are confronted with. The use of the native language ends up giving way to the language of the host country, here French. In the film, this transition, manifested in the linguistic interferences between Kurdish and French, is not only seen as an integration process. Thus, in the following sequence where Çeto dictates to Mîna what she should cook:

Çeto: Zimanê xwe bibire/bi pîvaz/û bexdenûs/û îsotê çêke/wek tu hizdikî/bo îşev/ baş e?
Mîna [hesitating]: C'est moi qui coupe ta langue!
Çeto: Hein?
Mîna: J'ai dit oui/d'accord/je vais couper ma langue/ger tu wer dixwazî?

Azad: Take it easy/we stick to our Kurdish names and we speak in French/this way everybody can understand.

Çeto: Malmîrat/elle a appris le français.[19] [01:02 :32 – 01:02:55]

Çeto does not believe in his ears upon hearing Mîna speaking French. What is more, he is astonished to hear his humiliating remarks return directly to himself. Nevertheless, he must submit to the evidence that Mîna has learned French! The expression 'malmîrat' (bloody/hell) says a lot about the foreseeable consequences of this learning. Here, learning French for a Kurdish woman is presented as a possibility for her liberation, her emancipation from the man. In the second sequence where the women, among them Mîna and Leyla, are in the Hammam getting themselves massaged, the transition from Kurdish to French is considered 'desirable':

> Mîna: Jineka fransî heye/ji min re negot/ji wî re jî negot.
> Leyla: C'est la vérité des hommes/ce sont leurs mensonges.
> Mîna: Bi kurdî bibêje!
> Leyla: Na/bi kurdî/naxwazim tu êdî bi kurdî qisebikî/nexwe fransî fêr nabî.
> Mîna: Dis-moi!
> Leyla: La vérité des hommes/ce sont leurs mensonges.[20] [01:02:55 – 01:03:38]

Leyla's feminist commitment pushes Mîna to abandon Kurdish completely so that she could learn French better. Beginning from that sequence, Mîna starts to speak exclusively in French, even to Çeto. As a matter of fact, the more she learns French, the more independent she gets to be in her life. This learning enables her construct a new identity; from a shy and closed young woman, as she was at the beginning of the film, she ends up being able to rely on herself in all domains of her life. She no longer needs Çeto for her accommodation, for her food, for working nor for her papers. On the contrary, she uses make-up, takes care of herself and becomes more and more beautiful. This situation creates an alienation/detachment between them: while Mîna was dependent on Çeto at the beginning of the film, it is now Çeto, witnessing helplessly the metamorphosis of Mîna, who needs her. This helplessness is even intensified since his girlfriend, Christine, left him. The inversion of power in the film is thus presented as a consequence of learning French.

---

19 Çeto: Cut your tongue/cook it with onion/with parsley/chilli and/as you like/for this evening/ok?
    Mîna [hesitating]: I cut your tongue!
    Çeto: Eh?
    Mîna: I said yes/I agree/I will cut my tongue/if you like?
    Çeto: Bloody hell/she has learned French.
20 Mîna: He's got a French wife/he didn't tell me/he didn't tell her.
    Leyla: This is men's truth/these are their lies.
    Mîna: Say it in Kurdish?
    Leyla: No/in Kurdish/I don't want that you to speak in Kurdish/otherwise you won't learn French.
    Mîna: Tell me!
    Leyla: Men's truth/is their lies.

Identity Construction in Exile

The representation of language and culture contact thus leads to new forms of identity. As a matter of fact, exile and the diaspora are the best contexts for individuals, driven away from their native land yet obliged to adapt to the culture of the host society, to put a lot of themselves into a process of identity reconstruction. In the Kurdish context, identity reconstruction takes on a particular dimension in the diaspora: the exiles, free from the restrictions and interdictions imposed on them and their language in their native country, can freely reappropriate their native language and culture. This reappropriation also leads to the questioning and rediscovery of oneself. For many Kurds who arrived in France at a young age, the diaspora is an enriching experience allowing them to take a step back and obtain a different perspective on the language and culture, to construct their identity. Various sequences of the film represent the developments that characterise the identity reconstruction processes in the uprooting of the exile. I will investigate particularly one aspect, the one that places the name of a character (Fayaz) at the heart of a linguistic identity conflict.

Changing Name to Build a New Identity

The problem with the Fayaz' name is shown in various sequences. Fayaz is one of Çeto's close friends and a committed member of the association. Each time that his friends use the name *Fayaz*, the holder of the name shows a fierce reaction:

> Azad: Toi/tu n'as toujours pas de papier/toi?
> Fayaz: Parce que j'ai demandé de changer de prénom.
> Çeto: Oh/Fayaz!
> Fayaz: Ça me fait chier.[21] [07:25–07:30]

Fayaz is not happy with his name. For him, this is a name that he received from the Turkish language, even if it has an Arabic origin and a rather appropriate meaning ('extremely generous'). His friends call him by the nickname 'Maşko' and they use *Fayaz* only to annoy him. Up until three years ago, it was forbidden to attribute typically Kurdish names to children. As a result, Kurdish children were identified by Turkish names (Akin 2004). It was imperative to obey this interdiction within the official frontiers of Turkey, yet it makes no sense in the diaspora, where individuals enjoy the freedom of changing names, which Fayaz actually does and applies to French authorities to change his name. In the following sequence where he is busy copying the papers, he is faced with the astonishment of his friend Misto:

> Fayaz: A cause du changement de mon prénom.
> Misto: Ça fait trente ans que tu t'appelles Fayaz/et tu veux t'appeler Marc-Maurice/ c'est nul!

---

21   Azad: You/you still have no residence permit/have you?
     Fayaz: Because I asked to change my first name.
     Çeto: Oh/Fayaz!
     Fayaz: It pisses me off.

Fayaz: Moi/ça fait trente ans que je rêve de me débarrasser de ce putain de prénom turc/Fayaz/Fayaz![22] [39:46–40:00]

Misto does not make sense of Fayaz's intention to change his name because he has had it for such a long time. However, Fayaz retorts that he has always wanted to get rid of his name. This desire to change his name implies what is at stake when it comes to the social usage of the names. As a matter of fact, the name is not a simple label to identify individuals. It assigns the individuals into classes, gives information about them. The names are also bearers of discourse, and loaded with judgements and connotations regarding social positioning. As a consequence, they cognitively influence the individuals and participate in their identity construction processes. Thus it is actually the Turkish identity marked and transferred by the name that Fayaz wants to change by changing his name. Towards the end of the film, a sequence [01:19:44] presents the result of Fayaz's initiative, having finally obtained his French name, *Fernandel*. Yet the announcement of the change does not please Fayaz who receives it very timidly: we do not change our identity simply by changing our name. *Fernandel*, the new and virgin name, must be dressed up, empowered and finally turned it into an identity marker. This sequence ends on a song from the musical comedy *Ignace*, shot in 1937 by Pierre Colombier, the famous prewar comic. Interpreted by French singer and actor Fernandel (whose real name was *Fernand Joseph Désiré Contandin*) in the role of Ignace Boitaclou, the song shows all the affection that can be invested in a name:

Ignace, Ignace, c'est un petit petit nom charmant...
Ignace, Ignace, qui me vient tout droit de mes parents.
Ignace, Ignace, il est beau, il me va comme un gant,
Moi je le trouve plein de grâce, Ignace, Ignace,
Je n'm'en crois pas mais il me place, Ignace c'est un nom charmant![23]

Conclusion

Hiner Saleem's first feature film, *Vive la mariée* treats language and culture contact from a metalinguistic perspective in relation to the role of languages and the construction of an indivdual's identity in diaspora. The film places the conflict of linguistic identity in the context of diaspora, confirming H. Bozarslan's position on the conflicting nature of Kurdish immigration (Bozarslan 1995). The multilingualism intentionally shown is not only presented as a consequence of immigration, but also as a means of revealing the political conflict in the country of origin of actors. This

---

22   Fayaz: Because of my change of name.
     Misto: It's thirty years Fayaz your name/and you want to call yourself Marc Maurice/sucks!
     Fayaz: I/I have dreamed of getting rid of this bloody mess Turkish name for thirty years/Fayaz/Fayaz!
23   Ignace, Ignace is a charming little name ...
     Ignace, Ignace, that comes straight from my parents.
     Ignace, Ignace, it is beautiful, it fits me like a glove,
     I think it's full of grace, Ignace, Ignace,
     I'm not too proud but it gives me a position, Ignace is a charming name!

conflict is certainly represented in its various forms, but the contact and the status of languages, the role that languages play or should plays in the integration or in the struggle of a nation in search of recognition has been placed at the heart of the inter-actions. The fact that Kurdish is an endangered language in the Kurdish areas has undoubtedly contributed to the amplification of its filmic representation. However, the film also attacks so-called archaic traditions of the Kurdish society, which has its own contradictions and internal struggles. Furthermore, the representations of the perception of French language and culture by Kurdish exiles in the film constructs a depiction of France in which it appears especially altruistic and homely. Future re-search would benefit from further examination of this representation which is like-ly to be derived from the personal experiences of the director, but should perhaps be nuanced and assessed relative to current local context.

References

AKIN, S. (coord.) (2008), *La Langue Kurde, Études Kurdes*, n° 9, Paris: L'Harmattan.

AKIN, S. (2004), 'La dénomination des personnes et la construction identitaire: le cas des prénoms kurdes en Turquie', in: *Bulletin suisse de linguistique appliquée*, 80, 27–38.

ARSLAN, M. (2009), *Kürt sinemasi: yurtsuzluk, sinir, ölüm* [The Kurdish Cinema: Stateless, Border, Death], Istanbul: Agorakitapligi.

BLAU, J. (2006), *Manuel de kurde sorani*, Paris: L'Harmattan.

BOZARSLAN, H. (1995), 'L'immigration kurde, un espace conflictuel', in: *Migrants – Forma-tion*, 101, 115–129.

NAFICY, H. (2001), *An Accented Cinema. Exilic and Diasporic Filmmaking*, Princeton: Princeton U. P.

RAUFER, X. (2005), 'L'Union Européenne, la mafia turque et... l'Arlésienne', in: *L'outre-mer*, 10, 83–95.

WAHL, Ch. (2005), 'Discovering a Genre: The Polyglot Film', in: *Cinemascope – Inde-pendent Film Journal*, vol.1, 1–8.

IV. Post-Colonialism and Cultural Contact in French Migrant Cinema

Raymond Rajaonarivelo's Cinema:
Between Madagascar and France

Karine Blanchon

Madagascar and France are historically and economically linked, the former having been for many years under the domination of the latter, a fact still attested to today by linguistic and ethnic mixes in Madagascar.[1] In the cultural and cinematic spheres in particular, traces of this relationship are clear. Cinema was imported to Madagascar by the explorers Alfred Machin and Léon Poirier at the beginning of the twentieth century. The first Malagasy director, Philippe Raberojo, had access to a camera because of his close relationship with the French colonial administrators, which is how he managed to film a docu-fiction entitled *Rasalama martiora*[2] (1937). After the country declared its independence in 1960, Malagasy students were sent to France to be trained in cinematography. Raymond Rajaonarivelo was among them. Born in Madagascar in 1952, he was an assistant director before he made his own short film in 1974 called *Izaho Lokanga Ianao Valiha*[3]. But it was his first feature film, *Tabataba*[4] in 1988, that really helped him to make his name with a wide audience. He then made a documentary on the famous Senegalese sculptor Ousmane Sow before directing his second feature film, *Quand les étoiles rencontrent la mer*[5] in 1996. More recently, he co-directed with César Paes a 90-minute documentary on Madagascar through the epic story of a group of Malagasy musicians: *Mahaleo*. Influenced by the atmosphere of the films of Akira Kurosawa and Wong Kar Wai, Raymond Rajaonarivelo presents his interest in nature and childhood in his works of fiction. In that regard he is similar to other African film-makers such as Ousmane Sembène, Djibril Diop Mambéty or Idrissa Ouédraogo. Nevertheless, like many other African directors who have migrated to Europe, Raymond Rajaonarivelo sees his native country from the perspective of someone with mixed heritage. Though he has lived on the outskirts of Paris for many years, he returns to Madagascar for filming. This dual culture is reflected notably in his feature films.

---

1   Translation by Rebecca Willis.
2   *The Martyr of Rasalama.*
3   *I am 'lokanga', you are 'valiha'.*
4   *Rumour.*
5   *When the Stars Meet the Sea.*

Our article intends to show, through a description of his two main works of fiction, how Raymond Rajaonarivelo expresses this mixed background, which is not only inherent to his personal journey but also to the Malagasy society which gave birth to it. Mixtures manifest themselves in his films in choices of spoken language and in cultural practices, which are a source of nostalgia and then of rejection. To begin with we will see how the linguistic plurality of dialogues is used by the director to put Madagascar and France in opposition. Subsequently, we will look into the way in which multilingualism allows Rajaonarivelo to question his identity and that of his cinema.

An Exile's Perspective: *Tabataba*

In Madagascar, linguistic policy is complex because a multitude of dialects coexist along with three official languages: English, French and Malagasy. The last two are the most widely spoken within the country. Official administrative documents are bilingual, as are numerous national daily newspapers and television programmes. French is mainly spoken in towns, where there is trade and a lot of activity. It is not just the preserve of educated people but is acquired during exchanges between foreigners and workers, and used in tourism and prostitution.

Despite its relatively frequent use in daily life, Malagasy cinema stills give French a limited role. In the history of Madagascar, language has often been used to make political demands, as a way of affirming one's sense of belonging to a nation. This country is part of the French-speaking world, more because of a willingness to be part of an international political community than out of linguistic convictions. Films are, for the most part, in Malagasy, rarely released abroad, they target a local audience first and foremost. As well as certain literary works written in French by Malagasy authors, Malagasy national cinema does include some bilingual works. Raymond Rajaonarivelo arrived in Paris during a time when Madagascar was going through a serious political crisis. The majority of his fellow film-makers who stayed in the country had either to stop working or to adhere to the censorship brought into force. Because of his geographical distance, Raymond Rajaonarivelo had greater freedom of expression. In his first feature film *Tabataba*, he used this distance to express his nostalgia and affection for his country of birth through his mother tongue and his visual depiction of ancestral traditions.

The Film of Memory

For his first feature film, Raymond Rajaonarivelo took a major event in Madagascar's history as his theme: the independence uprising which took place in 1947 in the south of the country. For several months, part of the Malagasy population revolted against the French colonial army in a bloody struggle. The repression in villages that followed was terrible, leading to fires, arrests and torture. Women, children and the elderly were the indirect victims of the conflict and suffered particularly from famine and illness. This subject had already been dealt with in the cinema two years previously by the Malagasy director Ignace Solo Randrasana in his film entitled *Ilo tsy very*[6] (1986), as well as acting as the inspiration for several novels. Realising there was a reality that had been hidden for a long time, Raymond Rajaonarivelo positions himself as a director who was close to his roots despite his geographical distance. Beyond a historical description of these events, this film-maker justifies his choice of theme by what he calls the 'duty of memory'.[7] His father told Raymond Rajaonarivelo about certain episodes in this uprising when he was 12 years old, and, having never forgotten what he had been told, he decided to write a script to tell these tales to the Malagasy people:

> Après mon deuxième court métrage, je suis retourné dans la région où avait eu lieu l'insurrection de 1947. Pendant trois mois, j'ai interviewé les gens qui avaient vécu cette époque. J'ai aussi beaucoup lu de livres sur ce sujet, je me suis documenté. Mais je voulais créer ma propre histoire en m'appuyant sur ces faits. Tout le monde me racontait une histoire, jamais la même. Cela a donné lieu à une rumeur, Tabataba, qui me paraissait refléter ce que j'avais entendu là-bas. Ce sont toutes ces mémoires qui m'ont servi à faire le scénario que j'ai écrit ensuite.[8]

Moreover, the first name of the main character of *Tabataba* is significant because 'Solo' means 'the replacement'. He will replace his brother as head of family after his relatives' death and keep alive the memory of those who died during the revolt. Not only is this child a unifying link between all of the film's characters, he above all symbolises the collective memory that he represents and of which he is the beneficiary. This is still a very sensitive subject between France and Madagascar. It was many years before historians dared to research it and before the survivors started to talk about it: 'In the years following the rebellion, the generation that lived through 1947 has learned, through certain subtle turns of mind, to avoid the topic' (Cole 2001: 224). It was only in July 2005, during an official visit, that the French President Jacques Chirac acknowledged '[the] unacceptable nature of the repression born of the excesses of the colonial system' (Chirac 2005: 2).

It took Raymond Rajaonarivelo six years to complete this project, from the initial idea to the film's release in cinemas, notably because of the care he took to give a specific meaning to each image: the film evoked the 1947 uprising as a rumour. During the event, everyone involved predicted their own imminent victory, and peddled false reports on the arrival of reinforcements and canons, so as to destabilise or motivate the troops. The imaginary world built around this revolt is clearly evoked throughout the film, from the title to the final scenes when the insurgents' weapons are discovered to be nothing more than pieces of wood in the shape of guns. It is the story of a small Malagasy village during the uprising. Solo is still too young to fight but sees his brother and most of the men in his clan join up. He hopes his el-

---

6   *Eternal Blessing.*
7   Raymond Rajaonarivelo, personal interview conducted in Paris in 2003.
8   'After my second short film, I went back to the area where the uprising had taken place in 1947. For three months I interviewed people who had lived through that period. I also read a lot of books on the subject. But I wanted to create my own story based on these facts. Everyone told me a story, but never the same one. That gave rise to a rumour, Tabataba, which seemed to me to reflect what I had heard there. I used all those memories to then write the script' (Rajaonarivelo, interview 2003).

der brother will return a hero, but instead he sees the French army arrive to put down the rebellion. Raymond Rajaonarivelo deliberately took the side of the Malagasy insurgents by placing the camera in the heart of the village. Furthermore, in showing the community's resistance to the oppressor, he encourages the spectator to take the side of those who are fighting for their freedom. He relates some particularly deadly events but without ever showing bloody images on screen, with the exception of the first battle scene. Violence is latent and omnipresent without being visible, which makes the subject more penetrating. It is palpable in the proverb read out at the beginning and the end of the film, which leads the spectator to foresee an imminent threat: 'Hiran'ny ala maitso, hiran'ny riana, ny hazo tapaka tsy mitovy halavana, hoatra ny haren'olombelona'[9] [02:23–02:33; 01:14:06–01:14:17]. Making use of such an adage is not insignificant because such proverbs, which often have several meanings as well as a moral, play an integral part in the everyday life of the Malagasy and are difficult to understand for those who do not speak their language. It is therefore a way for the director to reaffirm his attachment to his mother tongue. Moreover, positioned in these key parts of the story, namely the prelude and the conclusion, this sentence also allows the director to reinforce the film's political viewpoint.

A Patriotic Film

Tabataba is fiction, and, even if it has a real historical subject, its message is coloured by the feelings of the film-maker for his native country given that the dialogues are in Malagasy and only the colonial soldiers speak in French. The mutual lack of understanding between the two countries is accentuated by the use of wordplay, which is intended to ridicule the colonists and again to encourage the audience to side with the rebels. The most obvious example is a retort by Solo's grandmother, Bakanga. When the colonial administrator brings voting papers to the community, she speaks to him in Malagasy: 'Taratasy anaty boaty: ny tonon-kira any an'ala.'[10] The *aide-de-camp* then translates this into French for the colonist, who doesn't understand Malagasy: 'Elle a dit: Vive la France!'[11] [18:01–18:11]. This sentence allows Bakanga to get the upper hand over the representative of the colonial administrators by pointing out the linguistic gap separating the Malagasy from the French:

> Many Westerners have tried to convince the non-occidentalized Malagasy through a logical reasoning based on syllogistic thinking. The Westerner tries through concise and logical arguments to express the reasoning as clearly as possible, only to arrive at breakdown. Then a couple of words from a Malagasy quoting a proverb or a slogan that to the European has nothing to do with the problem at stake persuade the listeners at once. The Malagasy have used the technique of reasoning through comparison. The use of striking metaphors convinces the Malagasy. (Dahl 1999: 144)

---

9   'Listen to the leaf, listen to the waterfall, not all timber is cut to the same length like the wealth of mankind.'
10   'Papers in a box are wind in the trees.'
11   'She said: Long live France!'

Thus, linguistic differences become a political argument, since to refuse to speak or to understand French during colonisation was an act of resistance. This refusal to give in to the cultural pressure exercised by the French also appears in the lessons of the schoolmaster who makes the pupils repeat 'Madagasikara Tanindrazana' in Malagasy, which means 'Madagascar, Land of the Ancestors' [04:35 – 04:45] and not 'France, our Homeland' as the colonial administrator says [17:38].

Raymond Rajaonarivelo also highlights the resistance of the Malagasy people to the oppressor who wants to forbid traditional practices. When in exile, either enforced or voluntary, the linguistic and cultural practices of the country of origin are often maintained. The director shows his attachment to his native country through his depiction of traditional ceremonies such as one in which a line of trees is covered by a white sheet. The trees represent those killed in the uprising and whose bodies have not been found, because custom dictates that the deceased be buried in the family tomb so that they may join their ancestors. Likewise, the film-maker emphasises the fact that the Malagasy continue the tradition of '*tavy*' which consists of scorching the earth before planting to make it more fertile, despite this being banned by the colonists. The colonial administrator, when he learns this custom is still being carried out, is heard to say to the villagers: 'Au tavy? Je croyais avoir déjà dit que cette pratique est interdite. C'est mauvais pour le sol. Si vous brûlez la forêt, les sols ne tiennent plus. La pluie les emporte. D'abord, vous devez cultiver du café.'[12] He says this in French and the translation into Malagasy by the *aide-de-camp* underlines once again the mutual lack of understanding between the two countries: 'Voarara ny tavy! Tsy fanao ny mandoro ala'[13] [17:10 – 17:28]. These fires are also a symbol of resistance as they 'are the expressions of the anger, the resentment felt towards power or any abusive authority' (Alexandre 2007: 44).

It is during one of these fires that Solo's brother decides to join the insurgents. The representation of these traditions is equally a way of denouncing the economic exploitation of Madagascar by foreigners. The population was encouraged to grow coffee for exportation rather than to grow products for local consumption. Moreover, this patriotism is felt in a more formal way in the political ideas revealed in the dialogues; the rebels mention the arrival of American soldiers several times, who may come to their aid to overthrow the oppressor just as they did for the Jews during the Second World War [32:56 – 33:05; 37:45 – 38:00]. However, the outcome of this story shows a certain weariness since *Tabataba* is above all a film about a defeat. Hopes of liberation were dashed as the rebels once again failed in their fight to have their rights recognised in 1947, just as they were during previous Malagasy revolts against the colonisers. The leaders of the uprising were arrested and numerous Malagasy perished during this time. The revolt is still a very sensitive topic in the collective memory, as is the whole period of colonisation. In the same way as the Senegalese

---

12 'Tavy? I told you: that's forbidden! It ruins the land. If you burn the forest, the soil won't hold. Rain washes it away. You must grow coffee.'
13 'Tavy is forbidden. Anyone caught burning the forest will be shot.'

director Ousmane Sembène had great difficulty with *Camp de Thiaroye* en 1988, Raymond Rajaonarivelo great difficulty financing *Tabataba*:

> J'ai cherché des producteurs et je me suis heurté à beaucoup de refus car c'est une histoire assez tragique et pas très glorieuse vis-à-vis des Français. Mais je ne pouvais pas uniquement chercher des producteurs à Madagascar car ce n'était pas rentable. Je suis donc allé démarcher des producteurs en Suisse, en Europe, un peu partout en fait et j'ai fini par trouver Jacques Leglou qui a trouvé cette histoire incroyable.[14] (Rajaonarivelo, interview 2005)

This audacious French producer agreed to finance the film which went on to appear at several international film festivals, winning various awards. It was also chosen for Directors' Fortnight at the Cannes International Film Festival in 1988, for the Taormina Film Festival in Italy and for the FESPACO a year later. However, although the film deliberately took the side of the Malagasy insurgents, it was nevertheless not allowed to be shown in Madagascar:

> On m'avait fait déjà pas mal de difficultés pour tourner ce film. Finalement, il a été diffusé à Madagascar par l'intermédiaire du Centre Culturel Albert Camus qui organisait un festival de cinéma à Madagascar et qui a choisi de projeter mon film malgré tout. Ensuite, le gouvernement malgache ne pouvait plus s'opposer à sa diffusion dans l'île. Il y a alors eu des files d'attente incroyables devant les salles de cinéma où passait le film.[15] (Rajaonarivelo, interview 2005)

Thus, the difficult chain of events linked to the making, the release and even the subject of the film demonstrates the very strong relationship connecting the director to his country of origin and his adopted home. This mixture of cultures is characteristic of a mixed background, born of the movement of people and ideas in a more or less violent way as Serge Gruzinski explains in his book (Gruzinski 2008: 22). Nevertheless, although he takes the side of Madagascar in his first feature film, Raymond Rajaonarivelo seems to distance himself from his native country in his second work of fiction. Doubts are seen to appear with relation to the continuation of certain ancestral customs, and multilingualism is used once again. While his first feature film clearly makes use of Malagasy for the majority of the time, in the second film it is on an equal footing with French. Raymond Rajaonarivelo is viewing his country from a more personal and at the same time a more distant perspective.

---

14 'I looked for producers and came up against a lot of refusals as it's quite a tragic story and not very glorious with regards to the French. I couldn't only look for producers in Madagascar because it wasn't profitable. So I went canvassing producers in Switzerland, in Europe, everywhere actually and in the end I found Jacques Leglou, who found the story incredible.'

15 'It had already been very difficult for me to make the film. In the end it was shown in Madagascar through the Centre Culturel Albert Camus who organised a film festival in Madagascar and who chose to show the film despite everything. After that, the Malagasy government couldn't oppose its release on the island. There were incredible queues outside the cinemas where it was screened.'

A Film of Mixed Race: *Quand les étoiles rencontrent la mer*

As has just been demonstrated, Raymond Rajaonarivelo's first film was tinted with nostalgia, whereas in his second feature film, *Quand les étoiles rencontrent la mer*, his vision of his native country is more modern, even though it deals with an ancestral tradition. He defends the idea that, in order to develop, a country must adapt and leave behind certain aspects of its culture and language. This film is the product of exchange and mixing. The population of Madagascar is made up of migrants from Europe, China, India, the African continent and neighbouring islands. Besides the mixture of communities, Malagasy vocabulary, whose origins are in the Indonesian language from the south of Borneo, also borrows from Bantu, French, English and Arabic. Furthermore, Raymond Rajaonarivelo migrated to France and is therefore imbued with another culture. In this film French and Malagasy are used in turn in dialogues as, beyond the denunciation of an ancestral belief, the director evokes above all themes of difference and the search for identity in the immigration process.

The Dilemma of Immigration

Quand les étoiles rencontrent la mer is a colour film which starts by presenting a Malagasy tradition, according to which a child born on the day of an eclipse is given a strength which might be dangerous for the community in which he or she lives. To neutralise this evil power, the newborn must undergo the trial of the zebus. For one night, the baby will be trampled by the zebus, and if he or she survives, will be able to stay in the community. In the village of Ambohimanao, in the south of Madagascar, Kapila is born on the day of an eclipse, and, as tradition dictates, his father puts him in the zebu pen. However, a young woman sees this and saves Kapila. She takes him far away from the village and raises him as her own son. He is nevertheless scarred by his time in the pen; he has a limp, and his classmates make fun of him because of his disability. Once he is an adult, Kapila stays in the capital, Antananarivo, with his adoptive mother, who makes '*lamba*' (pieces of fabric), while he collects empty bottles to resell at the market. One day, Kapila meets an old woman who tells him the truth about the day of his birth. He decides to return to his village to get his vengeance.

The film underlines the mixing of ideas that has taken place within the director because of his geographical distance from his native country and his integration into another culture, noticeable in the metaphor of movement. Journeys allow the director to define his characters, and those who move are associated with those who are marginalised, as is the case of the main character given that he leaves his native village for the city and then returns there. In Madagascar, the rural exodus is a sizeable phenomenon, because migrants believe that they will be able to leave behind their poverty and make their fortune in the city. Kapila's case is one of flight towards anonymity and the promise of a new start, where no-one knows of his past. Travelling is alluded to several times through images of trains and through Kapila and his friend's shared longing to go and see the sea. The main protagonist does finally make a journey, not to the ocean but to his native village. This return to his roots takes on a great importance, as much for its position in the middle of the film as for its duration. It takes approximately thirteen minutes of the story [37:00–50:50]. Moreover, the marginality of the main character is evoked in dialogues, through the word 'alone', for example when his adoptive mother tells him: 'Aujourd'hui chacun de nous est seul à sa manière mon fils. Mais maintenant *toi* tu seras vraiment seul'[16] [36:17–36:26]. She also confirms he is different when she says to him: 'J'ai tout fait pour que tu deviennes un homme comme les autres mais quel genre d'homme pouvais-tu devenir?'[17] [33:44–33:51]. It is precisely this break from the norm that creates imbalance and exclusion, in a society based on the concept of '*fihavanana*', which in Malagasy culture means solidarity and mutual aid. This concept, difficult to translate, implies that there are moral obligations between members of the same community who, for example, must attend traditional ceremonies so as to maintain social cohesion within the group. But '*fihavanana*' tends to get lost amid urban individualism:

> People who have moved to the city expect to be treated as members of the extended family. But communal life as it was lived in the village compound is not possible in the city. The market economy particularly favours individualism and core family myopia, which is inconsistent with the expectations of the rural family. (Dahl 1999: 162)

Whereas in the West identity is often linked to the individual, in Madagascar the identity of an individual is first defined by his belonging to a group. According to Dubois, the Western man favours the 'personal self' while the Malagasy man lends more importance to the 'collective self'. Many Malagasy films show several main characters belonging to the same circle of friends, the same family or even the same community (a religious one, for example) and it is their union which makes their eventual success possible. In *Quand les étoiles rencontrent la mer* the newfound peace between the villagers and Kapila is made apparent through the romance between a young villager and the main protagonist.

Malagasy films attract a local audience because they appeal to social connections that unite the members of a community, through '*fihavanana*'. However, the proliferation of American and Asian films broadcast on television channels has gone some way to influence the viewer, who is now conditioned to seeing, perpetually, foreign behaviour and ways of life. On average, between three and four foreign feature films are broadcast daily on each of the six terrestrial channels. At the weekend, this number rises to five or even six. 99 % of these are American action films, dubbed into French even if 'only ten percent of the Malagasy population is really francophone' (Rasoloniaina 2000: 355). Immigration therefore brings with it a cultural break and at the same time a linguistic mix that is very apparent in *Quand les étoiles rencontrent la mer*.

---

16 'Today every one of us is alone in our own way my son, but now *you* really will be alone.'
17 'I've done everything I can for you to become a man like any other, but what kind of man could you become?'

Two Cultures and Plurilingualism

Raymond Rajaonarivelo's second film is the product of a mixed background in the very conception of the film and in its dialogues. *Quand les étoiles rencontrent la mer* was written in collaboration with Santiago Amigorena, financed by French producers, and the music was composed by a French musician originally from Côte d'Ivoire and Haiti. Aside from these numerous collaborators, the Western influence is clear in the rhythm given to the film; whereas in his previous film shots could last several minutes, in *Quand les étoiles rencontrent la mer* they are very much shorter. In making this change the director distances himself from the 'slow' label often attributed to African films because of shot lengths. Nevertheless, even if the form is westernised, the content is Malagasy. The film bears the mark of its creator: 'C'est toujours très personnel un film, il raconte toujours plus ou moins une partie de ma vie'[18] (Rajaonarivelo, interview 2005). The director's personal involvement in the film is even apparent in the story itself, given that he is physically present in it and speaks in Malagasy to the protagonist, showing him the way [45:27–45:50].

> Pendant tout le film Kapila est perdu, dans son voyage initiatique, il ne sait plus où il est et ce qu'il doit faire: doit-il vraiment y aller vers cette montagne qui soutient le ciel, ou continuer à se perdre? La seule personne qui pouvait le ramener dans le film ou dans l'histoire c'est celui qui a écrit l'histoire et qui mène le film, et c'est moi, voilà pourquoi c'est moi qui lui indique le chemin du film ou le chemin de LA FICTION.[19] (Rajaonarivelo, interview 2005)

There are therefore very strong connections between the story and its author, which is also perceptible in the film's bilingual dialogues. Like the director, Kapila speaks French and Malagasy and can use either one of them, depending on the situation. He speaks in French to his adoptive mother but she sings him lullabies in Malagasy to help him fall asleep as a child. He learns French at school but as the years go by he expresses himself more and more frequently in Malagasy, all the more when he returns to his native village. This gives rise to a bilingual discussion between Kapila and his friend, a thief: 'Tu sais toujours pas parler en français?'[20] Kapila asks him in French; 'Tsy nianatra aho fa amin'izao'[21], the thief replies in Malagasy. The rest of the conversation is in Malagasy [12:57–13:16]. French is therefore put in the same category as education and modernity while Malagasy is the mother tongue, the language of tradition. It is, in addition, not just by chance that the character of the old blind woman, who is a metaphor for his conscience, addresses Kapila in Malagasy. She reminds him who he is. The same is true elsewhere for his father who first addresses his son in French but

---

18 'A film is always very personal, it always essentially tells the story of a part of my life.'
19 'Throughout the film Kapila is lost. During his initiation journey he doesn't know where he is anymore nor what he should do: should he really go towards that mountain that is holding up the sky, or get even more lost? The only person who can get him back into the film or into the story is the one who wrote the story and who is directing the film, and that's me, that's why I show him the film's direction, or FICTION's direction.'
20 'Can't you speak French?'
21 'I didn't go to school like you.'

then asks him in Malagasy, 'Ary ianao, fantatrao ve izy ianao?'[22] [58:48–58:53]. He then continues in French: 'Mon fils, quel est ton nom?'[23] 'On m'appelle Kapila'[24], his son replies. His father gets close to him and whispers in his ear: 'Kapila? Ce n'est pas un nom, c'est une infirmité!'[25] [59:28–59:45]. Through these alternate uses of French and Malagasy, we see more clearly the character's instability in his search for identity. Here again the relationship with the director's personal tale is apparent, because the French language was forced upon him for the dialogues although

> Je ne peux pas tourner en français [...] Ce n'est pas ma culture. Ce n'est pas là où j'ai vécu l'enfance, où j'ai senti le vent dans mes pieds ou dans mes cheveux, où j'ai vu les paysages. [...] Les impondérables économiques imposent de se plier à certaines choses [...], mais il faut être fin pour ne pas détruire l'histoire. Le vrai combat est devant la feuille blanche: ça ne passera pas; alors il faut le dire autrement pour que ça passe...[26] (Interview Raymond Rajaonarivelo in Barlet 1996: 220–291)

Balance is regained at the end of the film, as Kapila's father will from then on speak to him in Malagasy, which shows that he has once again been accepted as part of the community [01:12:00–01:12:38]. *Quand les étoiles rencontrent la mer* had a mixed reception on its release, probably because of what it had borrowed from two cultures:

> Plus que jamais, les cinéastes sont condamnés à lutter contre les fantasmes qui voudraient les enfermer dans un espace traditionnel territorialement déterminé. C'est pourquoi ils revendiquent l'errance comme caractéristique de leur place dans le monde. Plutôt qu'un cinéma métisse, c'est un cinéma nomade qui cherche à s'imposer, sans jamais renier ses origines mais en les considérant comme un passage.[27] (Barlet 2005: 3)

Immigration, which has spread unbalance, finally becomes a claim for identity.

Raymond Rajaonarivelo's Nomadic Perspective

Up to now Raymond Rajaonarivelo has made only two 35mm Malagasy films. This article has attempted to show that multilingualism and the cultural contacts present in his cinematography reflect his mixed background:

> La culture africaine est volontiers syncrétique, sa force étant d'opérer sans cesse un habile tri de ce qu'elle veut prendre ou ne pas prendre dans ce qui vient la traverser.

---

22 'And you, do *you* only know who you are?'
23 'My son, what's your name?'
24 'They call me Kapila.'
25 'Kapila? That's not a name, that's an illness!'
26 'I can't film in French. [...] It's not my culture. That's not where I grew up, where I felt the wind on my feet and in my hair, where I saw the landscape. [...] Uncertain economic situations force you to conform to certain things [...], but you have to be astute so as not to destroy the story. The real struggle is against the blank page; that won't work, so we'll have to say it differently to make it work...'
27 'More than ever before, film-makers are condemned to fight against the fantasies that would like to confine them to a territorially determined, traditional space. That is why they claim that wandering is characteristic of their place in the world. Rather than being mixed race cinema, it is nomadic cinema that seeks to impose itself, without ever disowning its origins but seeing them as a step/ passage.'

Ce n'est pas un métissage, c'est une appropriation de ce qui vient l'enrichir culturellement.[28] (Barlet 2005: 1)

So, in Raymond Rajaonarivelo's filmography, appropriation has not yet been fully achieved, as much on a cultural level as on a linguistic one. In his first feature film *Tabataba*, traditions appear to be a tool with which to affirm Malagasy national identity. In his second work, in contrast, the topic is more nuanced, owing to the director distancing himself from his native country. Likewise, while he chooses to use French and Malagasy in his dialogues, they exist side by side but are not mixed. Contrary to dialogues in films currently being shot in Madagascar which combine standard Malagasy with slang and foreign vocabulary within single sentences, the dialogues in *Tabataba* and *Quand les étoiles rencontrent la mer* are either in French or Malagasy. This distinction is discernible in the first film discussed in this article, in which Malagasy is reserved for the Malagasy and French for the French. In his second film, *Quand les étoiles rencontrent la mer*, assimilation is highlighted as the dialogues alternate between French and Malagasy, more because of the situation than because of the person addressed. The multilingualism present in Raymond Rajaonarivelo's films is a way of underlining the communication problems that exist between the Malagasy, both within the country and outside of it. Through the examples of these two films it can therefore be concluded that Raymond Rajaonarivelo's cinema, influenced as much by Madagascar as by France, is nomadic.

References

ALEXANDRE, C. (2007), *Violences Malgaches*, Antananarivo: Foi et Justice.

BAKARI, I. & M. CHAM (eds.) (1996), *African Experiences of Cinema,* London: British Film Institute.

BARLET, O. (1996), *Les Cinémas d'Afrique Noire: le regard en question*, Paris: L'Harmattan.

BARLET, O. (2005), 'Du cinéma métisse au cinéma nomade: défense du cinéma', in: *Africultures*, URL: http://www.africultures.com/php/index.php?nav=article&no=3727 (21 July 2010).

BLANCHON, K. (2007), 'La pluralité langagière et ses contraintes dans le cinéma malgache francophone', in: *Glottopol*, 12, Université de Rouen.

BLANCHON, K. (2009), *Les Cinémas de Madagascar, 1937–2007*, Paris: L'Harmattan.

CHIRAC, J. (2005), 'Discours de Monsieur Jacques Chirac, Président de la République lors du dîner offert en son honneur par M. Marc Ravalomnana, Président de la République de Madagascar', in: URL: http://www.elysee.fr/elysee/root/bank/print/30784.htm (21 July 2010).

COLE, J. (2001), *Forget Colonialism? Sacrifice and the Art of Memory in Madagascar*, Berkeley: University of California Press.

DAHL, O. (1999), *Meanings in Madagascar. Cases of intercultural communication*, Westport: Bergin and Garvey.

HALL, S. (2007), *Identités et cultures. Politique des Cultural Studies*, Paris: Éditions Amsterdam.

GRUZINSKI, S. (2008), *Planète métisse*, Paris: Actes Sud.

---

28 'African culture is willing to reconcile different practices, its strength being constantly to sort carefully through what it wants to take and what it does not from what crosses its path. It is not hybridisation; it is an appropriation of that which will enrich it culturally.'

MALKMUS, L. & R. ARMES (1991), *Arab and African African Film Making*, London: Zed Books Ltd.

MANNONI, O. (1984), *Le Racisme revisité. Madagascar, 1947*, Paris: Denoël.

MULLEN KREAMER, C. & S. FEE (2002), *Objects as Envoys, Cloth, Imagery, and Diplomacy in Madagascar*, Washington: University of Washington Press.

PFAFF, F. (2004), *Focus on African Films*, Bloomington: Indiana U. P.

RASOLONIAINA, B. (2000), 'Le 'Variaminanana': Négociation d'une Appartenance Biculturelle', in: Allibert C. & N. Rajaonarimanana (eds.), *L'extraordinaire et le quotidien: variations anthropologiques*, Paris: Karthala, 351–359.

SHAKA, F.O. (2004), *Modernity and the African Cinema*, Trenton: Africa World Press.

SHARP, L. A. (2002), *The Sacrificed Generation. Youth, History and the Colonized Mind in Madagascar*, Los Angeles: University of California Press.

TRONCHON, J. (1986), *L'Insurrection malgache de 1947. Essai d'interprétation historique*, Fianarantsoa/Paris: Éditions Ambozontany Fianarantsoa/Karthala.

Memory, the Body, and the Transformation of Migrant Subjectivities in Lâm Lê's film *Vingt nuits et un jour de pluie*

Hélène Sicard-Cowan

Introduction

Generally considered to be the first Franco-Vietnamese film-maker to make films in France, Lâm Lê migrated to France in the 1960s after attending a French lycée in Saigon and witnessing his family's split along political party lines in the aftermath of decolonisation (Blum-Reid 2003: 39). Recently, Lê fictionalised this migrant experience in his autobiographical film *Vingt nuits et un jour de pluie*[1] (2006). Forming the third and last chapter of a trilogy devoted to Vietnam after his films *Rencontre des nuages et du dragon*[2] (1981) and *Poussière d'empire*[3] (1983), the film narrates a chance encounter between an unnamed Vietnamese man living in Paris and an equally anonymous German woman raised in the South of France by her grandmother. Both protagonists left countries torn by war and political division. Whereas he chose to live in the capital of Vietnam's former colonial ruler, she elected to settle on the island of Java. At the onset of their relationship, he seems struck by cultural amnesia. She, for her part, is plagued by an unnamed traumatic event in her past that prevents her from visiting her old Parisian apartment, located directly above his.

Lê is committed to making cinema which seeks to convey experiences, knowledge, fantasies and memories that may otherwise be lost to translation in the migration process. As Laura Marks indicates, the differences between cultures' regimes of sense knowledge mean that untranslatability is an integral part of the postcolonial experience (Marks 2000: 116). In Lê's film, spectators are given the opportunity to experience this aspect of the postcolonial condition since Lê's characters speak several languages, including French, Vietnamese, German, Indonesian and English. Moreover, Lê's decision not to provide his viewers with a systematic translation of enunciations uttered in languages other than the protagonists' main idiom of exchange (French) also needs to be understood in conjunction with his stated intent not to fall into the trap of colonialist, exoticist filmmaking which lays bare his subjects' souls, reducing their complexity in

---

1   *Twenty Nights and One Day of Rain.*
2   *Where Clouds and Dragon Meet.*
3   *Dust of Empire.*

the process. His gesture is thus one that aims at preserving the opacity, or integrity, of his characters, as will become clear below. To come back to the film's plot, both protagonists undergo psychological transformations that offer them a way out of their initial predicaments, as their relationship unfolds during the three weeks they spend as lovers in his Parisian apartment. In what follows, I want to explore this transformation of migrant subjectivity in Lê's autobiographical film while paying particular attention to the connections the film draws between language(s), memory and the body.

The Male Protagonist

Considering that Lê describes *Vingt nuits et un jour de pluie* as a fictional rendering of his own experience as a Vietnamese migrant overinvested in the Western world, it is not surprising that his male character is obsessed with France. Lê's Franco-Vietnamese protagonist is a divorced, lonely, and work-absorbed architect who describes Paris as his only home and the most beautiful city in the world, consumes only French food and wine, and sees Java only as an exotic travel destination. We also learn that he only believes what he sees from behind his glasses, that he arrives at airports exactly two hours prior to his flight departure, and that he dismisses the Asian tradition of making offerings to one's ancestors as mere superstition. In other words, the film's protagonist aspires to embody French ethnocentrism and the Cartesian man *par excellence*: self-controlled, rational, and ocularcentrist. However, in the sequence in which he is first introduced to the spectators, the actor's deliberately mediocre acting suggests that the character's exclusive identification with Frenchness and Cartesianism is forced; from the woman's point of view, we watch the character entertain a phone conversation with his mother in Vietnamese, promising her to honour his dead father by lighting candles [04:45 – 05:17]. Although he shows contempt for his mother's request in front of the female intruder after having hung up the phone, we later discover that he owns a small altar hidden behind a row of books. Similarly, during his phone conversation, he switches from Vietnamese to French as soon as he meets the woman's gaze. Such details suggest that this character's seemingly negative relationship to the Vietnamese world derives from shame.[4] Put differently, this character embodies the untenable position occupied by colonial subjects who are, in the words of Homi Bhabha, 'almost the same, but not quite white' (Bhabha 1994: 89). When his female guest asks him to talk about his native country, Lê's character is unable to do so. He explains instead that the twenty years he has spent in France have rendered his memory defective. However, the film suggests that it is the male character's ocularcentrism, and not exile, that is responsible for the latter's apparent memory loss.

---

4   According to Karl Britto, '[t]he sense of inferiority experienced by many Vietnamese as a result of their position as subjects of the French empire was exacerbated by the colonial educational system, which actively affirmed the cultural superiority of the French via its program of assimilation' (Britto 2004: 25 – 26).

In his attempt to remember his past life at the onset of the film, Lê's male protagonist relies solely on an old black and white photograph featuring himself as a
child sitting on his father's shoulders. But photography turns out to be completely
inadequate as a catalyst for memory since this character has absolutely no recollection of the moment captured by the camera. He is forced to rely on his mother's narrative about the individuals visible on the photograph to make sense of what he sees
there. Like Roland Barthes before his own childhood photo, Lê's protagonist thus
experiences the certainty of photographic evidence for a former life mixed with a
complete lack of Proustian recollection (Barthes 1980: 99–113).

Not only is the male protagonist plagued by shame and memory loss in relation
to his native country, but his body is also a site of conflict claimed by both Vietnam
and France. As he tells the woman in the opening sequence, his body is the only
thing he owns from there (Vietnam), yet the very same body is simultaneously a
painful reminder of French colonialism and cultural assimilation:

> La France, c'est un corps grand comme ses colonies. La France n'envoyait pas de
> troupes dans ses colonies, c'était son corps qui s'en allait et ce corps, les peuples sou-
> mis devaient l'ingérer pour devenir les enfants de cette mère d'outre-mer. Et je suis
> ce corps [...]. Je fais corps avec la France.[5] [19:13–20:26]

The excessive quality of the male protagonist's identification with Frenchness is suggested in the film when we learn that he broke his own ankle in order to be granted
political asylum in France, a gesture which marked his definitive physical separation
from the loved ones he left behind in Vietnam.

This traumatic episode in the male protagonist's past life in Vietnam is not
voiced until the outcome of the film. Indeed, although completely fluent in French as
a result of his colonial education, Lê's Vietnamese protagonist does not talk about
this highly traumatic moment with his lover. At the same time, Lê does give a voice
to his Vietnamese character, albeit an English one, thereby highlighting the divide
between conventional representations of colonised subjects as voiceless beings, and
his own representations: at the very end of the film, the Vietnamese character is
shown opening up and unburdening himself from his trauma during a conversation
in English with an Indonesian woman he meets while travelling in Java. By contrasting the relationship of the male protagonist with his lover and his relationship with
the Indonesian teacher, Lê therefore raises the question whether his male protagonist's inability to talk about his trauma in French has to do with the French language
itself, i.e. language of the former coloniser, or with his interlocutors, or both.

Interestingly enough, until the scene during which the trauma is finally expressed,
Lê nonetheless renders such trauma perceptible by using a rattling sound similar to
that produced by Rumpelstiltskin, a midget found in the German eponymous folktale
and referenced in Lê's film. Every time we hear this sound, the male protagonist reach-

---

5   'France is a body as big as her colonies. France didn't send troops to her colonies, it was her body
    she sent, and that body, the subjected peoples had to ingest it in order to become the children of that
    mother overseas [...]. And I am that body. I make one body with France.' (Translations by the author.)

es for his ankle, his facial features distorted by acute pain. By alluding to the trauma of colonisation through his staging of the body in pain of an Asian man, Lê offers a response to the ways in which his predecessors Alain Resnais and Marguerite Duras represent Asian masculinity in *Hiroshima, mon amour*, both the film and the eponymous script written by Duras herself.[6] Resnais' film narrates the brief love affair that takes place between a French actress and a Japanese architect in Hiroshima in the aftermath of the nuclear bombing of this city by the US near the end of World War II. Commenting on the representation of the male protagonist in Duras' script, Rey Chow states in her article titled 'When Whiteness feminizes…:'

> [R]ealism and referentiality, being scorned mimetic orders, are no longer good enough for a progressive, avant-garde representation of the French woman, who embodies a profound, psychologically individuated reality. But realism and referentiality, she [Duras] seems meanwhile to say, remain adequate for the representation of yellow people, whose reality, being less profound, can continue to be treated as a mere group event […]. All in all, whether hierarchically organized (in which case it is disparaged as mere referentiality) or disavowed (in which case it should be forgotten in favour of a modern, internationalist humanism), cultural difference – "Japan" – is there simply in order for the subjectivity – the existential survival, the attainment of individual being – of the French woman to be performed. (Chow 1999: 157–158)

In *Hiroshima, mon amour*, the trauma experienced by the French woman's Japanese lover and his family never finds expression, be it verbal or non-verbal. This aspect of the film suggests not only a lack of psychological depth on the part of the Asian man, as Chow argues, but it could also undermine the horror of the event itself, i.e. the nuclear bombing of Hiroshima. As Sharon Willis aptly remarks in her description of the film script, Duras' writing exhibits a 'fascination with its own textual practice' that could result in an 'endless deferral of the subdiscursive' (Willis 1987: 34). In contrast to Resnais' film, Lê highlights the psychological trauma experienced by his Vietnamese protagonist as a former colonial subject by foregrounding the latter's physical suffering, all the while refraining from extorting from him a confession in a language used by the French to 'injure' the Vietnamese during the colonial era. I borrow the term 'injure' from Judith Butler who, in her book called *Excitable Speech*, defines the effects of 'injurious speech' as follows:

> One need only consider the way in which the history of having been called an injurious name is embodied, how the words enter the limbs, craft the gesture, bend the spine. One need only consider how racial or gendered slurs live and thrive in and as the flesh of the addressee, and how these slurs accumulate over time, dissimulating their history, taking on the semblance of the natural, configuring and restricting the doxa that counts as 'reality'. (Butler 1997: 159)

---

6   In the chapter 'Diaspora and Cultural Displacement: Linda Lê and Tran Anh Hung', Jane Winston relies on Roland Barthes' notion of literary fields of struggle to argue very convincingly that Vietnamese diasporic artists cannot do otherwise but to confront themselves with Duras' canonical vision of Indochina in their works (Winston 2001: 183–212). In the case of a film such as *Vingt nuits et un jour de pluie*, it would be very difficult to overlook references to Resnais' film. A detailed analysis of Lê's borrowings and deviations from *Hiroshima, mon amour* is, however, beyond the scope of this paper.

Butler's reflections are very pertinent for the analysis of colonialism as a process that claims both psyches and bodies through the deployment of injurious discourses on the identity of colonised peoples. It is especially relevant to the discussion of a film such as *Vingt nuits et un jour de pluie* since this film can be read, in part, as a representation of the male protagonist's successful attempt to exorcise the colonial vision of the Indochinese man that he has come to embody. And as will become clear in what follows, the transformation of the male protagonist's identity entails a redefinition of his relation to both the French and Vietnamese languages.

The Female Protagonist
So far, my discussion of Lê's film has focused on the male protagonist's interior transformation. However, the film also deals to a great extent with the female character's own predicament and psychological transformation, most specifically her coming to terms with her beloved grandmother's death as well as male sexual violence. This character's defining feature stands in a stark opposition to the Vietnamese character's initial Cartesian outlook. Indeed, Lê's female protagonist adopts a mimetic relationship with the world that surrounds her. Drawing on the Frankfurt School, Marks defines mimesis as 'a form of yielding to one's environment, rather than dominating it' (Marks 2000: 141). To take an example of mimesis drawn from Lê's film itself, the religious men and women who seek to appease the erupting volcano on Java by 'resonating' with it embody an extreme form of mimesis since they go to their deaths in the process. Were it not for the scientist who relies on visual data to predict the volcano eruption, the Franco-German woman would have died too since she longed to be united with the volcano. That both protagonists exhibit traits that do not fit squarely with what viewers might expect may be surprising at first. One might indeed expect the Franco-German woman to be Cartesian and her Asian counterpart more attuned to a mimetic mode of relating to the outside world. But this is not the case. In fact, by frustrating his viewers' expectations, Lê manages to avoid the trap of cultural essentialism, and he also uses his male protagonist to show how cultural assimilation 'succeeded' under French colonial rule in Vietnam, whereas his female protagonist embodies a successful subjective cultural reordering away from Western culture codified as disenchanted and oppressive through her unconditional adoption of Indonesian culture and language as her new 'home'.

Even though Lê's female protagonist differs from her lover in her way of being in the world, her psychological transformation mirrors his own since it also entails a revisiting of the past. At the beginning of the film, she is unable to enter the apartment that she inherited from her grandmother. As she confides to her lover, the grandmother once made the trip from the South of France to visit her in that very same apartment. However, they missed each other on that particular day, and the old woman died before she could ever see her granddaughter again. What is left untold in the protagonist's narrative is made visible to viewers through a series of flash-backs: nobody came to the door to greet the old woman because the granddaughter was pinned down to a bed in what is clearly depicted as a scene of non-consensual sex since we witness her struggle to break free from the man who is penetrating her from behind. The details of the rape are highly significant since they evoke one of Gauguin's first Tahitian paintings discussed at several points by the two lovers in the film. Entitled 'Manao Tupapau', which can be translated either as 'l'esprit des morts veille'[7] or 'elle pense au revenant'[8], the painting depicts a nude Tahitian woman lying on her stomach on a bed, as well as an older female figure clad in black who is sitting on a chair next to the bed. In the flashback to the missed encounter between the female protagonist and her grandmother, the fantasy of sodomy that imbues Gauguin's painting materialises in the suggested rape of the Franco-German woman by a white male, while her grandmother is waiting to be let in.

In the scene under discussion, Lê's unobstructed close-up of the female character's exaggeratingly protruding buttocks is all-revealing and seems at first to cater to male erotic fantasies. However, the film-maker stops short of showing us sexual intercourse. Lê's deviation from his respectful way of filming his actress can thus be read as a parody of Gauguin's vision through which he comments on male/female relations in transcultural colonial and post-colonial contexts. Indeed, whereas Gauguin spoke for the voiceless Tahitian woman depicted in his painting by way of the caption he had devised for this piece, Lê's female protagonist has a voice of her own. Her lover, for his part, does not take advantage of her offered body, as her previous lover-turned-rapist had done. Thus, her lover's unexpected nurturing attitude is what enables the female protagonist to overcome her fear of men and to ultimately share with him a traumatic event from her past, namely the loss of her revered grandmother in a moment already marked by great distress for her. However, in the same manner as her lover keeps his trauma to himself, she refrains from revealing her rape to him. Here again, we are forced to ask ourselves whether it is her adoptive language (French), her fear of masculinity, or her perception of her lover that hinders her from sharing with him.

Coming Together – Language as a Liberator

As they open up to each other, both protagonists learn to come to terms with their respective pasts – even if they are still unable to articulate the most traumatic moments they contain. Still, she plays an instrumental role in helping him overcome his cultural amnesia by making the French language hospitable to Vietnamese identity, while he helps her to move beyond her fear of masculinity through his knowledge of the German culture and language. Moreover, the characters' appropriation of languages as tools for self-emancipation mirrors Lê's own appropriation of one of the legacies of French colonialism in Vietnam: cinema.

---

7   'The spirit of the dead looks on.'
8   'She thinks of the ghost.'

Describing *Vingt nuits et un jour de pluie* in an interview, Lê states that the film 'raconte mon histoire d'homme trop habitué à l'Occident'[9] (MpM 2006). His desire to balance out what he perceives to be his overinvestment in the Western world is apparent in many aspects of his film, both at the formal level and in its content. At the formal level, the film challenges the aesthetic conventions of classical Western cinema in several respects, including traditional forms of dialogue such as the confessional mode, as we have already seen. First, the film displays a distinct desire to undo the linearity of classical narrative, an aspect visible in Lê's complex use of flashbacks and flash-forwards. In addition, through his emphasis on the sense of touch at the expense of Cartesian ocularcentrism, Lê attempts to forge a haptic cinema of the kind described by Laura Marks in her study *The Skin of Film*. Third, Lê adopts the Chinese symbolic construction of the universe. In an interview he gave for *Cahiers du Cinéma* shortly after the release of his first long-feature film *Poussière d'empire* in 1983, Lê foregrounded the importance of the geometrical figures of the square and the circle:

> Toute la première partie est déterminée par le carré qui avec le cercle compose ce symbole chinois de l'univers; toute la seconde partie est composée par le cercle. Le carré impliquait un espace fermé où je passe du bois au feu, puis à la terre comme autant de relais. Au début c'est l'emprise du ciel, du spirituel, du religieux, tandis que la seconde partie est consacrée à la terre. La première partie est ainsi faite sur le chiffre 4, la deuxième partie sur le chiffre 3 [...]. La deuxième partie, c'est la terre, la procréation.[10] (Philippon/Lardeau 1983: 30)

The structural organisation highlighted by Lê in this paragraph also characterises *Vingt et un jours de pluie*: in the first part, which takes place in the confines of a small Parisian apartment, both protagonists are confronted with their traumatic pasts in which death, religion and self-destructive impulses played a major role; on the other hand, in the second part which features the lush Javanese countryside, Lê emphasises notions of personal rebirth and empowerment, as well as procreation. Significantly, the use of the French language dominates the first part, whereas it is completely absent from the second part since all dialogues are in English. It will therefore come as no surprise that it is also during the first twenty days of the male protagonist's encounter with his female counterpart that Lê makes the latter experience, at the symbolic level, the complete history of colonialism in Vietnam. In other words, Lê conflates a personal story with Vietnamese collective history by condensing the colonial history of Vietnam into a three-week time span: on the one hand, the juxtaposition between the menacing planes and the pouring rain undoubtedly raises the spectre of the decolonisation war through a thinly veiled evocation of napalm; on

---

9   'tells my story as that of someone who has grown too accustomed to the West.'
10 'The first part is entirely determined by the square which, along with the circle, constitutes this Chinese symbol of the universe; the second part is entirely constituted by the circle. The square implied a closed space where I moved from wood to fire, and then to the earth as if these were relays. At the beginning, the sky, spirituality and religion have a hold, whereas the second part is devoted to the earth. The first part is thus determined by the number 4, the second part by the number 3 [...]. The second part represents procreation and the earth.'

the other hand, we need to recall that the filmic narrative begins on 24 June, a day on which the advent of the summer solstice is celebrated in France. Originally a pagan celebration, it became part of the Christian tradition under King Clovis's reign. It is therefore no coincidence that Lê chose to have his story begin on such a day since it conjures up the memory of the earliest attempts by the French to colonise the Vietnamese through the use of Christianity. In this context, the burning sensation that spreads from the male protagonist's ankle to the rest of his body during the first part of the film denotes the male character's trauma as a survivor of the Vietnam War. In light of these circumstances, it is understandable that the latter suffers from amnesia. However, it turns out that his condition can be reversed through the presence of what Marks calls a 'souvenir object', on the one hand, and the use of French in the love game they engage in on the other.

In *Vingt nuits et un jour de pluie*, the 'souvenir object' defined by Marks as 'that stubborn survivor from another place-time that brings its volatile contents to the present' (Marks 2000: 77) is constituted by a mosquito net. Indeed, the male protagonist's mere striking of it – an object he grew up with – projects him back to colonial Vietnam, as evidenced in the scene in which he tells the woman about the dream he had while sleeping under the net next to her. In this dream, the woman was his schoolteacher in the French colonial education system, and he was a young boy fantasising that he had come into contact with her skin simply by touching her leggings. According to Marks, most of the memories left untranslated in the migration process are those derived from 'peasant practices', 'the women's practices', and 'the sensory practices' (Marks 2000: 90). In his film, Lê seeks precisely to salvage tactile memories and knowledge through his recurring emphasis on fabric and the sense of touch. For instance, the male protagonist is shown making several attempts at drawing the Javanese volcano on his lover's naked breasts until she tells him that he finally got it right without even looking at any of the shapes he had drawn [46:42–47:39]. In yet another scene, the male protagonist is shown without the glasses he had been wearing since the beginning to witness the transformation of the wall of his apartment into a screen on which Javanese shadow theatre is projected in a tribute to the Eastern roots of cinema [33:19–33:43]. Both scenes suggest that not only is Cartesian vision inadequate to bring forth memories, but it stands in the way of recollection altogether. The relinquishing of Cartesian vision is therefore necessary for the male protagonist to be able to reconnect with his past, to connect to the Asian world beyond Vietnam, and to redefine his relationship to both the Vietnamese and French languages in the process.

The male protagonist's embracing of bodily sensations, especially the sense of touch, is what ultimately enables him to put an end to his cultural amnesia. This is most apparent in the scene in which he has a vision of his dead father, while his lover sucks on his big toe [48:50–49:07]. When she tells him that he dreamt out loud in Vietnamese, he answers that his father was really there, talking to him. This scene inaugurates the male protagonist's break away from his former Cartesian self who only believed what he saw through his glasses and always remained self-contained.

Indeed, whereas he was reluctant to expose his lover to his native language at first, here he shares it willingly, correcting her laughingly as she mispronounces his father's words.

The male character's new attitude toward the Vietnamese language mirrors his changing relation to the French language as well. At the beginning of the film, Lê's character uses the language of the former coloniser to dismiss the Asian tradition of honouring one's dead relatives as mere 'superstitions'. However as the film progresses, the love game that unfolds between the protagonists leads to a positive reappropriation of the French language by the male character. In the film, the woman introduces her lover to Java in French, especially Javanese mythology. She does so by making him step into a Javanese sultan's skin whenever they have sex, while she masquerades as his lover Ratu Kidul, the Javanese Goddess of the Southern Sea. In addition to embodying Ratu Kidul and the sultan, Lê's characters imitate the Hindu transcultural sacred symbols of *linga* and *yoni*[11] by using sex to be fully regenerated. Beyond the role it plays in the plot, Lê's positive referencing of Asian religious and cultural traditions on the one hand, and his oblique critique of Judeo-Christian perceptions of selfhood and sexuality on the other hand, can be read as a 'displacement [of] our understanding of colonization as a 'purely spatial praxis' (as Lucien Lefèbvre would have put it)' to 'a conflict over the 'sacred', which was one of the most effective ways in colonizing the imaginary of the Vietnamese people,' as Panivong Norindr remarks in his article 'The Postcolonial Cinema of Lam Lê' (Norindr 2001: 151).

Through his impersonation of the Javanese sultan, the male protagonist, who otherwise suffers from self-destructive impulses, not only gains a sense of sexual potency, as he jokingly indicates, but he also begins to express his emotional attachment to pre-colonial Vietnam, as if he had taken 'a step back to [...] a presubjective, preoedipal space in which he might manage to redefine himself in relation not to a colonial *imago*, but to an image proffered by his motherlands, his personal ad culture origins', to borrow the suggestive words used by Jane Winston to describe Linda Lê's Vietnamese protagonist in the fiction piece *Vinh L.* (Winston 2001: 194). This is apparent in the scene in which he deplores the disappearance of Chinese ideograms in Vietnam through the introduction of romanised script by French Catholic missionaries in the 17th century. Still in the same scene, Lê's male character writes ideograms on his lover's body, thereby saying the French meaning of the words out loud: one word is 'femme' (woman) and another is 'petit bois' (little forest) – the nickname given to him by his late father. This moment of self-inscription in a language other than French can be read as a gesture through which this character 'expropriat[es] the discursive means of its own production' as colonial subject, to borrow Butler's terms (Butler 1997: 159). The next step in his renewed relations to both Vietnamese and

---

11 *Linga* and *yoni* are two transnational, transcultural Hindu sacred symbols which represent the male and female sexual organs.

French consists in the *détournement* of the language of the former coloniser to make the latter amenable to things Vietnamese: the male protagonist indeed uses French to characterise Vietnam as a 'home' ('chez nous'), a word he previously reserved only for Paris. This gesture echoes, once again, Butler's following description of the liberating appropriation of a language harbouring 'injurious speech': 'The appropriation of such norms [performative uses of language that can both do and undo subjects] to oppose their historically sedimented effect constitutes the insurrectionary moment of that history, the moment that founds a future through a break with the past' (Butler 1997: 159). Such a break with the past takes various shapes in the film: for instance, it is apparent in the conspicuous display of the altar which the male protagonist had previously hidden behind a row of books, as well as in his desire to travel to an Asian destination (Java), and to use languages other than French to talk about himself, i.e. English. The protagonist's psychological transformation culminates on the twenty-first day of his encounter with his lover: he is indeed shown welcoming the rain that pours down on him through the open skylight, while military planes race noisily in celebration of the national French holiday. In short, the playful impersonation, in French, of a sea goddess and a sultan in a love story contained in the *Book of Centhini*, the Javanese equivalent of the Mahabharata, serves as a tool for self-empowerment and the redefinition of his identity by the male protagonist, who begins to connect in a different way to his native country, as well as his Vietnamese relatives. An important part of this character's inner transformation indeed consists in his newly acquired ability to no longer see his father as an adamant supporter of the French colonial regime, as Lê portrays him, but first and foremost as a father. This is evidenced in the scene in which the male protagonist describes the following dream to his lover: his father is building himself a house deprived of proper foundations and supported only by the names of his children. Clearly, this scene should be read as the emergence of filial loyalty on the part of the male character, who had callously dismissed the tradition of honouring one's ancestors as 'mere superstition' at the beginning of the film. In the dream in question, the protagonist's father also cautions his son 'ne prends refuge qu'en toi-même'[12], inviting him to give up the hollow framework of France, and possibly his lover as well. The love game that both protagonists engage in the film thus leads the male protagonist to emancipate himself from a self-destructive obsession with Frenchness to establish a non-judgmental relation to Asianness.

In *Vingt nuits et un jour de pluie,* we witness not only the Vietnamese character's inner revolution and its ramifications, but also the psychological transformation undergone by Lê's female character as well. As already mentioned above, the latter struggles both with her fear of masculinity, as well as her grandmother's passing without being able to say goodbye to her because she was having sex when the latter came to visit her. To punish herself for not being there for her ancestor, the fe-

---

12   'take refuge only within yourself.'

male protagonist relinquished her sexuality, as evidenced in the immaculate outfit she wears and her overall austere appearance when she meets her lover for the first time. To represent her inner revolution, Lê rewrites the German folktale 'Rumpelstilzchen' ('Rumpelstiltskin'). The tale narrates the encounter between a poor woman and a dwarf (Rumpelstiltskin) who both suffer from their respective subjective positions in patriarchal society; whereas she is to be married to a king who believes her father's lie that she can spin straw into gold, he is excluded from the circulation of erotic desire and condemned to loneliness in light of his physical difference. However, he knows how to spin straw into gold. Under the threat of losing her life at the hands of the cruel king, the woman agrees to give away her first newborn to Rumpelstiltskin in exchange for his help. For the fairy tale scene, Lê made his actress crouch behind the balcony railing to convey her character's sense of entrapment, and her face clearly displays a sense of deep fear. Is the man she is staying with going to turn against her like her previous lover did? Is she indeed at his mercy like the heroine in 'Rumpelstilzchen'?

As with Gauguin's painting, however, Lê rewrites this tale by ultimately removing from it the fear, cruelty, greed, and stigmatisation of female sexuality it exhibits; as the woman continues to narrate the Grimm story, her lover arrives to reveal that he not only knows the fairy tale, but can recite it in her native language of German. As a result, the woman's fear of her lover's masculinity gives way to loving complicity, as illustrated by her affectionate nicknaming of him 'mon petit Rumpelstilzchen'[13]. Significantly enough, after he is done reciting the tale, his lover wraps her in a dark shawl reminiscent of the one worn by the old female spirit depicted on Gauguin's painting. Such a gesture can be interpreted as a sign that the nurturing intimacy she shared with her grandmother is possible with a male stranger, and Lê's female character comes to this realisation in the scene that follows: having overcome her fear of masculinity, she indeed conveys her loss to her lover. Interestingly enough, her body is shown as such since the woman's breasts and genitals are conspicuously put on display. Such a vision offers a sharp contrast to Gauguin's painting in which all traces of the Tahitian model's femininity are erased from view. Moreover, Lê's celebration of a different kind of sexuality through his allusion to the sacred symbols of *linga* and *yoni* constitutes a radical departure from the ways in which female sexuality is represented in 'Rumpelstilzchen': there, the dwarf's request that the heroine gives him her first child can be read as punishment for her engaging in sexual activity. Lê's rewriting of 'Rumpelstilzchen' in *Vingt nuits et un jour de pluie* thus gives birth to a post-colonial tale that binds its intercultural male and female protagonists together in a relationship where sharing, love, female sexuality, and life are celebrated, reflected in the mingling of language and voice.

---

13   'my little Rumpelstiltskin.'

Breaking Apart – Finding a Voice

Towards the end of the film, the female character leaves her lover without warning to return to Java where he ultimately goes to look for her at the end of the film. This unexpected flight allows them both to complete their inner transformations, and to articulate their new sense of self in a 'neutral' country. In other words, Lê's multi-layered references to Java paint a picture of this island as a space of empowerment and regeneration for both protagonists, things they could find neither in France nor in their respective countries of origins. For Lê, in particular, who refused the temporary visa granted to him by the Vietnamese government to film the second film of his trilogy out of protest against the political regime in Vietnam, the image of Java appears to function as a substitute for an imaginary Vietnam. Arguing that Indonesia and Vietnam share similar historical and political legacies, spiritual beliefs, and cultural realities, Lê has described Java as 'mon Vietnam par procuration'[14] (MpM 2006). *Vingt nuits et un jour de pluie* may therefore be read as Lê's own personal attempt at remembering Vietnam through his relationship with writer and journalist Elizabeth Inandiak, who gave the first translation of the *Book of Centhini* and also co-wrote the script for *Vingt nuits et un jour de pluie*.

Not unlike his creator, Lê's male protagonist, even though he can only interact with the locals in English, remarks that the Indonesian drink he is served tastes like a drink he used to savour while growing up in Vietnam [01:10:7 – 01:12:04]. Equally important, since Vietnam and Indonesia share similar political histories, their respective peoples exhibit similar self-destructive behaviours. When an Indonesian schoolteacher tells the Vietnamese tourist that her husband broke his own ankle in order to avoid being drafted into Suharto's army, the protagonist replies that he did the exact same thing [01:13:11 – 01:13:23]. He is finally able to give voice to a traumatic past experience (his self-indicted injury and its symbolic significance) that had been plaguing him for many years of exile in France.

In an interview in which he discusses Western cultural imports into Vietnam, Lê notes that the West brought cinema to Asia, most specifically what he considers to be the very first cinematic image: that of the trace of Christ's body on his shroud.[15] He further adds that all of his films attempt to reinvest such a vested image with new meanings. In *Vingt nuits et un jour de pluie* in particular, the body that comes to replace Christ's body on the screen at the end of the film is that of the male protagonist. In a highly theatrical scene, we witness his arrival at the Carmelite convent where he hopes to find his beloved who has left him without warning. But the significance of such a scene goes beyond his quest for his lover. Rather, it serves to dramatise the birth of an empowered Asian man. At the beginning of the scene, two nuns are shown hanging a set of bed sheets to dry. Upon hearing the protagonist enter the convent however, the nuns draw open the bed sheets as if they were theatre curtains,

---

14 'My Vietnam by proxy.'
15 See note 2. Panivong Norindr (2001) offers a very convincingly argued analysis of the use of the screen in Lê's films.

and his revealed body fills up the centre of the screen. He asks them, in English, about his lover's whereabouts. Significantly, Lê's staging of a truly self-empowered, post-colonial Vietnamese man coincides with his appropriation of the English language as a language in which his self comes to be expressed, since French disappears almost completely in the second part of the movie: indeed, only the volcanologist whom the female character meets during her first stay on the island speaks French. However, it becomes clear that the scientist is a double[16] for the Vietnamese protagonist, which means that his ability to speak French does not reflect an authentic practice. The disappearance of the French language, combined with the protagonist's appropriation of the English language, thus seems to signify that there is a way for the Vietnamese to connect to Asia and themselves without being subjected to the potentially hurtful mediation of French in the post-colonial era.

As far as the female protagonist is concerned, the final images of the film show her freeing birds from spaces of confinement, as well as making a jar that Lê juxtaposes to her belly, thereby highlighting that she is expecting a child. Through these final shots, in which the movement and sound produced by the spinning of the clay serve to assert life, we are made to understand that she has put behind her sorrow and fear to embrace and create life.

It is not the first time in the movie that movement, together with sound (including voice), is used by Lê to convey meanings relative to the various subjects he represents such as the celebration of life, but also trauma, change, survival, and identity. In that respect, Lê's cinema contrasts with other visual arts referenced throughout the movie, most specifically colonial painting and photography. Such a contrast is most striking in Lê's contextualisation of the black and white photography which features his Vietnamese alter ego as a child sitting on his father's shoulders. As is also the case for Gauguin's painting, the photograph does not convey the emotions felt by the subject represented on it. In his article on Lam Lê, Norindr indicates that Lê saw the potential of cinema as a powerful conveyor of emotions, when he realised that painting lacked the dimension of time (Norindr 2001: 148). In *Vingt nuits et un jour de pluie*, the intensity of the trauma experienced by the male protagonist is precisely rendered through Lê's animation of the voiceless, motionless child on the picture into a crying child who urinates on his genitor out of sheer terror for the menacing display of French military prowess. By so doing, Lê highlights the fact that his Vietnamese protagonist is endowed with a full-fledged subjectivity, i.e. the ability to have feelings and a voice with which to express them, features that are still rarely discernible in mainstream representations of immigrants and their offspring in France. With this knowledge, it is possible to read Lê's *Vingt nuits et un jour de pluie* as partaking of indexical cinema, or as 'une émanation du référent'[17] (Barthes 1980: 126), an expression Roland Barthes uses to characterise photography after André Bazin's own def-

---

16 In *Le Jeu des quatre coins* by Philippon and Lardeau Lê indicates that he shares German expressionist film-makers' interest for the theme of the double.

17 'an emanation of the referent.'

inition of photographic art forms such as cinema (Bazin 1967: 9–16). Barthes also compares photography to a shroud, namely St. Veronica's (Barthes 1980: 129). As a matter of fact, *Vingt nuits et un jour de pluie* can be called indexical in the extent to which it bears the trace of Lê's own life story as one of the few French Vietnamese film-makers who have had first-hand experience of French colonisation. In *Le Jeu des quatre coins*, Lê indeed indicates that:

> Je sais que ma génération est la dernière à avoir vécu la présence française [...]. Il y a peu de films qui ont été faits sur l'Indochine. La 317ème section de Pierre Schöndorffer, c'est le meilleur film sur l'Indochine, mais c'est toujours le point de vue du Blanc, de l'Européen. Alors pourquoi ne pas faire un film sur cette époque, mais senti de l'intérieur, donnant le point de vue du colonisé?[18] (Philippon/Lardeau 1983: 29–30)

In his film, departing with colonial and neo-colonial representations of colonised subjects and immigrants, Lê thus bears witness to the transformed existence of a former Indochinese, and of his doubly 'Other' (the French-German woman) as historical subjects endowed with a voice and a soul, all the while keeping the latter's integrity intact by resorting to aesthetic devices such as the filming of the actress from behind various filters (the mosquito-net, water, etc.). Interestingly enough, Lê's narration of the protagonists' respective psychological revolutions foregrounds their redefinition of their relationship with the various languages they speak – the most striking feature of such a redefinition being their relinquishing of French in favour of English for him, and Indonesian for her.

Jarring Voices – Discord and the Conflict between Language and the Message
In spite of the fact that both protagonists appear more confident and empowered as they relinquish French for other languages (English and Indonesian), there are aspects of the film that force viewers to question how perfectly it all falls together. As a matter of fact, how are we to interpret the fact that the female protagonist never mentions her rape to her lover? And what should we think of her intention to donate the money she makes from selling her grandmother's apartment to a by-product of the Dutch colonial legacy – a Carmelite convent located on Java? The male protagonist questions her motivation, visibly unsettled by the idea. However, his question remains unanswered. In a previous scene, she had compared him to Gauguin's female Tahitian model, describing him half-jokingly as a 'savage'. He hadn't reacted. Such interactions between the protagonists seem to suggest that the unreflected legacy of Western imperialism and colonialism lies at the root of negative attitudes towards cultural and/or ethnic Others on the part of former colonised and non-colonised subjects alike. And it is perhaps the lingering of such attitudes that keeps the protagonists from communicating even more freely.

---

18   'I know that my generation is the last generation who has experienced the French presence [...]. Only a few movies have been made on Indochina. The best film on Indochina is Pierre Schöndorffer's *317th Section*, but it is still the perspective of a white man, of a European man. So why not shoot a movie about that period from the perspective of the colonised, felt from the inside?'

Conclusion

In *Vingt nuits et un jour de pluie*, Lam Lê stages the psychological, cultural and linguistic reordering accomplished by two immigrants in France through their brief love affair. The latters' bodies and senses other than sight play a fundamental role in the redefinition of their respective subjectivities, and of their relation to their native and adopted languages. As they open up to each other, they share their native languages with one another, and unburden themselves from traumatic past experiences. And at the end of the film, they both emerge as self-empowered subjects in languages other than French and their native languages: Indonesian for her, and English for him. In fact, Lê's male protagonist manages to render the French language hospitable to his native country of Vietnam on the one hand, and to circumvent the mediation of French when he opens up to an Indonesian woman on the other. However, the trauma he suffered as a former colonised subject remains unsaid throughout the film. In a similar fashion, the female character never reveals her rape to her lover, even though she does manage to verbalise, in French, the trauma of losing her grandmother. She also interprets her lover's knowledge of German and of the German folktale tradition as proof that it is possible to develop intimate, nurturing relationships across gender lines. Although he highlights the failure of language to express deep-seated traumas, Lê still suggests the intensity of his protagonists' difficult experiences by using sound and a black-and-white 'film within the film'. By so doing, Lê highlights his Vietnamese protagonist's full-fledged subjectivity. In addition, he films his doubly 'Other' – a white woman – in a non-voyeuristic fashion (except in the scene in which he parodies Gauguin), thereby distancing himself from colonial and neo-colonial representations in which women are usually exoticised and objectified without further reflection. Lê therefore renews representations of Asian men and women in general, as well as the relationship between Asian men and white women: whereas the lovers in Marguerite Duras's *Hiroshima, mon amour* part and never meet up again, Lê leaves room for cautious optimism by giving an open ending to his film.

Filmography

Lê, L. (1980), *Rencontre des nuages et du dragon*, Vietnam/France.

Lê, L. (1983), *Poussière d'empire*, Vietnam/France.

Lê, L. (2006), *Vingt nuits et un jour de pluie*, France/Germany.

RESNAIS, A. (1959), *Hiroshima, mon amour*, France/Japan.

References

BARTHES, R. (1980), *La Chambre claire. Note sur la photographie*, Paris: Gallimard.

BAZIN, A. (1967), *What is Cinema?*, Berkeley: University of California Press.

BHABHA, H. (1994), *The Location of Culture*, London: Routledge.

BRITTO, K. (2004), *Disorientation. France, Vietnam, and the Ambivalence of Interculturality*, Hong Kong: Hong Kong U.P.

BLUM-REID, S. (2003), *East-West Encounters. Franco-Asian Cinema and Literature*, London: Wallflower Press.

BUTLER, J. (1997), *Excitable Speech. A Politics of the Performative*, New York: Routledge.

CHOW, R. (1999), '*When Whiteness Feminizes ...: Some Consequences of a Supplementary Logic*', in: *differences* 11, 137–168.

MARKS, L. (2000), *The Skin of the Film: Intercultural Cinema, Embodiment, and the Senses*, Duke: Duke U.P.

MPM (2006), 'Buzzz', URL: http://www.ecrannoir.fr/films/filmsb.php?f=2019 (1 February 2010).

NORINDR, P. (2001), '*The Postcolonial Cinema of Lam Le*: Screens, the Sacred, and the Un-homely in *Poussière d'Empire*', in: Winston, J. & L. Ollier (eds.), *Of Vietnam. Identities in Dialogue*, New York: Palgrave, 143–157.

PHILIPPON, A. & Y. LARDEAU (1983), 'Le jeu des quatre coins. Entretien avec Lâm Lê', in: *Cahiers du Cinéma* 352, 30–34.

WILLIS, S. (1987), *Marguerite Duras. Writing on the Body*, Urbana and Chicago: University of Illinois Press.

WINSTON, J. (2001), *Postcolonial Duras. Cultural Memory in Post-War France*, New York: Palgrave.

V. POLYGLOT FICTION AND NONFICTION: NARRATIVES FROM SPAIN AND PORTUGAL

Immigration and Plurilingualism in Spanish Cinema

Cristina Martínez-Carazo

The displacements associated with globalisation and the resulting encounters/mis-encounters between subjects immersed in this dynamic force us to reflect upon the instability of identity and about the anxiety that such a reality generates. The figure of the immigrant is perhaps that the one which most clearly exhibits and suffers the tension between imagining one's self as the subject of a community, as Benedict Anderson indicates, and reinventing one's self in the bosom of the other (Anderson 1991: 6). Communications media and cultural products in general, inserted in their historic matrices, mirror the situation and open a space for reflection in which these questions of identity are debated. But it is film in its illusory mimetic capacity and in its social scope that is the artistic manifestation most capable of constructing and questioning with great efficiency the images that float in and profile the collective imaginary of otherness. Beyond its inherent visuality, cinema derives its meaning from the convergence of visual and verbal discourse and it is precisely this terrain of the verbal in which my study is anchored. Taking language as a point of departure I propose to explore how plurality and the linguistic complexity of Spain, associated with the presence of Spanish, Basque, Catalan and Galician as well as the languages spoken by immigrants, projects and duplicates the tension the country experiences between the desire to preserve its homogeneous national identity and the necessity of reinventing it to take into account the presence of the other. I include in this linguistic exploration questions as diverse as the absolute ignorance of the language on the part of the immigrant, the process of learning, the manipulation of the language as an instrument of occultation and its impact as a catalyst for the interaction between the Spaniards and those recently arrived in the Iberian Peninsula.

To the decentralising effect derived from the autonomic process and the tottering of identity as a stable and uniform structure we add the impact of immigration as a phenomenon that visually and factually invalidates the illusory homogeneity inherited from the Franco era.[1] Along with these questions of identity, I will analyse the mechanisms that film activates to reflect this linguistic diversity, the implications of dub-

---

1   As Stuart Hall does well to point out, national identity is 'a production, which is never complete, always in process, and always constituted within, not outside, representation' (Hall 1989: 68).

bing or its absence, subtitles, voice-off, written texts, accents in speech and other verbal markers which mediate the impact of this chorus of voices to the spectator.

There are many critics who have studied the function of film as a creator of the new image of Spain and as an instrument for making this transformation visible, among them Nuria Triana-Toribio (2003), Marsha Kinder (1993), Barry Jordan and Rikki Morgan-Tamosunas (1998), Peter Evans (1999), Mark Allinson (2001), Isolina Ballesteros (2001), Rob Stone (2002), Isabel Santaolalla (2003) and Steven Marsh and Parvati Nair (2004), but the function of language in this equation has merited scant attention. Language as an identity marker reflects clearly the difficulties that surround negotiating these pluralities and the impact of knowledge/ignorance of the Spanish language in the process of integration. The immigrant, when speaking his or her own language is inaudible: she or he has no voice and is enclosed in an impenetrable circle, which attacks the assimilation project proposed by the Spanish government and blocks integration in the society. Language emerges as an instrument of resistance and subversion, as a weapon used to preserve one's own space, hermetic, inaccessible to the receiver and as a means of blocking the process of acculturation. However, the protection that this provides is inseparable from the vulnerability that miscommunication creates, since the survival and the negotiation of differences among cultures are arranged by way of language. The ample corpus of movies and documentaries centered on immigration affords a wide platform of reflection about the implications of this crossing of languages and cultures that remains outside official history. Among the filmic texts that discuss the problem, several stand out: *Las cartas de Alou* (Montxo Armendáriz, 1990), *Saïd* (Llorenç Soler, 1999), *Bwana* (Imanol Uribe, 1996), *En la puta calle* (Enrique Gabriel, 1996), *Menos que cero* (Ernesto Tellería, 1996), *Susanna* (Antonio Chavarrías, 1996), *En construcción* (José Luis Guerín, 2001), *La sal de la vida* (Eugenio Martín, 1996), *Cosas que dejé en La Habana* (Manuel Gutiérrez Aragón, 1997), *El sudor de los ruiseñores* (Juan Manuel Cotelo, 1998), *Flores de otro mundo* (Icíar Bollaín, 1999), *Tomándote* (Isabel Gardela, 2000), *Salvajes* (Carlos Molinero, 2001), *Poniente* (Chus Gutiérrez, 2002), and *Princesas* (Fernando León de Aranoa, 2005).

If it seems excessive to affirm that this repertoire of films constitutes a genre, it can be stated that it shares a series of registers with what Hamid Naficy defines as 'accented cinema' (Naficy 2001: 4), understanding by this the cinematographic work of exiled or diasporic directors, whose productions share formal traits and narratives, themes, questions of identity and modes of production. To this list Raymond Williams would also add shared 'structures of feeling'.[2] Although in the case of Spain, almost all of the movies centred on the theme of immigration have been di-

---

2   For Raymond Williams the 'structure of feeling' is a conjunction of personal and social experiences, with internal relationships and tensions, that 'is still in process, often indeed not yet recognized as social but taken to be private, idiosyncratic, and even isolating, but which in analysis has its emergent, connecting, and dominant characteristics, indeed its specific hierarchies. These are often more recognizable at a later stage, when they have been (as often happens) formalized, classified, and in many cases built into institutions and formations' (Williams 1977: 132).

rected by Spanish film-makers (an exception is *Al otro lado: un acercamiento a Lavapiés* by Basel Ramsis, 2001), we can trace many registers common to those directed by exiled or emigrant subjects – as Naficy points out –, among them the presence of the voyage as a motif, acculturated characters with identity problems as protagonists, feelings associated with liminality and not belonging (nostalgia, fear, insecurity), and plurilingualism.

With respect to language use, the displaced characters oscillate between two linguistic codes: their mother tongues and Spanish with a marked accent, an accent that, besides its phonetic peculiarities, carries a social charge. Behind the communication is hidden a series of added values such as social class, level of education, degree of integration, ethnicity and place of origin. The sensation of alienation that is derived from language is thus doubled: on the one hand we hear the accent of the immigrant when he/she speaks Spanish, and on the other, the presence of the mother tongue of the characters, generally still incomprehensible to the Spanish audience. In this way, tension arises between the distancing effect created by the presence of the foreigner with his/her languages, races, and/or accents, which incites the spectator to pay special attention to the subject represented and to try to decipher his/her enigma. The film thus oscillates between proximity and distance, duplicating the essence of the relationship between the immigrant and the Spanish citizen. The fact that the films, which are mostly narrated from the perspective of the emigrated subject and centred on her/his victimisation, asking the audience to empathise with the character, only adds to this tension.

The Voiceless Other

One of the situations that reflects the immigrant experience with great clarity is the inability to communicate in the language of the receiving country. *Bwana*, directed by Imanol Uribe, narrates the story of an African, Ombasi, recently disembarked from a raft, along with the corpse of his travelling companion, on a semi-deserted beach in the south of Spain. Ombasi is completely ignorant of the language. His encounter with a Spanish family of the lower economic and cultural class and with a band of 'skinheads' provides the focus of the film and determines the course of his short and unfortunate experience in Europe. The character speaks only Bubi, one of four dialects of the Bantu language of the island of Bioko, belonging to Equatorial Guinea, which serves as the basis for his discordant encounter with the family of the taxi driver.[3]

The few words which the protagonist utters are left untranslated, and in this way we only gain access to his thoughts by means of these short subtitles that are translated in a dream in which he converses with his drowned friend: 'Te matarán. No sueñes con ella. Quiero prevenirte de la gente blanca. Nos tiraron al mar', says

---

3   I take this fact from the unedited thesis of Pablo Marín Escudero (2006: 88), *Construcción de la identidad del inmigrante en el discurso fílmico y literario español de los 90*, directed by Domingo Sánchez-Mesa, University Carlos III, 2006.

the corpse.[4] Ombasi responds, ingenuously: 'Estás furioso porque estás muerto. Esta familia es diferente. Me llevarán con ellos.'[5] This oneiric dialogue foreshadows the dénouement and the excuse that unravels it – his supposed desire for the white woman. The lack of synchronisation between the speaker and the message – the drowned travelling companion only appears on the screen as a phantasmagorical shadow and his voice sounds like an echo – makes the text unreal while it reveals the inability of the immigrant to read the 'white man' correctly. The perception of Ombasi as enigmatic derives from his linguistic limitations, in contrast with the transparency of the white man, whose characteristics mark him as being lower-class, xenophobic, mistrusting of the 'other' and who lacks mystery for the spectator. Besides that, Ombasi's ignorance of the Spanish language is interpreted as a sign of primitivism. Jesi, the daughter, surprised that Ombasi only says two phrases in Spanish – 'Induraín' and 'Viva España'– asks her mother, '¿Por qué siempre dice lo mismo? ¿No sabe hablar más?'[6] Her mother responds, 'Estas personas negras son muy incultas.'[7] Isabel Santaolalla refers to this simplistic reading of otherness and affirms: 'The black man, who speaks no Spanish, is unable to make himself understood, a failure that sparks the group's racial prejudice, and that leads to his stereotyping as a primitive cannibal' (Santaolalla 2003: 155). Ironically, the two words that Ombasi utters in Spanish echo the nationalist will which, as a response to peripheral regionalisms and to globalisation, floats in the collective Spanish imaginary – a will which he himself threatens by being an immigrant. Depriving him of words makes a double reading possible in this context; on the one hand, it explains the fear felt by the white family, forced to spend the night on the beach with Ombasi and incapable of communicating with him; on the other, it accentuates his vulnerability since being deprived of language removes his ability to create meaning, guaranteeing with it his subordination. As Olga López Cotín indicates, 'La ausencia de un lenguaje común convierte los intercambios lingüísticos en cómplices de una realidad menos articulable, donde los personajes se enfrentan a sus miedos internos más reprimidos'[8] (López Cotín 2007: 148).

The recurrence of impossible dialogues due to the ignorance of the language on the immigrant's part – the taxi driver, Antonio, demands of him in Spanish that he go away, Dori, his wife, relates her marital misadventures to him – reduces effective communication to gestures and metaphorically duplicates Spain's inability, as a nation, to open up a dialogue with otherness. The innermost part of the character is shown only partially through his facial expression; fear, sadness, loneliness, pleasure, are thus reduced to a punctual reaction, far from any reflection. This results in

---

4   'They'll kill you. Don't even dream about her. I want to warn you about white people. They threw us into the sea.' (All the translations by the author.)
5   'You're just angry because you're dead. This family is different. They'll take me with them.'
6   'Why does he always say the same thing? Doesn't he know how to say anything else?'
7   'These black people are not very cultured.'
8   'The absence of common language converts the linguistic exchanges into accomplices of a reality that is less easy to articulate, where the characters face their most repressed inner fears.'

the objectifying of the character, shown as an object of terror for the family in general and of desire for the woman in particular, who agrees to go swimming nude at the beach with him. The camera and lighting intensify this perception through shots taken from below that magnify his body and envelop him in a warm light produced by the reflection of the sun on his dark, wet skin.

This small transgression – swimming nude with a white woman – serves as a justification for the aggression of the 'skinheads' who add another level of linguistic complexity to the film by communicating among themselves in English and German. The violence and the threat of castration and death are expressed in another language, allowing the spectator to distance him- or herself from this extreme xenophobia. In the same way, the taxi driver's extreme racism, his cowardice, his lack of cultural awareness and especially the comic effect that they produce detach the spectator from this reality, and thus distanced, she/he feels no ethical responsibility. The choice of these narrative strategies on the part of Imanol Uribe, the foreign languages and extreme lack of culture awareness assigned to violence ends up limiting the efficacy of the text and clouding its message.

Bwana, whose protagonist lacks a voice due to true ignorance of the languages, could be considered a polar opposite of *Salvajes*, directed by Carlos Molinero, to the degree that the director portrays African characters who hide their proficiency in Spanish as a defense mechanism. The development of the story, the violence inflicted by a group of neo-Nazis against a Senegalese man, places the spectator in front of a series of fragmented images, filmed with a hand camera, in which an African is beaten without pronouncing a word. The police investigation attributes the attack to drug trafficking, when in reality the crime of this character is, ironically, the illegal trafficking of immigrants. When the wife of the immigrant is interrogated by the police, we hear the dialogue that she holds with her son in an African language and the translation that he gives to the police officers, alleging that his mother doesn't understand. 'Mi madre no habla español. Es una buena madre,'[9] says the boy. But after the interrogation concludes, we hear the woman speaking Spanish, thus demonstrating the power of language as an instrument of concealment.

The faked ignorance of the language as a means of protection is amplified in the numerous silences, real and metaphorical, that run through the text. In one instance we see the trafficker in the hospital, after having been assaulted, connected to an artificial respirator that prevents him from speaking. This same character resorts again to silence when after recovering, he is taken to the police station in order to identify the assailants. On this occasion he also chooses to remain silent, despite the fact that he recognises his attackers. The presence of a group of illegal immigrants who are getting out of a truck in silence has the same meaning, although, paradoxically, at the end of the film they monopolise the dialogue. Santaolalla summarises this epilogue as follows:

---

9   'My mother doesn't speak Spanish. She's a good mother.'

El director intenta reparar la falta de protagonismo concediéndoles la voz a las vícti-
mas al final, en una especie de epílogo de estilo documental, en el que unos cuantos
africanos en situación irregular hablan directamente a la cámara, expresando sus
miedos y sus necesidades.[10] (Santaolalla 2005: 133)

This cinematographic strategy abruptly interrupting the narration integrates the
spectator into the story by turning her/him into a witness and a direct recipient of the
immigrants' complaints. The fact that these Africans express themselves in perfect
Spanish reduces the distance even more for the spectator, who, besides confront-
ing the problematic present, finds him/herself obliged to remember Guinea's past
as a Spanish colony and to reflect upon historical responsibility. Ethnic otherness
becomes diluted before the linguistic affinity, which by contrasting with the film's
premises – the African 'other' speaks an 'other' language – destabilises the dialectic
between the spectator and the characters. If this ending seems abrupt aesthetically, it
is ethically effective in the sense that it includes a double message: the denunciation
of injustice and the evocation of the colonial burden.

Also in contrast to *Bwana*, Icíar Bollaín's *Hola, ¿estás sola?* positions us in front
of a Russian who does not know the Spanish language. His linguistic limitations
grant him in this case, the privilege of freedom, since, shielded by his inability to
communicate verbally, he maintains a fleeting romantic relationship with the two
protagonists (Trina y la Niña) at the same time. Olaf, what they call the Russian, not
knowing his real name, who is capable only of repeating words and phrases uttered
by his friends, floats through the text with total autonomy, as a presence and an absence. Exempt from giving explanations by nature of his linguistic incompetence
and far from any emotional compromise, he limits his action to his sexual relations
with both girls. Susan Martin-Márquez interprets the Russian's presence in the film
in these terms:

> Thus while Olaf's linguistic isolation results in a radical decontextualization of his
> character, the film does begin to problematize that decontextualization by implying
> that Olaf's character will always manage to escape the imperialist/Orientalist clichés
> according to which he tends to be delimited. (Martin Márquez 2002: 260)

The fact that his monologues in Russian are not subtitled, his name is never known,
and that he appears and disappears fleetingly convert him into an enigmatic character, inapprehensible, who unfolds in light of the problematic global reality of the
century's end with great ease. Desire rather than rejection are in his case the nex-
us between the immigrant and the receptive culture, inverting with it the dominant
structure of the relationship between immigrants and receptive cultures.

---

10   'The director attempts to remedy the lack of protagonism, granting voice to the victims in the end,
      in a sort of documentary-style epilogue, in which several Africans, in an irregular situation, speak
      directly to the camera, expressing their fears and their needs.'

In Search of a Voice

The representation of the immigrant's language learning process is more common. Both *Saïd* by Llorenç Soler and *Las cartas de Alou* by Montxo Armendáriz take as a theme the acquisition of the new language as a barometer of the process of integration. Saïd and Alou, the Arab and Senegalese speaking protagonists of the films, arrive in Spain without knowing the language and the films' narration shows the evolution from the impossibility of communication to their domination of the language. The language barrier that they face upon their arrival intensifies the sensation of strangeness that the protagonist and the spectator experience. As John Mowitt indicates, 'Language operates most effect-fully when its obstruction of understanding is the explicit topic of exchange' (Mowitt 2005: 85), so that the reflections on language during the first classes that Alou gets from his compatriots, who kindly teach him how to ask for work in Spanish, clearly mark the function of language as a catalyst for the migratory experience. As the title announces – *Las cartas de Alou* – letters, written and read by the protagonist in his mother tongue, Senegalese, and subtitled on the screen, constitute the structural axis of the film.[11] He sends the first from Senegal to his friend Mulai already settled in Spain, the second and third, written from Spain, are addressed to his mother, residing in Senegal; and the fourth is sent again to Mulai after having been deported, communicating his intention to return to Spain. Within the markers of the epistolary communication – absence, complicity, desire – the dislocation of the emigrated subject, his divided subjectivity, his fragmentation, are accentuated by the fact that these letters are not created in order to receive answers. The reading of the letters is reduced to a voice-over, not linked to Alou's image, generating with it an agile exploration of his subjectivity. The fact that the mother's voice is omitted also forces the spectator to infer her feelings according to the few comments that she makes. The voice is a key piece in this affective fracture of the immigrant, as the first letter that Alou sends to his friend shows. In it he narrates the pain that it causes his mother to lose him and the answer that she gives when he reminds her that she still has several other children, 'Ninguno tiene tu voz'[12]. As Isabel Santaolalla points out, the inclusion of the letters as a narrative strategy generates an:

> Efecto paradójico que combina un acercamiento (con el contenido confesional e íntimo de las cartas) y distanciamiento (mediante la alienación lingüística del público, sólo superable con la lectura de los subtítulos). De esta forma la película logra un delicado equilibrio: por un lado invitando a la empatía, y por otro, alimentando un cierto sentimiento de extrañeza – una combinación verosímil y apropiada tratándose de una dramatización del encuentro con la diferencia.[13] (Santaolalla 2005: 123)

---

11 The work of Linda Kauffmann (1986) and of Gurkmin Janet Altman (1996) on the presence of letters in a literary text also brings to light their function in the film that concerns us, *Las cartas de Alou*.
12 'None of them have your voice.'
13 '[...] a paradoxical effect which combines proximity (with the confessional and intimate content of the letters) and distance (through the linguistic alienation of the audience, only surmountable by reading the subtitles). In this way the film achieves a delicate balance: on the one hand, inviting

At the same time, the temporal dislocation between the present of the story and the moment of the letter writing, if it indeed interrupts the diegesis and attacks the illusion of reality, also opens a space for reflection that endows the text with profundity, ensuring that the apparent simplicity derived from Alou's linguistic limitations does not take away from the psychological complexity of the protagonist.

The text resorts to the character's mother tongue, Senegalese, to give voice to his emotivity. Besides reading the letters, Alou uses it, this time without translation in a sort of religious chant to express the pain of the death by gassing of his flatmate, also an immigrant. With this a difficult balance is achieved between the sensation of authenticity, respect for privacy and empathy with the spectator who accepts what is hidden as an integral part of the character's subjectivity.

In addition to the protagonist, there are several plurilingual characters and voices who refer to present day Spain. Alou interacts with a group of immigrants, mostly Arabs, who live in a subterranean tunnel and who communicate with each other in Arabic; with a group of Africans with whom he speaks a rudimentary French and with another African who does not speaks the same language, obstructing the cohesion among immigrants. To this is added the presence of a Catalan voice, which announces the arrivals in the train station in Barcelona. This linguistic incompetence is associated with abusive situations: the character takes up residence in an infrahuman space: he is the victim of labour exploitation by those who manage the street vendors and of the robbery of his luggage in the train station. The figure of the other in search of a voice that will allow him to find his place in a strange space is installed in the space between idiomatic competence and incompetence.

In *Saïd*, linguistic plurality is portrayed as a marked monopoly of Arabic in opposition to Spanish, since the foreign language dominates the soundtrack as much at the level of spoken communication as a musical track. Additionally, Catalan also alternates with Spanish. The documentary style of the film and the sense of veracity that it transmits are joined by the omnipresence of Arabic as a vehicle of communication, always subtitled. El Raval, a neighbourhood emblematic of the impact of immigration on Barcelona, becomes the scene of antithetical attitudes, racism and harmony, molded, respectively, in the attacks by groups of 'skinheads' and in the performances of the Arab band in which Saïd plays.[14] The underlying presence of Catalan, also charged with ethical and political connotations, functions as a backdrop to this plurality. Ana, Saïd's friend, girlfriend and protector, speaks Catalan with her parents, who, alarmed by her relationship with the Moroccan, try to discourage her from seeing him. Cultured and human, but a paradigmatic example of the benevolent racism that prevails in Spain, her father helps Saïd after he is beaten in the street, but rejects the relationship his daughter has with him. Catalan is also the language of communication

---

empathy, and on the other, feeding a certain feeling of strangeness – a credible and appropriate combination dealing with the dramatisation of an encounter with difference.'

14   The documentary *En construcción* (José Luís Guerín, 2001) is also set in the El Raval neighbourhood and explores, among many other themes, that of immigration.

between Ana and her lawyer, the latter committed to the immigrant cause and more open to plurality. Significantly, the most xenophobic characters in the film, the police inspector, incompetent as well as racist, and the 'skinheads', only speak Spanish, marking off a space of tolerance and social compromise which is reserved for Catalan. Beyond the extrapolations that the narration provokes, associated with the ethical slant that the change of idiomatic register adopts, it also underlines the cosmopolitan and plural character of Barcelona, which, if not entirely devoid of xenophobic subjects, has managed to open small spaces of acceptance.

One of the achievements of this film is to propose a valuing of otherness, taking music as a point of departure. Allowing the opening of dialogue above and beyond words, the Arab music that dominates the soundtrack of the film appeals to a universal sensibility that transcends ethnic markers, allowing for a communication not restricted to language. The valuing of a plural culture capable of bringing differences into harmony is installed in the parenthesis opened by the music. Giovanni Sartori refers to this, defending pluralism, which integrates, and setting it against multiculturalism, which disintegrates, creating a ghetto culture. According to this reality, Sartori states that:

> La variedad y no la uniformidad, el discrepar no la unanimidad, el cambiar y no el inmovilismo, sean 'cosas buenas'. Estas son las creencias de valor que emergen con la tolerancia, que se adscriben al contexto cultural del pluralismo y que tienen expresión en una cultura pluralista que haga honor a su nombre [...]. Y en la medida en que el multiculturalismo actual separa, es agresivo e intolerante, en esa misma medida el multiculturalismo en cuestión es la negación del pluralismo.[15] (Sartori 2001: 32)

Fitting into a larger framework, with respect to the search of voice, is *Poniente* by Chus Gutiérrez, in as far as it explores the phenomenon of immigration from divergent angles. To the presence of the recently arrived foreign immigrant is added the presence of Spanish emigrants to Europe who are returning to Spain and the round-trip journey of Spanish citizens in their own country. The feeling of uprootedness transcends the boundaries of nationality and impregnates the text with a sensation of not belonging that seems to infect the whole community. The inability to integrate otherness ends up fragmenting a community.

The function of language in the integration process is especially complex in this film. Adbembi, the most visible immigrant in the greenhouse area, is the leader for labour relations and functions as a bridge between the locals and the recently arrived workers, thanks to his fluency in Spanish. Compelled by the infrahuman work conditions of the immigrants and frustrated by the inefficiency of his negotiations with the owners of the greenhouses, he addresses his compatriots in Arabic to propose a work stoppage. The owners respond by firing everyone and contracting new

---

15 'Variety and not uniformity, disagreement, not unanimity, change and not immobility, would be 'good things'. These are the value beliefs that emerge with tolerance, that ascribe to the cultural context of pluralism and that find expression in a pluralistic culture that does honour to its name [...]. And as the current multiculturalism separates, is aggressive and intolerant, so is the multiculturalism in question the negation of pluralism.'

hired hands. The Spaniards formulate their proposal as follows: 'Que vengan peruanos o ecuatorianos que son más dóciles y además hablan en cristiano.'[16] The language factor, while it does make verbal understanding possible in the case of Latin Americans, again evokes the memory of the colonial past and the dialectic between dominance and submission. If in the case of Adbembi the domination of the language gives him a certain power, the inefficiency of his discourse returns him to his marginal position. Nevertheless, he is the only one given a voice and as Verena Berger indicates:

> Es Adbembi quien pronuncia con toda claridad la opinión estereotipada que la sociedad española parece tener de los inmigrantes. A la vez es también la figura que rompe con el estereotipo del inmigrante como el 'otro' inferior, sumiso, al enfrentarse al creciente rechazo que manifiestan los habitantes locales y al oponerse a la injusticia y a los mecanismos de exclusión.[17] (Berger 2007: 192)

His verbal and intellectual superiority prove ineffectual when the time comes to establish relations between the recently arrived immigrants and the receiving society. Nevertheless, what the text does show is the necessity of redefining the interaction between developed and underdeveloped countries and the burden that the colonial past carries. Regarding this question, Yen-Soo Kim points out that 'While natives are still caught in the worldview shape by a colonial order, immigrants operate in a postcolonial, global frame' (Kim 2005: 175). The impossibility of forgetting the relationship between coloniser and colonised and the will to cling to the old order and provide ballast for this dialectic between immigrants and their receivers inverts the logic of progress anchoring the developed countries in the past and positioning the underdeveloped ones toward the future. The fact that a majority of the dialogues among immigrants are in Arabic without subtitles, but are clearly contextualised (fights, money issues, annoyances...) shows their most simple side, that which refers to survival, limiting the exploration of their subjectivity. This simplistic perception of the figure of the immigrant connects with what Gayatri C. Spivak considers a risk in the representation of the other, his homogenisation and and the undifferentiated portrayal of him (Spivak 1990: 63).[18]

Moving in the same space as the Arabs are the Sub-Saharans, whose linguistic, racial and cultural distance alienates them even more than the North Africans. The text associates their ignorance of the language with their submission: they work in silence, do not assert their claim to better working conditions and are susceptible to being controlled. Again the historic past crops up when it becomes time to differen-

---

16 'Let the Peruvians or Ecuadorians come instead, they're more docile, and besides, they talk like Christians [they speak Spanish].'

17 'It is Adbembi who pronounces with complete clarity the stereotyped opinion that Spanish society seems to have of immigrants. At the same time he is the figure that breaks the stereotype of the immigrant as the inferior 'other', submissive, on facing the growing rejection shown by the local inhabitants and on opposing the injustice and the mechanisms of exclusion.'

18 Spivak warns of the risk of 'constructing the Other simply as an object of knowledge, leaving out the real 'Others'' (Spivak 1990: 63) owing to the fact that the representations are mediated by the vision of those who access to power.

tiate between Sub-Saharans and Moroccans, the latter evoking the ghost of the Arab conquest and protagonists of persistent tense encounters between Spain and North Africa. As Daniela Flesler reminds us, 'Es a partir de la reificación del discurso de la invasión mora sufrida en 711 que la inmigración marroquí de hoy se percibe como 'invasion''[19] (Flesler 2001: 78–79). The intersection of languages that crosses over the text dissolves in a dramatic final scene in which the immigrants, falsely accused of having set fire to the greenhouses in which they work, abandon the town in silence. The beach that had functioned as a scene of encounter of languages and cultures, shaped into a 'multi-ethnic' fiesta among Arabs, Spanish and Africans, now operates as the backdrop of a failure, a flight in which expulsion is accompanied by the loss of voice.

The Other with the Same Voice

The language question becomes diluted and distorted when analysing the position of Spanish-speaking immigrants arriving to Spain from South America. Besides the aforementioned case of Guineans, the Spanish language spoken by the Latin American community diminishes their otherness and affords them a status that is in some ways advantageous. Here accent, lexicon and morphosyntax, and not language (nor even racial features in numerous cases), is the sign of otherness. Their speech, in addition to its phonetic peculiarities, carries a social and regional charge. Behind the concrete meaning of each word hides a series of added signifiers such as class, education, place of origin and degree of integration that determine the recently arrived immigrant's position in the social scale.

Beyond these social indicators, Spanish marked by a wide gamut of accents again brings the epoch of the Conquest into the present. The spectator then faces an 'other' heir to the Spanish language and culture that oscillates between familiarity and strangeness, an 'other', who, based on a common past, strives to be recognised and embraced as a child of the 'mother country'.[20] The colourful speech of Latin Americans acquires a notable protagonism in films featuring them. So, in *Cosas que dejé en La Habana* we hear the three Cuban sisters (Nena, Rosa and Ludmila), who have recently arrived in Madrid, comment that their aunt, who is also Cuban, but has been settled in the capital for quite some time, 'habla bonito'[21]. With this they allude to the acculturation process experienced by their aunt, who, far from her native Cuba, has changed her way of speaking, accent as much as vocabulary, as well as her gastronomic preferences. Accent will also be the detail that helps the protagonist, Igor, and Nena to identify each other as Cubans from the first sentence of their conversation.

---

19 'It is by way of the discourse's objectification of the Moorish invasion endured in 711 that today's Moroccan immigration is perceived as an 'invasion'.'

20 In *Cosas que dejé en La Habana* Igor, the Cuban protagonist, maintains a dialogue with his friend, also Cuban, about the 'mother country's' moral obligation to open up a space for them and its non-compliance with these optimistic expectations.

21 'speaks nicely.'

In Icíar Bollaín's *Flores de otro mundo*, language duplicates the dichotomy between the austerity of the Segovian village, Cantalojas, where Patricia (Dominican) and Milady (Cuban) arrive, and the exuberance of their native Caribbean. The fluid and colourful verbal exchanges between these two immigrants, characterised by its eloquence, musicality and Cuban and Dominican accents, are in opposition to the verbal aridity of the Castilians who minimise their verbal exchanges. Along the same lines in *Sobreviviré* by Alfonso Albacete and David Menkes, the optimism reflected in the Cuban woman's (Rosa's) speech contrasts with the monotonous and plain discourse of the Spanish Marga, a single mother immersed in a problematic sentimental relationship. It is language in these films with Hispanic protagonists that marks the disjunction between the clichés of optimism in the face of adversity that is ascribed to South Americans and the sordidness inscribed in their existence.[22]

However, the constant presence of Latin American actors (Cecilia Roth, Ricardo Darín, Héctor Alterio, Federico Luppi among others) in Spanish cinema as protagonists far removed from the issues of immigration has contributed to the normalisation of the presence of different accents. Hamid Naficy alludes to this when affirming that:

> Stressing musical and oral accents redirects our attention from the hegemony of the visual and of modernity toward the acousticity of exile and the commingling of premodernity and post modernity in the films. Polyphony and heteroglossia both localize and locate the films as texts of cultural and temporal difference. (Naficy 2001: 25)

Conclusion

The human displacements linked to globalisation have contributed to positioning the immigrant at the centre of political, social and economic discourses and granting the immigrant a strong protagonism in the communications media.[23] The impact of the immigration phenomenon on the media means we cannot ignore the problems associated with this new diaspora and obliges us to open a space for reflection on its implications at the beginning of the new millennium. Equally, film and television translate into images a central debate when tracing the dynamic of our changing national identity and specifically the cultural markers that help us to imagine it: language, race, religion, and cultural heritage. Iain Chambers describes the centre-periphery debate as follows:

> There is the emergence at the centre of the previously peripheral and marginal. For the modern metropolitan figure is the migrant: she and he are the active formulators of metropolitan aesthetics and life styles, reinventing the languages and appropriating the streets of the master. This presence disturbs the previous order. [...] All is

---

22   The film *En la puta calle* directed by Enrique Gabriel (1996) reflects the contrast between Caribbean Andy's upbeat personality, and the incurable pessimism of Juan, a Spanish failure.

23   Walter Mignolo's hopeful reading of the impact of the World Conference on Language Rights celebrated in Barcelona in 1996 alludes to this question. For him, 'The relocation of languages and cultures, finally, is creating the conditions for the emergence of an epistemological potential at the multiple intersections and interstices of the 'West and the rest' ' (Mignolo 1998: 51). This dialogue between the 'West and the rest' of the world points to a restructuring of the relationship between language and power that in the case of Spain still needs to be refined.

revealed in the dexterity of molding the languages of modernity and cultivating the city according to different rhythms, making it move to a diverse beat. It is to speak the languages – linguistic, literary, cultural, religious, musical – of the dominator, of the master, but always with a difference. Language is appropriated, taken apart, and then put back together with a new inflection, and unexpected accent, a further twist in the tale. (Chambers 1994: 23)

The plurality of languages present in contemporary Spain imposes and reinforces an image of change which helps the viewer to understand and consolidate the mobile nature of contemporary reality. The spectator faces an ample repertoire of voices and images that converse among themselves and force us to understand multiculturalism as something essential to our time.

In this context, plurilingualism simultaneously reflects the immigrant's inclusion in and the exclusion from the Spanish socio-political project. The aforementioned filmic texts bear witness to the absence of a sphere of power in which the multiple languages that sound in public spaces are made audible. The circuit in which these languages and these accents travel remains outside cultural production and, by extension, the exercising of power. Callaghan is referring to this when he indicates that:

A linguistic market is established as the only acceptable context within which persons can exchange what are recognized as legitimate expressions and ideas. [...] Those who have knowledge of and access to the dominant expressions are able to control the market and can circumvent others whose expressions or social identities are not affirmed by the rhetorical context. (Callaghan 1997: 67)

The fact that the immigrants who have arrived in Spain belong primarily to the first generation helps us to understand their limited presence on the cultural map of the country. Indeed, even if the efforts to give voice to these recently arrived are minimal and ineffective, the swift transformation that the Spanish population is experiencing allows us to believe that the dominant languages will have to share their public sphere with those of the recently arrived.

Filmography

ALBACETE, A. & D. MENKES (1999), *Sobreviviré*, Spain.

ARMENDÁRIZ, M. (1990), *Las cartas de Alou*, Spain.

BOLLAÍN, I. (1999), *Flores de otro mundo*, Spain.

CHAVARRÍAS, A. (1996), *Susanna*, Spain.

COTELO, J. M. (1998), *El sudor de los ruiseñores*, Spain.

GABRIEL, E. (1996), *En la puta calle*, Spain.

GARDELA, I. (2000), *Tomándote*, Spain.

GUERÍN, J. L. (2001), *En construcción*, Spain.

GUTIÉRREZ ARAGÓN, M. (1997), *Cosas que dejé en La Habana*, Spain.

GUTIÉRREZ, Ch. (2002), *Poniente*, Spain.

LEÓN DE ARANOA, F. (2005), *Princesas*, Spain.

MARTÍN, E. (1996), *La sal de la vida*, Spain.

MOLINERO, C. (2001), *Salvajes*, Spain.

SOLER, Ll. (1999), *Saïd*, Spain.
TELLERÍA, E. (1996), *Menos que cero*, Spain.
URIBE, I. (1996), *Bwana*, Spain.

References

ALTMAN, G. J. (1996), *Epistolarity: Approaches to a Form*, Columbus: Ohio State U.P.

ALLINSON, M. (2001), *A Spanish Labyrinth. The Films of Pedro Almodóvar*, London: IB Tauris.

ANDERSON, B. (1991), *Imagined Communities*, London: Verso.

BALLESTEROS, I. (2001), *Cine (ins)urgente*, Madrid: Fundamentos.

BERGER, V. (2007), 'Los movimientos migratorios y el miedo al otro', in: Pohl, B. & J. Türschmann (eds.), *Miradas glocales*, Madrid: Iberoamericana/Vervuert, 185–197.

CALLAGHAN, K. A. (1997), 'Symbolic Violence and Race', in: Kramer, E. M. (ed.), *Postmodernism and Race*, Westport/Connecticut/London: Praeger, 65–77.

CHAMBERS, I. (1994), *Migrancy, Culture, Identity*, London/New York: Routledge.

EVANS, P. (ed.) (1999), *Spanish Cinema. The Auterist Tradition*, Oxford: Oxford U.P.

FLESLER, D. (2001), 'De la inmigración marroquí a la invasión mora: discursos pasados y presentes del (des)encuentro entre España y Marruecos', in: *Arizona Journal of Hispanic Cultural Studies* 5, 73–88.

HALL, S. (1989), 'Cultural Identity and Cinematic Representation', in: *Framework* 36, 68–81.

JORDAN, B. & R. MORGAN-TAMOSUNAS (1998), *Contemporary Spanish Cinema*, Manchester/New York: Manchester U.P.

KAUFFMANN, L. (1986), *Discourses of Desire. Gender, Genre and Epistolary Fictions*, Ithaca/New York: Cornell U.P.

KIM, Y.-S. (2005), *The Family Album*, Lewisburg: Bucknell U.P.

KINDER, M. (1993), *Blood Cinema*, Berkeley: University of California Press.

LÁZARO REBOLL, A. & A. WILLIS (eds.) (2004), *Spanish Popular Cinema*, Manchester/New York: Manchester U.P.

LÓPEZ COTÍN, O. (2007), 'Desde la mirada oscura: geografías fílmicas de la inmigración en España', in: Cornejo Parriego, R. (ed.), *Memoria colonial e inmigración: La negritud en la España postfranquista*, Barcelona: Ediciones Bellaterra, 143–156.

MARÍN ESCUDERO, P. (2006), *Construcción de la identidad del inmigrante en el discurso fílmico y literario español de los 90*, thesis directed by Domingo Sánchez-Mesa, University Carlos III.

MARSH, S. & P. NAIR (eds.) (2004), *Gender and Spanish Cinema*, Oxford/New York: Berg.

MARTIN-MÁRQUEZ, S. (2002), 'A World of Difference in Home-Making: The Films of Icíar Bollaín', in: Ferrán, O. & K. Glenn (eds.), *Women's Narrative and Film in Twentieth-Century Spain*, Hispanic Issues, vol. 27, New York/London: Routledge, 257–272.

MIGNOLO, W. (1998), 'Globalization, Civilization Processes and the Relocation of Languages and Cultures', in: Jameson, F. & M. Miyoshi (eds.), *The Cultures of Globalization*, Durham/London: Duke U.P., 32–53.

MOWITT, J. (2005), *Re-takes. Postcoloniality and Foreign Film Languages*, Minneapolis: University of Minnesota Press.

NAFICY, H. (2001), *An Accented Cinema*, Princeton: Princeton U.P.

Santaolalla, I. (2003), 'Behold the Man! Masculinity and Ethnicity in *Bwana* (1996) and *En la puta calle* (1998)', in: Rings, G. & R. Morgan-Tamosunas (eds.), *European Cinema: Inside Out*, Heidelberg: Universitätsverlag Winter, 153–163.

Santaolalla, I. (2005), *Los otros. Etnicidad y raza en el cine español contemporáneo*, Zaragoza: Prensas Universitarias, 2005.

Sartori, G. (2001), *La sociedad multiétnica*, Madrid: Taurus.

Spivak, G. C. (1990), *The Post-Colonial Critic*, New York/London: Routledge.

Stone, R. (2002), *Spanish Cinema*, London: Longman.

Triana Toribio, N. (2003), *Spanish National Cinema*, London/New York: Routledge.

Williams, R. (1977), *Marxism and Literature,* Oxford: Oxford U.P.

Identities Adrift: Lusophony and Migration in National and Trans-national Lusophone Films

Carolin Overhoff Ferreira

Introduction

Portugal's colonial and postcolonial history is a European exception. It was one of the first European colonial powers and one of the last to let go of its African colonies after its peaceful revolution in 1974, which ended five decades of dictatorship and five centuries of empire. Due to its journeys of discoveries and its many colonies spanning Brazil to Macau, but even more because of its weak socio-political and economic situation from the eighteenth century onwards, Portugal has always been a country of massive emigration. Accordingly, its cinema has been more interested in this subject than in portraying the relatively recent impact of migration into the country. While the decolonisation process after 1974 was an important factor for movements to Portugal, it was only when the country joined the European Community in 1986 that it become more attractive for immigrants. Since it remained distant from the social and economic standards of first world nations, Portuguese emigration to Brazil, richer European countries or the United States of America did not cease.[1]

The first migrants to Portugal came mainly from the Cape Verde islands in the 1960s when they were still considered Portuguese ultramarine territories. Its inhabitants were thought of as assimilated Africans and were allowed to work in the mainland's construction and manufacturing industries. As a result of its colonial history, the influx of migrants since the mid-1980s until today originates largely from the PALOP (*Países de Língua Oficial Portuguesa*[2]) that became independent in 1975 and suffered the consequences of brutal civil wars for a long period.[3] The second

---

1 Decolonisation led, in fact, to an inverted migration process since Portuguese citizens who had migrated to the African colonies now returned in large numbers. In terms of non-Portuguese citizens, immigrant numbers remained rather small, so that, in 1981, only 54,414 foreigners, of which thirty per cent came from Europe, were registered with the Service of Foreigners and Frontiers. This number had more than quadrupled by 2003 when immigrants with resident permits represented 2.3 % of the population to which should be added the temporary permanence permit holders who accounted for a further 1.7 % of Portugal's inhabitants (Malheiros 2002).
2 Countries with Portuguese as their official language.
3 According to Malheiros (2002) Angola represents 9.9 %, Cape Verde 22.3 % and Guinea-Bissau 7.6 % of legal immigrants.

largest group of migrants now derives from Brazil with which Portugal retained strong emigrational ties after independence in 1822, while the third place in the immigration rankings is occupied by Ukrainians due to migration after the end of the Soviet Union (Malheiros 2002).

In contrast to many other European countries, except France and Great Britain, contact between migrants and the Portuguese population results primarily from historical, cultural and linguistic ties. Moreover, Portugal has sustained a post-colonial discourse in which language plays a significant if not fundamental role: the concept of *Lusofonia* (Lusophony) suggests cultural homogeneity and harmony among the Portuguese-speaking world and is based, unlike the paternalistic Francophone or the arrogant Anglophone discourses, on an imaginary brotherhood. By constantly invoking a common language and memory it thus turns a blind eye to colonial and post-colonial conflicts.

The Portuguese literary critic Eduardo Lourenço (1999) was one of the first to challenge and demystify this symbolic power of the Portuguese language and its theorisation through the concept of 'Lusofonia'. Although the concept is used as reference for a common history, culture and language, this authoritative voice on Portuguese culture questions the idea of a unified idiom, stressing the misuse of Fernando Pessoa's famous phrase 'my country is the Portuguese language' and arguing in favour of recognising the diversity of Portuguese languages – and therefore cultures – that resulted from linguistic transformations in Africa and Brazil.

The author suggests that Pessoa's writing was a linguistic adventure that consisted primarily in pointing out that language had no subject and that the Portuguese language belonged rather to everybody and nobody. According to Lourenço it is absurd to use Pessoa in a neo-colonialist and nationalistic manner, since his expression was personal and unpatriotic:

> Isto não abre para nacionalismos tribais, para patriotismos de exclusão da universalidade alheia. A nossa relação com a lingua é de outra natureza e é outra a patria que nela temos ou donde somos. Por isso a tão famosa frase quer dizer apenas: a lingua portuguesa, esta lingua que me fala antes que a saiba falar, mas, acima de tudo, esta lingua que através de mim se torna uma realidade não só viva mas única, a lingua através da qual me invento Fernando Pessoa, é ela a minha patria.[4]
> (Lourenço 1999: 126)

In Lourenço's understanding, language played an extraordinary role in Portugal's cultural formation and has always been a source of feverish exaltation and secret suffering. While imperial in vocation, Portuguese has in fact been provincial and has never achieved the influence of other languages such as English and French

---

4   'This does not offer a basis for tribal nationalisms or exclusive patriotisms of a strange universalism. Our relation with language is of a different kind, as is the country that it offers us to inhabit. The famous phrase only wants to say that the Portuguese language, the language that speaks me before I learn to speak, and, even more importantly, that I turn not only into a living reality but also into the only reality – in other words: the language that I use to invent myself, Fernando Pessoa, this language is my country.' (Translation by the author.)

(Lourenço 1999: 131–133). Today, after decolonisation, Lourenço insists in the necessity of rephrasing Pessoa: one should not speak of one Portuguese language but of a plurality of countries, peoples and languages. The author believes that the unconscious neo-colonial attitude that suggests that sharing a language implies sharing a culture can only be avoided by this awareness. Since language is a privileged place for the formation of identity, Portuguese has to be seen as a pluralised language: it is not the language that the Portuguese people speak but the voice that 'speaks' the Portuguese and other peoples who share the same linguistic roots: 'A lingua portuguesa é menos a lingua que os Portugueses falam do que a voz que *fala* os Portugêses' (Lourenço 1991: 121). Consequently, any analysis of Portuguese films under the perspective of plurilingualism has to part from an open concept that not only considers the languages spoken in the former colonies – like the different Creoles – but also the diverse Portuguese accents and grammars. Indeed, the few Portuguese films that do deal with immigrants structure their narratives around cultural encounters between characters with various Lusophone backgrounds.

So far only three Portuguese film-makers have dedicated feature films to the subject: Pedro Costa, author as much of *Casa de Lava*[5], 1994, set mostly on the Cape Verdean Ilha de Fogo, as of the 'Fontainha trilogy' (*Ossos*[6], 1997, *No Quarto da Vanda*[7], 2000, *Juventude em Marcha*[8], 2006) about the lives of Cape Verdean immigrants and their descendants in the Lisbon slum Fontainhas; Teresa Villaverde, whose interest in the future of adolescents made her choose an African descendant as one of three main characters in *Os Mutantes*[9], 1998 (and, exceptionally, a young Russian woman in *Transe*[10], 2006); and Leonel Vieira who offers a mainstream portrait of the second generation of Angolan immigrants in *Zona J*[11] from the same year.

Additionally, there are some co-productions between Portugal, the PALOP and Brazil that tackle the subject of migration. They were directed by film-makers of diverse Lusophone backgrounds and tell stories about Brazilian and African migrants in Europe: *Terra Estrangeira*[12] (Walter Salles, 1995), *Fintar o Destino*[13] (Fernando Vendrell, 1998), *Nha Fala*[14] (Flora Gomes, 2002), *Tudo isto é Fado*[15] (Luís Galvão Teles, 2003) and *Um Tiro no Escuro*[16] (Leonel Vieira, 2005). This article aims to give an overview of these films and to show how they deal with the question of *Lusofonia* by analysing the film-maker's portrayal of the encounters between representatives

---

5   *Down to Earth.*
6   *Bones.*
7   *In Vanda's Room.*
8   *Colossal Youth.*
9   *The Mutants.*
10 *Trance.*
11 *J Zone.*
12 *Foreign Land.*
13 *Dribbling Fate.*
14 *My Voice.*
15 *Fado Blues.*
16 *A Shot in the Dark.*

of the different languages and accents that depart from mainland Portuguese. Its main objective is to understand what perspectives they develop on post-colonial Lusophone identities, that is, if they replicate the neo-colonial discourse on cultural and linguistic homogeneity and harmony or engage with the potential conflicts of a plurality of languages and countries.

Portuguese Cinema

Pedro Costa is one of the most internationally recognised Portuguese film-makers of his generation, and his discourse on Lusophony is varied, paradoxical and intriguing. The first film on the subject, *Casa de Lava*, engages with Leon, a Cape Verdean construction worker, who is accompanied by a Portuguese nurse, Mariana, back to his island after he falls into a coma due to a failed suicide attempt. Although money was sent to pay for his return, nobody takes an interest in him when he arrives and it takes Mariana some time to discover his relatives and his relationship with a Portuguese woman, Edith. This other Portuguese woman's story indicates a bigger picture of trans-cultural relationships since she also came to the island to accompany someone: a prisoner who was sent during the dictatorship to the legendary concentration camp Tarrafal.

The Cape Verdean Creole language is an important instrument to discuss the cultural encounters in this highly visual and elliptic narrative. Like other Creole languages, Creole with Portuguese as its base is a result of linguistic encounters during colonisation. From a grammatical point of view it is a differentiated and autonomous language, which, once it was formed, became the symbol of a proper identity in Guinea Bissau and Cape Verde. After the separation of the two countries in 1980, it was recognised as a written language in Cape Verde in 1998. Given that it is actually more common than Portuguese, there are initiatives to turn it into the only official language.[17]

In *Casa de Lava*, Creole is a means to manifest Mariana's struggle in dealing with what is seen as a different, even strange, culture and her changing relationship with it. Accordingly, she seems to understand everything said in Creole when she arrives, but her difficulties in getting a deeper understanding of Cape Verdean culture is then reflected in her oscillating relationship with the country's language. The film makes it clear that Cape Verdean culture and language remember only on the surface its Portuguese roots and lexica. Notwithstanding her initial comprehension, when circumstances become more complex, especially Leon's relationship with other characters, Mariana suddenly needs an interpreter. Interpretation is easily provided since everybody is bilingual and thus, linguistically a step ahead of Mariana. She also demands that the Portuguese characters speak to her in her native language, especially Edith, whose adaptation to Creole culture and lan-

---

17   See for further informations on the formation of Creole with Portuguese as its base: http://cvc. instituto-camoes.pt/hlp/geografia/crioulosdebaseport.html (30 April 2010).

guage and her role as Leon's former lover Mariana does not understand in the beginning. Yet when she has a passionate encounter with Edith's nameless son who was born on the island and speaks only Creole, Mariana asks him to speak to her in the native tongue, thus attributing to it and enjoying an erotic connotation of its strangeness. Most of the time Mariana takes up a rather aggressive stance towards Cape Verdean culture and also expresses her resentment by attacking its language: during a fight with Leon she denigrates him through his language by saying that she understands his cowardly language.

Thus, the film depicts cultural conflicts between Mariana and the Cape Verdeans or the Portuguese characters that live on the island as conflicts of language. It demonstrates the main character's unwillingness to integrate, while suggesting that she becomes more and more enchanted with the people's crude emotions, which are, in fact, not unlike her own. The open ending hints at the possibility that she will remain on the island and become a part of its culture, like Edith and her nameless son who, by only speaking Creole, ignore (or have at least forgotten) their Portuguese origin. Both Portuguese and Creole cultures are represented with a consciousness of their ambivalences. Mariana is overconfident (especially in her profession as a nurse), 'paternalistic' and intrusive, but also engaging and caring. Additionally, there are more stereotypical features related to the African culture which indicate a clear gender divide – on the one hand complicity among the hard-working women and on the other the lack of responsibility by the men who are absent, seductive and violent. But the Ilha de Fogo and its extreme and arid nature is also a metaphor for a more complex, but mysterious and – especially from Mariana's European perspective – incomprehensible culture, whose most striking characteristics are paradoxical: a close relationship between death and desire, but also a passive, gloomy, yet relaxed and festive attitude towards life. Although conscientious of the cultural differences that question the Lusophone imaginary of a unified culture and language, *Casa de Lava* repeats, at the same time, the myth of the aptitude of the Portuguese to submerge in another 'strange' and initially hostile culture. The famous *cafrealização* – an expression for the adaptation of the Portuguese to African values, institutions and means of production – has been used to stigmatise this involvement, but has equally been considered a Portuguese capacity to adapt to tropical cultures (Santos 2001: 54). Mariana, and before her Edith, are aware that they are getting lost in the new surrounding and, in particular Edith, in its language; yet they start enjoying a life away from European conventions and ideas after some resistance. One of the last shots shows Leon and Edith together in the house of lava (of the original title in Portuguese), suggesting that there is a shared place for Creole and Portuguese culture based on reciprocal passion – a possibility for a Lusophone communion in the daunting African environment. One of its main expressions can be found in its language that, although based on Portuguese, has taken on a proper, but, and this is Costa's point, mixed identity.

Ossos[18] follows up on *Casa de Lava*'s gender divide within African culture but offers an almost opposite perspective on intercultural communication due to the change of location: Pedro Costa now looks at the second generation of Cape Verdean immigrants in Lisbon who live in the shanty town Fontainhas, which was constructed in the 1970s by the first migrants. Even though all the characters now speak Portuguese, the cultural and, especially, economic barriers between the former coloniser and the descendants of the colonised are here impossible to be overcome. This is told through the story of Tina, a young mother who has no support from her boyfriend (simply called the 'father'). Her friends, particularly Clotilde, try to help her through her depression that makes her try to kill herself twice: firstly after giving birth and again when the father takes the child away in order to make money (by begging on the streets and later by trying to sell it). The baby becomes the link between the universe of a middle-class nurse and the marginal life of the poor Cape Verdean descendants. This nurse assists the father on the street with food and then at the hospital after he almost killed the child by feeding it with bread and alcohol. She gets interested in keeping the baby but is repelled by the idea of paying for it. At the same time, Clotilde tries to recover Tina's child, finds out the whereabouts of the father and gets Tina a cleaning job at the nurse's home. But the child is no longer with the nurse since the father gave it to a prostitute he is friendly with. Even though the nurse's apartment becomes the stage for Lusophone (dis)encounters, there is no such thing as the house of lava, that is, a metaphoric but also linguistic space in which the two cultures meet and unite in harmony. In fact, only the nurse is capable of moving freely between the two separate worlds. While she seems to engage with the immigrants – she gives the father shelter, would take care of the baby, and tries to be friends with Tina –, she is also treacherous due to her loneliness and trespasses moral limits by sleeping with Clotilde's husband (who is only interested in sex) on her first visit to the community. Tina, Clotilde and the 'father', on the other hand, can only pass the invisible borderline when they have something to offer: their low-paid labour or the baby.

Aesthetically, the film shows that the characters are incapable of getting in touch with the outer world, positioning themselves within a visual field that might serve to constitute their subjectivity. The cinematographic strategies concentrate on isolation and suffering and end up turning the characters into victims. Since their circumstances are not really explored, they often seem caught within the frame and not within their condition. Language plays again an important role. There is a generalised difficulty in communicating, which is apparent through the very little dialogue. Whereas the Creole community is again bilingual, Tina, Clotilde and the father speak exclusively Portuguese – also among each other. There are actually only two characters who speak Creole most of the time, although they are bilingual: Clotilde's husband, who is portrayed as a stereotypical macho, and her son, who en-

---

18   For a more complex discussion of the film see Ferreira 2005 and 2007.

ters in his father's footsteps when he prohibits his mother to enter their home while the father is sleeping with the nurse. Thus, Creole does not draw a line between Portuguese and Cape Verdeans as it does in *Casa de Lava*, but between the men and women of the migrant community. Whilst Portuguese is the main means of communication, dominated by everyone even if scarcely used, Creole is used to express an African chauvinist attitude.

The closure of the film underlines this shift from a discussion of the social relationship between former colonisers and colonised to that of the gendered relationship within the community: the last sequence shows Clotilde trying first to kill the father by opening the kitchen gas (in the same way that Tina tried to kill herself) and then moving in with Tina. Instead of a Lusophone brotherhood and adaptation to a language that draws equally on African and Portuguese culture, or a passionate intercultural liaison, *Ossos* presents an inter-communal sisterhood that shuts doors and windows to both Cape Verdean men and Portuguese society, notwithstanding the fact that they speak the same language.

The documentary *No Quarto da Vanda*, the second part of the Fontainhas' trilogy, enters radically into Vanda Duarte's (the actress of Clotilde) life in order to show a less melancholic yet cruder picture of the second generation's life depicted in *Ossos*. The film accompanies not only Vanda's drug habit, her job (selling groceries from door to door), her conversations with friends, but also other drug users and the destruction of their neighbourhood, which is being demolished to give space to social housing apartment blocks. Language features only in the background, yet when it comes to the fore at one point it puts forward a powerful argument on the reasons for the second generation's marginal lives. The movie was filmed with a digital camera in long static and extremely beautiful and dense shots that are reminiscent of paintings and allow the spectator a long reflection on the marginal world of Fontainhas. Inscribed in the romantic tradition, the documentary gives voice to the underdogs of Portuguese society whose unhappy lives are given 170 minutes of time and space, thus bestowing an importance to their troubles, drug addiction and social exclusion that they are usually denied.

In contrast to both *Casa de Lava* and *Ossos*, *No Quarto da Vanda* has no gendered discourse. Both men and women suffer from marginalisation, use or sell drugs, look for places to stay or tell their sad stories. The fact that Vanda is the daughter of immigrants is not even directly acknowledged; on the contrary, she identifies with language and culture and questions certain features of the Portuguese society as being typical for her country. Even though the characters assume Portuguese identity, communicate exclusively in Portuguese and are not explicitly characterised as having Cape Verdean roots, there is one scene in which their heritage is strongly remembered. While Vanda's mother and sister are skinning a rabbit in the yard, we hear a man's voice in off lecturing Vanda in Creole. He questions her lack of respect and tells her that she would have received a lesson in Cape Verde for her behaviour, because only in Portugal there was no justice and everyone did as they liked. There is a cut to Vanda's room where she is sitting on her bed and starts smoking crack. The voice goes on questioning her lifestyle – the fact that she spends all day in bed and does not work. Another cut shows in a medium close up part of the man's body – an arm, his violin and part of his dress – and, without revealing his face, his voice tells Vanda about the hardships on his island in Cape Verde where men and women get up at three o'clock in the morning and work all day. The man leaves by saying that it was useless to talk to her and the film cuts back to Vanda who goes on smoking and mumbles that he must have been mistaken in the door.

It is not clear if the man is her father or a father figure, but he introduces a moral judgment that is absent in the rest of the film where the drug habit is a natural gesture – like eating, drinking, working and talking – and its users complex, ill and unhappy creatures. Dissimilar to the usage of Creole in *Ossos*, *No Quarto da Vanda* suggests, not unlike *Casa de Lava*, that Creole culture is, literally, more down-to-earth and wiser than Portuguese culture. In the earlier film the lesson is learned by the Portuguese character Mariana, who becomes receptive to this wisdom, while in the non-fiction film the second-generation character Vanda seems to ignore it. The argument here seems to be that the adaptation process to European culture and language impoverishes and marginalises the African descendants, while Creole culture is, albeit its mysterious surface, not only more open but also more enriching. The fact that the second generation does understand but does not speak Creole is a means of expressing their alienation.

Juventude em Marcha follows up on this idea through its main character, a first-generation immigrant. The Creole language features strongly in the film and develops the perspective that Cape Verdean language and culture are a reservoir of traditional values and virtues. It extends on the thought already present in *Ossos* and *No Quarto da Vanda* that the values represented by this anonymous man are endangered due to the destruction of the neighbourhood. Neither a documentary like *No Quarto da Vanda*, nor fictional like *Ossos* or *Casa de Lava*, the film's hybrid structure reconstructs without temporal or spacial linearity the past and present life of Ventura, an immigrant from the times of the first influx in the 1960s. Ventura was a construction worker and helped to build one of the most important cultural institutions in Portugal, the Calouste Gulbenkian Foundation, which hosts a museum, a library and a centre for the arts, as well as other institutions related to the country's scientific and artistic development. He is mainly characterised by his relationships to young characters who he considers his children. It is not evident if these young people – including Vanda – who he visits or talks to are in fact his biological offspring or if he is a father figure to them, but they construct Ventura as a patriarchal reference that represents the now anachronistic Cape Verdean value system of hard work, solidarity and dignity. The film has no story but aims to paint a dignifying portrait of this immigrant who dedicated his life indirectly to the development of Portugal. Instead of presenting a plot on Ventura's social contacts, past experiences and misfortunes, *Juventude em Marcha* is a massive visual experience that turns the Creole

worker into a living monument. Notwithstanding the fact that the title refers to a slogan of the Cape Verdean liberation movement against colonialism, and the use of a
political song in Creole, 'Labanta Braço', in one of the scenes, the film's politics are
as much linguistic as visual. Critics have celebrated the film's aesthetics as outstand-
ing, arguing that its choice of angles, long shots and lightning challenge conventional perception (Gardnier 2006). Indeed, Costa creates an atmosphere in which the
shots of Ventura turn him and the other characters into masterpieces – a monumen-
talisation which becomes even more obvious when he visits his former work place,
the Gulbenkian Museum of Art, where the paintings in exhibition suggest a close
comparison with the film-maker's iconography and lightning.

Just like *No Quarto da Vanda*, a marginalised and unspectacular character is
given centre stage; only this time it is not the negative result of migration – a generation without perspective lost in drug consumption – but an earlier, diligent age
group. Nonetheless, resembling Vanda, Ventura is shown to be caught within a process of deteriorating identity that stems from his condition as migrant. And, in contrast to the visual celebration of his personality, this occurs on the level of language.
Ventura's longing to return to Cape Verde is introduced through a letter written to
a loved one on the islands – which already appeared in *Casa de Lava* and expresses the hope to return full of money and with gifts. It is repeated various times like
a leitmotif and is the most evident sign of how language expresses that his identity is adrift. When the letter is composed for a friend while they are playing cards, it
is first recited by Ventura in Creole and then repeated in Portuguese. It is then cit-
ed another five times – three of them in Portuguese –, as though the speaker would
try to overcome the distance created by the new life and language through repetition, at the same time as it manifests the impossibility to do so. The choice of language indicates clearly whether the character belongs or not to Portuguese society.
Vanda, who is now a mother and drug-free, tells the story of the birth of her child
in both Portuguese and Creole, depending on whether she is addressing Ventura or
is relating her dialogue with the Portuguese nurses. She is now more rooted – due
to her new home, working husband and child – and therefore more capable of dealing with her double identity as both Portuguese citizen and Cape Verdean descendant. Ventura, on the other hand, speaks mainly Creole and only the longing letter reminds us of his plurilingualism. He is rather in limbo, an in-between, and his
choice of Creole expresses that he does not belong to the two cultures as Vanda does.
Portuguese culture is again exclusive and mainly associated to the modernisation of
the neighbourhood and the construction of clean and anonymous apartment blocks
that extinguish the Cape Verdean culture and community life cultivated by Ventura.
The strongest metaphor for this loss is the new empty apartment in which Ventura
lives without any relatives, given that his supposed children have apartments of their
own, and, like Vanda, are coping much better with this change.

The film's aesthetic strategies try to counterbalance Ventura's limbo by attributing
to him and his generation the place that they deserve, that is, within the portray gal-

lery of distinguished personalities. Because of this feature the film-maker has been accused of elitism, given that the worker is being integrated into a bourgeois aesthetic sense of high art (Krivochein 2007). While being partly true, *Juventude em Marcha* is also of a striking beauty that attributes Ventura with an unquestionable dignity, and at the same time, goes beyond the rather naïve believe in Lusophone harmony that we encounter at the end of *Down to Earth* and that (as *Ossos* and *No Quarto da Vanda* equally suggest) seems only possible on African soil. In contrast to *Ossos*, where the women reject as much the Portuguese as the men of their own community, the film accepts ambivalence and does not try to resolve Ventura's paradoxical situation. Besides using intertextual references that assimilate the Cape Verdean migrant into a European iconographic system, it also points linguistically at the main character's difficulties to integrate, as well as at the contribution of the first generation of immigrants to Portuguese society.

The films by Teresa Villaverde (*Os Mutantes*) and Leonel Vieira (*Zona J*) are equally concerned with integration of African descendents who have no linguistic barriers or memories, but search less for ways of recognising them by means of their cinematography, than to express aesthetically their rejection in Portugal's reality.[19] However, the approaches of Villaverde, a highly acclaimed auteur like Costa, and Vieira, a producer of blockbusters[20], could not be more different. *Os Mutantes* tells the story of three adolescents, Andreia (Ana Moreira), Pedro (Alexandre Pinto), and Ricardo (Nelson Varela) who live in state-run institutions. In two parallel narratives the film-maker shows their desire to find an alternative to their obligatory homes by running away. While Andreia is pregnant and initially tries to meet the father of her child (who is part of the African diaspora), the boys are in search of adventures but are caught and taken back by the police. Then their paths separate: Pedro still has a father, whom he is allowed to visit after having been arrested; Ricardo runs away from the institution, lives on the streets and since he needs money, steals from a warehouse, where he is caught by a group of adult men who kick him violently to death. Although life is hard for all of them, the boy of African descent is the most vulnerable of the three: he is almost raped during their first escapade, in which they participate in the shooting of a German paedophilic film in order to get some money, and ends up paying with his life. The chronological stories are told through a structure that obeys a visual pattern and not a plot of cause and effect. This also results from the way Villaverde uses space. She rarely reveals where her characters are; although they move all over Lisbon, they seem imprisoned within the frame of the shots. It is more important to be close to them than to tell an easily accessible and coherent realistic narrative. Similar to *Ossos*, there is no affirmation whatsoever of the Lusophone

---

19   For a more complex discussion of the films see Ferreira 2005 and 2007.
20   *Zona J*, a co-production with the private television channel SIC achieved the highest box office takings in the year of its release, 1998. According to the Portuguese Film Institute ICAM (*Instituto do Cinema, Audiovisual e Multimédia*) (2002: 172), 246,073 spectators saw the film, placing it fourth in the ranking of the ten Portuguese films with the biggest audiences.

myth of a shared place, apart from the fact that all share the same language. The film clearly indicates that within Portugal's postcoloniality race is an issue that endangers Luso-Africans even more than the already vulnerable adolescents.

Zona J offers the same discourse in terms of the impossibility of integration of a different adolescent – who not only speaks Portuguese as his mother tongue but also holds Portuguese citizenship – yet believes naively in another myth: the luso-tropicalist idea that racial mixture is a solution to racism.[21] The film's protagonist is the eighteen-year-old António, son of hard-working immigrants from Angola who live in an apartment block at Lisbon's outskirts, the Zona J, part of the suburb Chelas. His relationship with Portuguese society is explored through his romance with Carla, a middle-class white girl, and through his involvement with his group of friends, who live from petty theft and are planning a major crime. Even though António comes from a stable home, his story ends just like Ricardo's: with his death. Due to some rather unbelievable plot points – Carla becomes pregnant, his father loses his job and gets involved in diamond smuggling to Angola – he decides to participate in a jewellery robbery where he gets wounded. The film actually presents criminality as the only possible survival strategy for both the second and the first generation of African immigrants. Portuguese society is literally black and white; and this is presented as permanent and unchangeable. It is also suggested that António never really wants to be part of Portuguese society and culture: his room is decorated with posters of Africa. When he is wounded during the assault, it is clear to him that he does not want to remain in Portugal and he tries to travel with Carla to Angola.

The box office success of *Zona J* is easily explained by the film's conventionality, its 'visually attractive' and 'engaging narrative', referred to by the critic Eurico de Barros (n.d.). Indeed, the film manages to present a demanding topic in an entertaining format, so that the spectator can easily escape the challenge to engage critically with the exclusion of Luso-Africans. Despite its denunciation of xenophobia, the closure effortlessly dismisses the second generation as a lost cause and passes on to the unborn third generation that Carla is expecting. The last sequence shows António dying in Carla's arms while she looks symbolically to the horizon, holding her hand over the unborn in her womb. Instead of offering a solution, this rhetoric of positive racial mixture puts forward the luso-tropicalist discourse in a different disguise. Language is by no means a form of unification, just a means of communication that does not imply a deeper relation to the Portuguese culture, which is hostile against its immigrants, mainly because of the colour of their skin.

---

21 The concept of luso-tropicalism can be traced back to the Brazilian anthropologist Gilberto Freire. Margarida Calafate Ribeiro cites Caeiro da Mata, who suggested that it consists in euphemisms since the concept turned five centuries of colonialism into five centuries of relationships between different cultures and people, the colonial society into a multi-racial society, the imperial nation into a multi-continental nation and Portugal's civilisational and religious mission into Portugal's integration into the tropics (Ribeiro 2004: 152).

Lusophone Co-Productions

Due to a diplomatic crisis in 1993, when Portugal signed the Schengen Treaty and started to block Brazilian and PALOP citizens at its airports, the Community of Portuguese Speaking Countries, CPLP (*Comunidade de Países de Língua Portuguesa*), was created in 1996. This supra-national organisation, which aims to foster cultural, political and economic relations, triggered the discussion on Lusophony referred to earlier. Since its creation it has not only revived the myth of Lusophone homogeneity and harmony but, in order to foster this idea, also revitalised existing agreements for cultural collaboration or stimulated new ones. I will now look at the resulting two Luso-African and three Luso-Brazilian co-productions that deal with contemporary migration and Lusophony and ask to what extent they remystify cultural and linguistic bonds or if they succeed, as one might hope for, to develop multilateral perspectives.[22]

Walter Salles' and Daniela Thomas' *Terra Estrangeira* was the first co-production in this context and reacted directly to the economic crises that resulted from president Fernando Collor de Mello's economic plan in 1990 to modernise the Brazilian economy according to the neo-liberal recipe of global capitalism. This not only deeply affected the cinema industry but also resulted in mass emigration. A young student, Paco, becomes one of the migrants when he accepts to smuggle diamonds to Portugal. The journey to Europe is, in fact, part of his plan to go to his mother's home town in Spain. In Portugal, Paco encounters a young Brazilian woman, Alex, whose husband Miguel was killed by trying to outwit the smugglers. In a rebellious act she steels from Paco the violin in which the stones are being smuggled and sets off a chase in which Paco becomes the victim. In the open ending, Alex is driving across the border with the wounded Paco on her lap and it is unclear if they will make it to the 'real' Europe.

The characters negotiate and articulate complex and contradictory perspectives on the issues of Lusophone brotherhood, linguistic ties and identity throughout the film. The avant-garde artist Miguel, for example, denigrates luso-tropicalism by calling Lisbon conceitedly a 'cabaret of colonies'. He is a cynic whose music, in an obvious contrast to Tropicalism's popularity, is not fashionable at all. He dislikes Portugal mainly for being economically and culturally underdeveloped; it is just a hole in the Fortress Europe through which he wants to make it into the richer countries. Conversely, his girlfriend Alex is completely disillusioned about Europe as the Promised Land and her desire to return home intensifies during the narrative. By stating that her Brazilian pronunciation creates frontiers rather than feelings of linguistic or cultural belonging, she demonstrates that Lusophony is a fraud. Alex most strongly expresses her frustration about Brazil as a country that went wrong. But, in contrast to Miguel, she does not blame the ancient coloniser but acknowledges respect for the courage of the colonial enterprise.

---

22   There have been a total of 35 Lusophone co-productions between 1995 and 2008, 12 of which are Luso-African, 21 Luso-Brazilian and two Luso-Afro-Brazilian.

The characters have in general no feelings of belonging to the former coloniser or its postcolonial imaginary, the Lusophone community, and they are quite conscious of the differences in linguistic terms. This is made evident in Paco's relationship with Loli, a friendly Angolan character. Loli not only helps Paco but tries to make him aware of his self-pity by telling him about his people's suffering during the civil war that followed Angola's independence from Portugal. Paco feels rather bothered by him at first. The European descendant changes his approach when he feels in need of a friend. Their friendship develops during a conversation in which they joke about the different meanings of certain words and idiomatic expressions in Angolan, Brazilian and mainland Portuguese. But their bond does not last long and the cultural differences and prejudices come strongly to the fore. When his violin is taken away from him, Paco violently accuses the African of being the thief, unaware that his real antagonist is the Portuguese character Pedro. Pedro, a friend of Alex and Miguel, is the only character who reminds us of the sentimental relationships between Portugal and Brazil. He is in love with Alex and helps her out, thus betraying his friend Igor. When confronted with violence, he ends up betraying Alex as well. Evidently, there are no enduring bonds. The transnational antiques dealer Igor, who travels easily between the two continents and switches from a Brazilian to a Portuguese accent, is an unmistakable example of the fact that Lusophony is used as a means to take economic advantages. His dominion of the varying accents and grammars is rather a sign of opportunism and corruption than of closeness. It is also no coincidence that Igor keeps up the habit of smuggling diamonds in statues of saints or other cultural objects as was common during the colonial period.

The sympathetic but conventional film *Fintar o Destino* offers a contrary discourse on Lusophony and linguistic belonging by revisiting Pedro Costa's idea in *Casa de Lava* that the Cape Verde islands are a place where African and European culture embrace in brotherhood. Based on a true story and directed by Portuguese film-maker Fernando Vendrell, its plot – mainly set on the island São Vicente – concentrates on a bar tender, Mané, who is unsatisfied with his culture – its laziness, lethargy, and alcohol consumption. When he was young, Mané was invited by one of Portugal's most important soccer clubs, Benfica, to be a professional player but declined in order to marry and stay in his country. His life and marriage are now poisoned by his regrets and the feeling that his life is a failure. In order to give his life some meaning and believing strongly in Portugal as a better place, he travels to Lisbon where he wants to suggest to Benfica a young player who he coaches. Despite the insistence in Portugal's receptivity, borderless communication in Portuguese and the absence of integration problems (Mané's son is happily married to a white woman and perfectly at home in Lisbon; and his friend who went in his place to Portugal and now lives in poverty has himself and his bohemian lifestyle to blame), this journey makes Mané realise that he misses his country' culture, its sociability and happiness. He returns from the trip in peace with himself and certain of the strong bond with Portugal.

The main character's plurilingualism – he speaks Creole and Portuguese with the same ease and chooses it according to the country he is in – and his sense of belonging to Portuguese culture (he was invited when Cape Verde was still an ultramarine province) – which make him travel and allow him to move with some ease in Lisbon (although he does not like the big city and is cheated on when purchasing a ticket for the season's cup final) – extend at the end of the film into an acceptance of both cultures. While the film acknowledges their differences, it also emphasises the strong links (the soccer club being the strongest) that make it possible for Mané to encounter positive sides in his own culture. Since his idea that Portugal is the better place for soccer is not shattered, he insists that his young athlete leave the country and play at Benfica. Mané keeps on living the Lusophone dream of cultural harmony and linguistic unity: he believes that he and his successor can live in both worlds at the same time.

It is quite striking that there are no references whatsoever to the Cape Verdean colonial history and fight for independence in Vendrell's film and resentments towards Portuguese as official language are equally inexistent. While *Nha Fala*, a colourful and optimistic musical made by the Guinea-Bissauan film-maker Flora Gomes, also develops a discourse on intercultural and linguistic exchange, it at least remembers one of the central figures of colonial resistance in what is now the PALOP, the Cape Verdean Amilcar Cabral. Quite the reverse of his earlier films like *Udju azui di Yonta*[23] (1992) or *Po di Sangui*[24] (1996), in which cultural conflicts are central to the narratives and Creole is the only language spoken, Gomes' last film offers the possibility of overcoming obsolete African cultural elements like superstition, as well as European racism and ideas of superiority, in the encounter of African graciousness with Western language and technology. Although the two languages spoken in the film are Creole and French (instead of the official language Portuguese), the main character, the beautiful Vita, dominates French like her mother tongue and switches between them with ease, demonstrating the same cosmopolitism present in *Fintar o Destino*. Indeed, Vita only finds her own voice, referred to in the title, as well as her identity as a woman, after moving to France and by singing in its language.

The film's protagonist leaves Guinea Bissau in order to study in this richer European country that also co-produced the film. Before her departure, at the beginning of the film in which she says farewell to her family and friends, musical numbers – composed by famous Cameroon musician Manu Dibango – present the wide range of contemporary social problems that Guinea Bissau is facing: the difficulty in dealing with the memory of the heroic fight for independence, corruption, the coexistence of Animism and Catholicism, and the unemployment among young people with university degrees.[25] The songs sung in Creole express the ambiguities that the young African nation is still facing after three decades of independence. In Paris,

---

23   *Yonta's Blue Eyes.*
24   *Tree of Blood.*
25   The film was actually shot in Cape Verde due to the political conflicts in Guinea Bissau.

Vita falls in love with a French music producer. After their first night together Vita sings and thus breaks with an old family superstition which says that any female descendent of the family who sings will die. Singing in France has a completely different significance from singing in Guinea Bissau: not only does it express Vita's new-found freedom from obsolete traditions but it also implies financial success and independence. When she becomes a famous singer in Europe, Vita returns with her boyfriend and sound equipment to her home in order to deal with the offence. With the help of family and friends she stages her funeral, simultaneously respecting and transcending her mother's belief in the superstition. According to its genre, the film portrays a vibrant and utopian Africa, which, by embracing European culture, becomes capable of constructing a hybrid identity.

Notwithstanding its reference to Amilcar Cabral and his anti-colonialist resistance (his statue is carried around throughout the film and grows all the time), Portugal's colonial presence in Africa is only shortly recalled through an eavesdropping Portuguese cleaner in Paris. This character stresses the country's contemporary status as provider of cheap labour for rich European countries, and, in a very light fashion, the end of the hegemony of ancient colonisers. Vita is presented as a modern African woman who goes beyond her bilingual Creole/Lusophone background by speaking perfect French and conquering her place in the European music market. Neither language nor culture are obstacles and represent no boundaries. Everybody understands literally everybody, especially after the cultural problem of superstition is playfully overcome: Vita's boyfriend does not speak but understands Creole and her mother understands but does not speak French. It is quite obvious that the choice of language and the inoffensive discourse on Afro-European harmony and easy linguistic encounter are thought to gain a greater European audience, especially the French market that has a long tradition of absorbing African art house cinema.

Fado Blues by Luís Galvão Teles engages, like *Terra Estrangeira*, with three different Portuguese accents from Africa, Europe and South America. Yet, in contrast, the comedy puts forward a Lusophone discourse that not only unites the former coloniser in harmony with the ex-colonies, but also attributes a paternalistic role model to Portugal. All the characters in the film have an allegorical dimension: the Brazilian Leonardo who works in a video store in Rio de Janeiro but wants to follow in the footsteps of his idol Reis, a Portuguese writer of detective stories; the African Amadeu who, in a neo-colonialist attitude is considered Portuguese although he has an African accent, and lives with Leonardo in Brazil because he wants to make big money but does not get far by cheating on tourists; Reis's sensual daughter Lia with whom both young men fall in love but who only gives in to the equally white and more romantic Leonardo; and, finally, Reis, the father figure who does not want to assume his role but ends up uniting everybody in the goodhearted theft of a painting which had been stolen from Amadeu's former boss and friend, Salvador, and is now worth a lot of money. According to another Lusophone myth, all the characters, including Lia, are '*malandros*', inoffensive little crooks with a big heart. The story is as simple as its politics: Leonardo and Amadeu leave Brazil because it is a country with no economic perspective. Since they have Reis's address they invade his property and meet Lia who suggests to her father the plan of the perfect robbery. They steal the painting on the night of the finals of the World Cup in which Portugal and Brazil dispute the title. Given the Lusophone discourse of the film it is no surprise that they manage to steal the painting – with the important intervention of Reis –, Portugal wins the World Cup and all the characters celebrate the Luso-Afro-Brazilian harmony under Portuguese patronage on the streets.

It is important to add that the film is no satire at all, but, although it is a comedy, is serious in its perspective on Brazil as an economic fiasco and Portugal as the winning team in all instances. While Portugal embraces the other cultures – there is one light comment each to dismiss the factual discrimination of Brazilians and Africans (Leonardo's accent and Amadeu's skin colour) –, it is in fact superior, economically, culturally and even in terms of sports – which is the most absurd statement of them all. The wishful thinking of the film, in which all Africans are Portuguese – just like in colonial times –, and the Luso-Brazilian love-story is inevitable due to the unconditional Brazilian passion for its matrix, reflecting exactly the delirious Portuguese discourse that Eduardo Lourenço describes when he speaks about the factual absence of links between Brazil and Portugal and the Portuguese perception of proximity with Africa. This 'delirious' discourse not only ignores reality but, particularly, the linguistic and cultural differences between the three continents involved (Lourenço 1999: 140–141). While there are slight cultural and especially economic differences, the Portuguese language is the glue that holds the characters together. This is especially manifest in the importance that Leonardo attributes to the literary skills of Reis, whose name reminds of one of the famous heteronyms of Fernando Pessoa.

Um Tiro no Escuro, Leonel Vieira's second film on migration, also presents elements of Portugal's image of Brazil, although it offers a critique of the country itself. The film begins again in Brazil: a young woman, Veronica, leaves her four-month-old daughter for a moment with a stewardess on the airport toilet. The woman kidnaps the baby and we reencounter Veronica a year later in Lisbon in a stripper bar where she earns her living. After and during the shows she goes to the airport in order to spot the stewardess and thus find her child. The film is unclear on the reasons for her profession: we never know if she was a stripper before or if she chose to work exposing her body – as many female migrants do – so that she has a chance to return to Brazil with her daughter. The melodrama turns into a crime movie when Veronica is fired and Carlos, the bar's bodyguard takes her side and has to leave as well. His brother is a criminal who has just been released from prison and they end up forming a gang that starts robbing banks. As they are being hunted down by the police, the detective who is working on the case turns out to be the husband of the stewardess who kidnapped the baby and is finally spotted by Veronica at the airport. The suspense reaches a climax when the gang members shoot each other during the last robbery, which Veronica uses to mislead the detective and to get her daughter back.

As a final twist, the detective reaches the airport just before boarding, recovers the child, realises his wrongdoings and returns the girl. Veronica can finally leave with her daughter for Brazil.

Um Tiro no Escuro develops, just like *Tudo isto é Fado*, a stereotyped and strongly gendered idea of both Brazil and Portugal. However, the roles are now inverted: the Brazilian character is sensual (there are many scenes of Veronica stripping, taking a bath or having sex with Carlos), while the Portuguese are sterile, immoral and self-destructive (the stewardess and the detective lost their child and steal another one, the detective tries to use his position in order to conceal his wife's crime, and the gangsters are not only ignorant machos, but also incompetent and end up killing one another). Whereas the comedy unites light-hearted little crooks from three continents through language, *Um Tiro no Escuro* underlines (similar to *Terra Estrangeira*) the dark side of migrating from Brazil to Portugal, as well as the power structure below the supposed unity. Accordingly, the cultural proximity suggested by the common language is questioned: literally, when Veronica's accent is imitated by Carlos' brother and the other gangster, and indirectly by her exploitation by the stewardess and later by the bar owner who demands 5,000 Euros in return for her passport. Although the film is submerged in platitudes, it has a point when it suggests that Brazilians are seen by the Portuguese with either envy (by women), or aggressive desire (by men). The supposed proximity between Portugal and Brazil only hides deep resentment and, in contrast to *Tudo isto é Fado*, the film at least hints at the fact that the idea of economic and moral superiority expressed by the detective ('Maria is much better off with us than with a stripper') is an unconscious cover-up for both.

Conclusion

The Lusophone discourse is of Portuguese origin and possesses an unconsciously neo-colonialist character. This is to say, it is a unilateral discourse directed from Portugal towards the other members of the Portuguese speaking community. It aims to guarantee the country's place within the world outside its small postcolonial territory. One of the conclusions that we can draw from the films analysed above is that this one-sided discourse has a hard time incorporating the topic (and reality) of migration. In all the Portuguese films language is no unifying factor at all and the majority of Luso-Brazilian films share this perspective. Only the Luso-African films and one Luso-Brazilian production (*Tudo isto é Fado*) develop positive views on the possibility of Afro-European cultural bonds and easy plurilingual communication. In fact, from the eleven films studied only these three suggest that African and Brazilian migrants have a chance of being integrated into Portugal's society. Indifferent to their nationality, supporting perspective or aesthetics (author films or blockbusters) the film-makers of this study have no doubt that their migrants (both first and second generation) are not welcomed or are either marginalised or feel alienated. In three cases migration to Portugal (or being a descendant from migrants) is actually fatal (*Os Mutantes, Zona J* and *Terra Estrangeira*).

The Portuguese film productions have a pessimistic perspective on the possibility of integrating the second generation of migrants from Africa into Portuguese culture, even though language is no obstacle at all. The reasons for exclusion and alienation are to be found elsewhere: in the loss of traditional values (*No Quarto da Vanda*), racism (*Os Mutantes, Zona J*) and machismo in the Cape Verdean community (*Ossos*). Pedro Costa presents, indeed, quite different perspectives on language. In *Casa de Lava* he shows that the Portuguese, in sharp contrast to all other Cape Verdean characters in his films, are capable of adapting to another culture and language, albeit with initial resistance. When plurilingualism is a cultural given, as in the case of the Cape Verdeans, it has varying effects. While for the first generation of migrants being bilingual becomes a symptom of alienation from the native culture (*Juventude em Marcha*), the second generation learns to deal with this double identity from film to film: at first plurilingualism expresses female discrimination (*Ossos*), then marginalisation and, by ignoring the African language, also a sign of alienation (*No Quarto da Vanda*); yet, in the last film, it is a sign of increasing adaptation as well as of an acceptance of one's roots (Vanda in *Juventude em Marcha*).

Both Luso-African productions, one by a Portuguese film-maker and one by an internationally acclaimed African director, show how the European languages and the contact with its cultures empower their characters who become able to enjoy their respective cultures more fully after the intercultural exchange and due to their plurilingualist skills. The Luso-Brazilian productions are less light-hearted: only one comedy, made by a Portuguese film-maker, believes in Lusophone harmony, while the other two (one Portuguese and one Brazilian director) have a much more pessimistic – and perhaps more realistic – perspective on multicultural encounters. Interestingly, all three Luso-Brazilian co-productions deal with crime, thus echoing either playfully or with a dark tone the history of offences and the breaking of laws that are part of the shared colonial history (one can think of slavery, exploration, Indian genocide, the Inquisition, etc.). Only once are the different cultures and languages seen as being compatible and the migrant characters as successful in striving for a better life in Portugal (*Tudo isto é Fado*). Linguistic and cultural differences are either mentioned (*Um Tiro no Escuro*) or explored (*Terra Estrangeira*), but always shatter the Lusophone dream by indicating a deep divide between Africa, Brazil and Portugal.

Co-productions are no guarantee for multilateral views on the complex bonds and historical relationships between Portugal and its ex-colonies that make Africans and Brazilians choose to migrate. Despite the multiplicities of perspectives on Lusophony and the overriding critical stance, many films still look for harmony and – one might guess – box-office success. Others distrust the old myths but take resort to stereotypes. The Portuguese productions, dominated by Pedro Costa, are, on the other hand, almost too sure about difference and exclusion. There are few films, *Terra Estrangeira, Os Mutantes* and *Juventude em Marcha*, that can be considered as being the finest examples of a cinema that is trying to come to terms with the burden of Lusophony.

References

BARROS, E. de (n. d.), 'Sangue novo no celulóide', in: URL: http://www.insituto-amoes.pt/arquivos/cinema/sangcine.htm (3 February 2004).

FERREIRA, C. O. (2006), 'The Limits of Luso-Brazilian Brotherhood – Fortress Europe in the Film Foreign Land', in: *Third Text*, 20.6, 733–743.

FERREIRA, C. O. (2005), 'The Adolescent as Post-colonial Allegory: Strategies of Intersubjectivity in Recent Portuguese Cinema', in: *Camera Obscura*, 59, 35–71.

FERREIRA, C. O. (2007), 'No future – The Luso-African generation in Portuguese Cinema', in: *Studies in European Cinema* 4.1, 49–60.

GARDNIER, R. (2006), 'Pedro Costa, Juventude em Marcha', URL: http://www.contracampo.com.br/82/festjuventudeemmarcha.htm (14 December 2008).

KRIVOCHEIN, B. (2007), 'Juventude em Marcha de Pedro Costa', URL: http://www.zetafilmes.com.br/criticas.asp?id=328 (14 December 2008).

LOURENÇO, E. (1999), *A Nau de Ícaro seguido de Imagem e Miragem da Lusofonia*, Lisbon: Gradiva.

MALHEIROS, J. (2002), 'Portugal Seeks Balance of Emigration, Immigration', URL: http://www.migrationinformation.org/Profiles/display.cfm?ID=77 (10 January 2010).

RIBEIRO, M. C. (2004), *Uma História de Regressos. Império, Guerra Colonial e Pós-colonialismo*, Porto: Ediçõs Afrontamento.

SANTOS, B. S. (2001), 'Entre Prospero e Caliban', in: Ramalho, M. I. & A. Sousa Riberio (eds.), *Entre Ser e Estar – Raízes, percursos e discursos de identidade*, Porto: Ediçōes Afrontamento, 23–85.

Going North: Language and Culture Contact in Spanish Emigration Cinema

Miya Komori

Introduction

A key scene in Carlos Iglesias' *Un Franco, 14 Pesetas*[1] (2006) exemplifies many of the themes centring around language use by migrants: failures in communication due to a lack of language skills; a translator/mediator; somewhat stereotypical characters; a mother who does not speak the language of her host country; the second-generation child who is fluent in both languages and cultures and forms a bridge between them. 'Hí-ga-do,' says the Spanish migrant Pilar loudly and slowly to the Swiss butcher. 'Hí-ga-do – ¡de aquí!' she says again, pointing to her own abdomen and then drawing in the air, to his bafflement. Frustrated, she turns to her son Pablo who has just come into the shop: 'Lo que me ha costado este hombre, por Dios, que es un poco lelo. Me lo ha visto pedir cuarenta veces.'[2] 'Sí, Mamá,' replies the boy, who is bilingual after five years at the local school in the Swiss town of Uzwil, 'y yo también te lo he dicho cuarenta veces en alemán y no lo sabes'[3] [01:10:38–01:10:57; 01:11:00–01:11:04].

In contrast to the other articles in this volume, which focus on migrants coming into Europe, this essay uses examples from three films based on the experiences of Spanish emigrants going north to find work in Switzerland, Germany and France respectively. All three films are set during the Spanish economic downturn of the 1960s and 1970s, but present very different reactions to language and culture contact and clashes. Despite – or perhaps through – the differences in style and content, Carlos Iglesias' *Un Franco, 14 pesetas* (2006), Pedro Lazaga's *¡Vente a Alemania, Pepe!*[4] (1971) and Roberto Bodegas' *Españolas en París*[5] (1971) offer an insight

---

1   *Crossing Borders.*
2   'Li-ver… li-ver – from here! […] This man is driving me crazy, honestly, he's a bit slow, isn't he? I've asked him for it forty times!'
3   'Yes, mum, and I've told you forty times what it is in German and you still don't know.'
4   *Come to Germany, Pepe!*
5   *Spaniards in Paris.*

into intra-European migration during the late Francoist regime. The variety of subjects portrayed in the three films and their different approaches to the emigrant experience provide rich material for analysing language and culture contact. Using an interdisciplinary approach drawing on linguistics, film aesthetics and cultural studies, scenes from the films showing the emigrants in everyday situations (such as eating, working or simply passing the time of day) will be used to illustrate the different levels of contact and conflict portrayed, from a complete lack of understanding to being able to get a message across and finally achieving various levels of fluency in both language and culture.

Going North: Spanish Emigrants to France, Germany and Switzerland

The economic situation in their homeland during the 1960s and early 1970s, the period in which the films are set, forced many Spaniards to seek work elsewhere. As Juan B. Vilar and María J. Vilar explain, migration to France and the German-speaking countries was at its peak at this point in the century, probably because of their geographical proximity and their need for unqualified manual labour after the liberalisation of their markets. The numbers for migration out of Spain vary depending on the source of the statistics, as Vilar and Vilar's figures show. They claim that the number of 'assisted' (i.e. official) emigrants was around one million people between 1960 and 1973, and the actual figure around twice that (Vilar/Vilar 1999: 25–28; see also Black 2010: 46; Cazorla Sánchez 2010: 108–109).

The characters in all three films are fairly typical of Spanish emigrants to northern Europe: lured by the experience of apparently successful friends and acquaintances, the demand for semi-skilled work and the host country's strong currency, but, crucially, without existing language skills. Stanley Black quotes a 1966 poll conducted by the Ministry of Labour, which gave 'to help their families, to improve their income, and to save money' as the three main reasons for leaving the country of over 90 % of Spanish emigrants, while others included buying a house or because they were unemployed at the time (Black 2010: 111). Each of the films mentions at least one of these reasons, although their different origins and styles give them a distinctly different focus. ¡Vente a Alemania, Pepe! is a fairly straightforward example of the *landismo* cinema named after its most popular actor (Alfredo Landa, 'Pepe') in which the influence of Franco's censorship can be easily felt. Though not the 'nation-building propaganda epic' that Spanish cinema under the dictatorship is often (misleadingly?) regarded to be (Marsh 2006: 1), it is typical of a genre that enjoyed immense popularity at the time. The rather serious topic of migration is used as a setting for what is primarily a slapstick comedy based around the misadventures of the eponymous Pepe with a heavy dose of deliberately silly innuendo and unfortunate situations arising from a lack of cultural and linguistic understanding. It also ends typically with the 'return to a relieved acceptance of an implicitly superior Spanish status quo' (Black 2010: 48). In contrast, despite being a contemporary of ¡Vente a Alemania, Pepe!, *Españolas en París* is a considerably more subtle film, with women's and domestic workers' rights as a leitmotif. At the end of the film, Isabel, the protagonist, decides to stay in France and raise her child there. The ultimate message of the film is, however, somewhat ambiguous, as attitudes towards her as an unmarried mother at the time of its release would certainly have been considerably different from those of its 21st century audience.[6] Finally, *Un Franco, 14 Pesetas* is a much later work, written and directed by Carlos Iglesias, who was himself born in Switzerland to Spanish immigrants. A slightly bittersweet comedy, it draws on aspects of both of the older films, tempering the protagonists' return to Spain with doubts as to whether it was the right decision.

Working with Plurilingualism: Subtitling Strategies

As can be seen throughout this volume, there are several means of dealing with a polyglot cast of characters. Three of the most common are dubbing, subtitling and voice-over, the latter still being relatively unusual in fiction film (Heiss 2004). In the films studied, only subtitling is offered as a way to aid audience comprehension (if at all). This may be because it is arguably the best strategy for maximising understanding while preserving the plurilingualism and thereby the authenticity of the original, since the film's viewers are clearly aware that they are receiving an '*overt translation*' (Reinart 2004: 74; 78). It is curious, therefore, that *Españolas en París* does not have subtitles in any language, in spite of having several sequences where a language other than Spanish is spoken. In fact, Bodegas makes no attempt to make the bilingualism of the film (French/Spanish) accessible to a monolingual audience. *¡Vente a Alemania, Pepe!* has limited subtitles in Spanish where it is important for the dramatic irony, e.g. of the sleeping pills in the milk the dancers give to Pepe [27:56–27:59], but largely relies on the viewer's intelligence to piece together the basics from the jumble of languages. It is true that, in contrast to the other films, there is is very little conversation between native speakers of the host language, and the audience therefore does not need to know what is being said. However, in some cases grasping the gist of what is being said is simply not enough to appreciate the film fully. As Sigmund Freud points out in his theories on the joke, humour relies on the joke being *received* as funny (Freud 1992: 158). The humour of scenes based around bi- or plurilingual wordplay, to which Freud devotes considerable attention (Freud 1992: 45–47), is completely lost when the audience literally only understands one side of the joke. It is therefore arguable that the lack of subtitles, while enhancing the impression of foreignness felt by the audience, detracts from the comedic value of many scenes. Since *¡Vente a Alemania, Pepe!* is intended to be a comedy, this can be regarded as an oversight of considerable importance. On the other hand,

---

6   Though the moral repression that stood at the heart of the Francoist regime had relaxed somewhat by the 1970s, Spain still purported to be a country based around strict Catholic teachings including the sanctity of marriage, which was only legally recognised if it took place within the Church, and the prohibition of both contraception and abortion (Grugel/Rees 1997: 129–135; Cazorla Sánchez 2010: 139; 170–171).

it is questionable as to whether such homophonic puns are translatable at all, an issue which is too large for the scope and focus of this essay (see, for example, Reinart 2004: 86; 92). Similarly, Ella Shohat and Robert Stam also point out that in the omission of subtitles, 'the spectator unfamiliar with the source language misses certain ironies and nuances' (Shohat/Stam 2006: 120).

As a more recent film, with more technical possibilities at its disposal, *Un Franco, 14 Pesetas* offers subtitles in Spanish, German, French and English. The English and French subtitles differentiate between Spanish and German by means of font, italicising the latter. When Italian is spoken, subtitles are omitted to elicit the same bewilderment from the viewer as is experienced by the Spanish characters in the film. Interestingly, the Spanish and German subtitles are clearly intended for non-native speakers, as only the parts spoken in the other language (i.e. Swiss-German and Spanish respectively) are subtitled. Even more interestingly, it is assumed that German native speakers will understand the strong Swiss dialect, as it is not subtitled in German, although programmes shown on television in German-speaking countries often do subtitle non-standard German such as Swiss and even certain Austrian dialects. In terms of the audience's reception of the plurilingualism in the films, therefore, it can be argued that the subtitling in *Un Franco, 14 Pesetas* reflects the original mix of languages quite closely while still facilitating understanding, whereas the general lack of subtitling in *¡Vente a Alemania, Pepe!*, though not necessarily a hindrance to basic comprehension, can be said to dull the humour of this comedy to a certain extent. In contrast to the films set in German-speaking countries, *Españolas en París* appears to be intended for an audience fluent in both French and Spanish.

Arrival: Non-Understanding, Non-Verbal Communication and the Expression of Foreignness

The impression that the migrating characters are very much in a foreign country is thrown into stark relief by a lack of comprehension at the beginning of all the films: not knowing the majority language of the host country leaves the migrant without any sense of orientation (Hu 2007: 1). In order to make themselves understood, both the immigrants and the locals use various strategies to get the basic message across without having to rely on linguistic ability. In many cases, vigorous non-verbal communication or the presence of a third person in the role of translator or informant compensates for the migrant characters' difficulties in expressing themselves verbally. Curiously, food is often used as a prop. Before Martín and Marcos, the protagonists of *Un Franco, 14 Pesetas,* arrive at the Swiss border, they are touched by the generosity of their fellow Spaniard in the train, who shares his *chorizo* sausage with them, explaining meat cannot be taken into Switzerland [16:08]. These cold cuts can be regarded as Barthesian 'totem-foods', the Spanish equivalent to what wine, according to Roland Barthes, is to the French, i.e. a food with which a community, in this case a nation, identifies and which in turn allows it to identify with other members of the nation; a symbol of the values of the community (Barthes 2009: 66–67). This 'imaginative' identification process, as Benedict Anderson calls it (Anderson 1991: 6), is enormously important to those living outside the basic geographic area of the community, as they no longer have any physical means of identifying themselves as belonging to that nation. It is significant that a considerable amount of the meagre luggage many Spanish emigrants took with them consisted of such 'valued sausages, hams and brandy' in a literal attempt to hold onto their own culture, although it was largely confiscated at customs for 'sanitary reasons' (Cazorla Sánchez 2010: 110). This can be seen in the encounter with the Spaniard in *Un Franco, 14 Pesetas* which cuts directly to the following scene where the customs officer puts a large chunk of sausage belonging to the man in front of them in the bin, explaining curtly and obviously incomprehensibly in French [19:36]. The action, however, is clear and the implications of the loss of the family-made *chorizo* are also unambiguous: this is a strange country and they have just made the first step into the world of the 'Other'.

For Isabel in *Españolas en París*, the first event in her new life is to prepare the breakfast, where the technology presented to her – an egg-boiler, a toaster, a blender and a juicer [09:10–09:48] – baffles her as much as her employer's French. However, with the aid of vigorous miming, neither language nor the toaster is an insurmountable problem, and she is only insulted when her employer's husband, Monsieur Lemonier, tries to 'help' her by talking very slowly and over-articulating his words in the belief that this will aid the Spanish girl's understanding. This phenomenon was denominated 'foreigner talk' by Charles Ferguson, a term he coined to describe the adjustments a native speaker makes (usually through simplifying the language he/she uses) when speaking to a non-native speaker (Ferguson 1971: 281–282). René Appel and Pieter Muysken later distinguished between 'foreigner register', i.e. grammatically correct but 'slower and clearer speech, shorter sentences, avoidance of idioms [...] etc.' and the non-standard grammatical forms (e.g. omitting articles and the incorrect use of verb forms and pronouns) which they defined as 'foreigner talk' (Appel/Muysken 1987: 140), although 'foreigner talk' is also often used simply as an umbrella term (e.g. by Gass/Selinker 2008: 305-309). Isabel's employer provides the best example of a speaker adjusting his language when speaking to a non-native speaker. At the same time, he also confuses Spanish and Italian in his attempt to make himself understood. It is curious that her two employers represent two different attitudes to the language/culture clash, which shall be explored in more detail later on. At this point, it is sufficient to mention that M. Lemonier sees the Spanish girl as rather provincial and mistakenly assumes that she is in awe of the electricity. Isabel, in fact, takes advantage of the language barrier to answer him back without fearing repercussions: 'No rezo por la electricidad, rezo por los huevos pasados por agua. Que no soy tonta'[7] [10:44].

Pepe, in contrast, is deliberately portrayed as a country bumpkin and Lazaga makes considerable use of this trope. His arrival in Munich is marked by bewilderment. From

---

7   'I'm not praying for the electricity, I'm praying for the eggs dropped in the water. I'm not stupid.'

a close-up of the German sign 'Schalterhalle'[8] [12:45] the camera swings down to the mass of people on the platform, a huge difference from the sleepy Aragonese village Pepe has just left. The boisterous pseudo-German-folksong soundtrack clashes with the announcements (in German) on the loudspeaker, while the fast, jolted sweeping of the camera backwards and forwards, cutting sharply between close-ups of a rather lost-looking Pepe and more German signs, increases the sense of sensory overload [12:47–13:47]. Pepe's attempt to ask a policeman for directions fails badly; ironically, like Pilar in the scene at the butcher's in *Un Franco, 14 Pesetas*, the immigrant Spaniard blames the native of the host country for their failure to understand each other and uses a 'foreigner register' to speak to the native speaker in a curious role reversal. In *¡Vente a Alemania, Pepe!*, the protagonist talks over the policeman's directions and tells him to be 'tranquilo'[9], enunciating the question very clearly while the local is already giving him the answer [16:00–16:36].

Settling In: Minimal Understanding and Unintentional Misunderstandings
Although it can be argued, as Wolfgang Falkner does, that there is never a 100% match between what is meant and what is understood (Falkner 1997: 2), there are certainly instances in which communicative 'accidents' ('*Unfälle*', Falkner 1997: 3ff.) occur, resulting in the recipient understanding something completely different to what the emitter intended. It is true that similarities between languages, such as Spanish and Italian, can be advantageous when attempting to communicate. However, they can also prove to be misleading, 'resulting in errors such as false cognates' (also known as 'false friends'; Odlin 1989: 153), thus creating greater confusion than if the migrant characters had not understood anything in the first place. Fortunately, the incidents portrayed in the films do not have serious consequences, and are presumably included for their humorous effect. In his examples of the 'Klangwitz'[10] (e.g. the Italian lady's revenge on Napoleon for his tactless remark about her compatriots: 'Tutti gli italiani danzano si male? – Non tutti, ma buona parte'.[11]), Freud shows that the removal, or non-understanding, of the context and the linguistic references in the joke render it completely irrelevant and no longer humorous (Freud 1992: 47). An example of such a plurilingual pun can be found in the following conversation from *Un Franco, 14 Pesetas* as the Swiss landlady takes the newly-arrived Spaniards to their room:

> Hanna: Le sue camera sono nel piano sopra.
> Marcos: Ha dicho algo de un piano, ¿no?
> Martín: No sé, puede ser, pero yo le he entendido que a ella le sobra un piano.[12]
> [25:07–25:14]

---

8   'ticket office.'
9   'calm down.'
10 Literally a 'sound-joke', i.e. a pun based on homophones.
11 'Do all Italians dance so badly? – Not all, but a large number (*buona parte*).'
12 Hanna (in Italian): Your rooms are on the floor above (*nel piano sopra*).
    Marcos (in Spanish): Did she say something about a piano?
    Martín (in Spanish): I don't know, maybe, I understood her to say that they have an extra piano (*le sobra un piano*).

Though Martín and Marcos believe they have understood something of what Hanna has said, the 'false friends' of '*nel piano sopra*' and '*le sobra un piano*' has led them to a completely wrong conclusion, adding to the general effect of foreignness. On the one hand, the straightforward linguistic difficulties highlight the lack of understanding in terms of language, while on the other, the peculiar customs the locals appear to have emphasise a cultural difference which does not really exist. In *Un Franco, 14 Pesetas*, the communication breakthrough as far as language is concerned comes through breakfast. Having succeeded in explaining to Hanna through gestures and a lot of vigorous miming that they are cold and uncomfortable at night and in understanding that this is because they are sleeping on top of the eiderdowns instead of under them [32:40–33:01], they now manage to ask, and learn that their breakfast is included in the price of the hotel [33:20–33:32]. The freedom with which they attack their breakfast the next day reflects to a certain extent the liberty and sense of possibilities that being able to communicate effectively will allow them. At Christmas, Martín shows off his language skills by asking Hanna for more coffee in German, to the admiration and amusement of all around. Naturally, it is almost a matter of course that with the added power of language and the means to communicate with Hanna comes the added responsibility of where their relationship is headed.

Isabel, in contrast, finds the locals considerably less friendly. Though M. Lemonier speaks broken Spanish, he comes across as rather arrogant, unlike the cheerfully hospitable Hanna. The vast majority of the communication between Isabel and her employers also involves food, or more particularly, their attempts to explain their seemingly peculiar customs to her. In consequence, the first 'interlanguage' (see Appel/Muysken 1987: 83–92) which Isabel uses as she begins the arduous process of learning French is food-centred: 'fromage... jamais... frigidaire'[13] [14:37]. It is curious that while M. Lemonier airily believes he is communicating with his mix of Italian, French and Spanish, Mme Lemonier takes the language contact between herself and her foreign maid much more seriously, and tries both to teach Isabel French (e.g. in this sequence in the kitchen, and later for answering the telephone [38:57–39:27]) and to learn some Spanish herself. In contrast, in the brief sequences with Emilia's employers, it is evident that while their maid has excellent command of both Spanish and French, they only speak French [01:04:12–01:04:16].

Unfortunately, however, having a limited level of language can also prove to be more of a disadvantage than having no understanding at all, as can be seen in a rather discordant scene based around the Lemoniers' dinner guests. Though Isabel does not understand everything that is said in French, she clearly understands enough to realise that he is talking about her salary when the male guest code-switches into Spanish and declares that 'setecientos... son casi nueve mil pesetas' and the comment his wife adds in French 'c'est énorme'[14] [34:55–35:00]. The image, a close-up of Isabel's

---

13   'cheese... never... fridge.'
14   'seven hundred... that's nearly nine thousand pesetas'; 'that's loads.'

rather tight-lipped face instead of the total image of the group having the conversation, betrays that she has both heard and understood what is being said. The sequence that follows portrays a lack of both linguistic and human understanding. Mme Lemonier, in her attempt to bridge the language gap by telling Isabel to bring 'vino tinto'[15] in Spanish, is displeased when Isabel brings a glass of their house red instead of the bottle of Mouton Rothschild the Lemoniers had in mind. The belief that Isabel is being paid too much certainly does not help here, but the problem is primarily linguistic with an underlying cultural conflict (culture here referring to class as well as nationality):

> Mme Lemonier: Mais Isabel, qu'est-ce que c'est, ça? Monsieur vous a demandé une bouteille de Mouton Rothschild.
> Isabel: Yo he entendido vino tinto.[16] [34:07–35:09]

Subsequently, Isabel makes her displeasure at the lack of respect afforded to her clearly, albeit non-verbally, by refusing to serve the dinner [36:29].

For Pepe, the language barrier is surprisingly unproblematic, though that may be largely due to the fact that his communicative needs are fairly basic. Misunderstandings are rife and largely to comic effect. However, they also illustrate a typical characteristic of immigrant language, which rapidly assumes certain expressions from the host language, particularly in the areas of officialdom, school, the workplace, and leisure (Krefeld 2004: 40). The following sequence, taken from Pepe's first session on the crane with his colleague the window cleaner shows the early stages of this:

> Colleague: Du darfst nicht runter schauen! Dir wird schwindelig. Fällst. Bums. Kaputt!
> Pepe: Ja, ja, ja, ja, ja. Por eso decía yo... que yo... limpiar... primer piso, y tú, ay, con esa cara de gilipuertas que tienes, limpias todos estos de arriba, y yo, no kaputt.
> Colleague: Ja, ja. Du nicht kaputt.
> Pepe: Eso.[17] [31:56–32:24]

As well as Pepe's assumption of the host language, we see here more extreme examples of the 'foreigner talk' mentioned previously. In this excerpt, the native speaker both imitates some of the features which he believes to be typical of non-native speaker language, and combines it with the repetition of what Pepe says ('yo no kaputt'/'du nicht kaputt') (Appel/Muysken 1987: 140–141; see also Gass/Selinker 2008: 305–307). This scene is also an excellent example of code-mixing and the possibility of hiding insults behind an unknown language as seen in *Españolas in París*.

---

15   'red wine.'
16   Mme Lemonier (in French): But Isabel, what's that? Monsieur asked you for a bottle of Mouton Rothschild.
      Isabel (in Spanish): I understood he wanted red wine.
17   Colleague (in German): You mustn't look down! You'll get dizzy. Fall. Boom! Broken!
      Pepe (in slightly simplified Spanish with German words): Yeah, yeah. That's why I said... me, clean, first floor. You... and your stupid face, you can wash all those up there, and me, not broken!
      Colleague (in German): You, not broken.
      Pepe (in Spanish): That's right.

A more successful instance of using extremely limited language skills to communicate can be seen in the use of stereotypical images of Spain to cross the language barrier and communicate identity: 'Sí, yo españolito, fuerte, toro, mmm...'[18] [28:19]; 'Sí, señora, yo español, flamenco, bravo, olé'[19] [48:25]. Marcos and Martín, in *Un Franco, 14 Pesetas*, are also shown mock-bullfighting to entertain their hosts [35:39]. These popular images, combined with gestures to ease the reception of the message, appear to be adequate to convince the German girls of the Spaniards' manliness.

Even more interesting from the perspective of language and culture contact is the card which Andrés, another Spaniard living in the boarding-house, gives Pepe to chat up German girls:

> Andrés: Los que no hablamos, no tenemos otro camino [...].
> Pepe: ¿Pero qué pones aquí?
> Andrés: No sé, pero a mí me entendió en seguida.[20] [42:09–42:27]

Curiously, as it is neither shown nor read aloud to the audience, even a German-speaking viewer remains ignorant of this mysterious but seemingly magical message. Ironically, when Pepe's fiancée Pilar appears out of the blue, she also has no trouble making herself understood in the bar where she finds work, as she wears a very skimpy dirndl and a huge vocabulary is presumably not essential. It is clear that although officially there was a huge difference between Spanish and northern European culture, as can be seen in Pepe's gawping at the posters of bikini-clad women [19:42], Martín and Marcos' astonishment at the family swimming naked in the lake [29:50–31:50], and even Isabel's surprise at the couple kissing openly in the tram [21:47], some things are understood almost universally.

Among Friends? Communication with Other Emigrants

The speaking of different languages in a community tends to correspond to 'a division in different communicative networks' (Appel/Muysken 1987: 138). For Isabel, her Spanish emigrant friends, Francisca and Dioni, are her lifeline. Not only can she speak freely with them, but Dioni has a ritual every Sunday of making breakfast 'a la española' – with *churros*, hot chocolate and a fairytale in Spanish for the children [16:55–17:44]. In this way, a mini 'community' is built up based on shared language and shared 'totem' foods. The only time Emilia, trying to create a life after a broken heart, opens up is when she invites the Spanish girls – Isabel, Francisca and Dioni – for afternoon tea and they share cake and their stories with each other. Furthermore, the Spaniards who come to Paris gravitate towards Emilia, who addresses them in Spanish, but pretends to be French, speaking in her mother tongue with a heavy French accent. In terms of interaction between Spaniards, Emilia's 'disguise' allows her tourist

---

18   'Yeah, me Spanish, strong, bulls, mmm...'
19   'Yeah, lady, me Spanish, flamenco, bravo, olé.'
20   Andrés: If we can't speak the language, we have no other choice [...].
      Pepe: But what does it say?
      Andrés: No idea, but she understood me immediately.

compatriots to experience her and to gain an insight into the life of what they perceive as the 'Other'. A brief incidental scene after a lunch date shows one of these Spaniard's astonishment at the cost of the meal. Although the director probably included it to show how reasonably Spaniards lived, with the benefit of hindsight it in fact draws attention to the weak peseta and reminds the audience of one of the main reasons why Spaniards emigrated to northern Europe: 'Ciento veintidós francos, o sea... cien francos son mil doscientas y algo... ¡mil quinientas pesetas! Es verdad que la vida en España es más barata'[21] [53:05–53:07].

In *Un Franco, 14 Pesetas*, Martín and Marcos quickly make friends with an Italian, Tonino, who speaks Spanish reasonably fluently, though he tends to code-mix Spanish and Italian, particularly when he is strongly moved. A striking example of this is when Martín buys their first television set and his wife, Pilar, comes home to find her husband, her son and Tonino in front of it eating a most peculiar food (spaghetti bolognese). Culture, language and even generation contact is brought into sharp relief as the three men are united in their admiration of the new technology, Martín's backhanded approval of the foreign food, and Tonino's excitement betraying itself in his lapse into Italian [01:06:08]. The only other person in the factory who speaks Spanish is a Catalan, who comes to the guesthouse to tell Marcos and Martín that they can work at the factory. Martín's delight at finding someone whom he can understand after several days of not being able to communicate is abruptly cut short by the Catalan's rather distant manner:

> Catalan: Vosotros sois dos españoles que queréis trabajar en la fábrica.
> Martín: Coño, ¿pero eres español?
> Catalan: De Barcelona.[22]

In contrast to Martín's euphoria at finding a compatriot, the Catalan neatly sidesteps the question of nationality. It would seem that the tensions between Catalonia and the rest of Spain, in part resulting from Franco's repression of Catalonian language and culture, exist well beyond geographical borders.[23]

Tensions between long-term exiles and the short-term working emigrants can also be seen in *¡Vente a Alemania, Pepe!*. Characteristically, these come to a head over the boarding-house dinner table. The strength of the discussions is possible because they all speak Spanish, but the polite boarding-house owner brings them their meal in silence, reminding the audience that they are not at home in any sense of

---

21 'One hundred and twenty-two francs, that's, um... a hundred francs are on thousand two hundred and something... one thousand five hundred pesetas! It's true that life in Spain is much cheaper.'
22 Catalan: You're two Spaniards who want to work in the factory.
    Martín: Dammit! Are you Spanish?
    Catalan: From Barcelona.
23 Franco's Spain had a strictly one-language policy, to the detriment of regional dialects and languages such as Catalan, Galician and Basque which only survived as clandestine languages until their reintroduction into the new constitution as co-official languages of their respective regions in 1978 (Grugel/Rees1997: 68–69; 139; Boix 2006: 33; 38; Black 2010: 16–17; 96–98).

the word. On the other hand, it is the sight – and smell – of the cold meats, cheeses, bread and wine Pepe has brought with him from Spain, and his sharing of it, that releases the tension at the dinner table on the night of his arrival, and brings the little community of emigrant Spaniards living in the boarding house together, encouraging them to talk to each other instead of just sitting in silence [25:29–26:15].

A Home Away from Home? Attaining Fluency

Since integration is a primary motivation for learning a second language, and has even been shown in some instances to result in more successful language learning (Gass/Selinker 2008: 426; Hoff 2009: 314), it is not surprising, given the transitory nature of almost all the characters' sojourn in Munich, that very few are shown speaking German in ¡Vente a Alemania, Pepe!. Out of the main characters, only Ángel, Pepe's friend from the village who has been in Germany for some time, is portrayed as having any fluency in the language. The elderly doctor, who is portrayed as having left Spain for political reasons, can be presumed to have a reasonable command as he has lived in Germany for many years and works in a hospital, but he is never shown speaking German. Even Miguel, one of the other Spaniards living in the boarding-house who has been in Munich for four years, has to be told that his wife has had an accident by one of his colleagues when it comes over the tannoy, as he does not understand the message in German [36:04].

In contrast, in both *Españolas en París* and *Un Franco, 14 Pesetas*, several characters are portrayed as speaking the second language with varying levels of fluency. The principal characters in each eventually learn enough to communicate adequately, and both Martín in *Un Franco, 14 Pesetas* and Emilia in *Españolas in París* are shown acting not just as translators, but as mediators between two cultures, in both cases adding something to or omitting something from the original statement in order to emphasise the message. Emilia's fluency is evident in an early scene, which shows her negotiating Isabel's salary. Although she appears to be translating what Isabel and Mme Lemonier are saying to the other, Emilia's 'translation' in fact leaves both parties ignorant of what has been said:

> Emilia: Aquí no saben ni una gota de español. Así que avívate porque tienes que hablar francés.
> Isabel: Debe ser muy difícil.
> Emilia: Elle dit qu'il ne faut pas vous inquiéter. Elle apprendra vite.[24] [04:36–04:47]

Iglesias presents Martín in a similar role of mediator between a Swiss-German native speaker and a newly-arrived Spanish immigrant towards the end of *Un Franco, 14 Pesetas*. Having been shown stumbling through the process of learning the language, Martín is now able to communicate more than adequately, even though he

---

24   Emilia (in Spanish, to Isabel): They don't speak a word of Spanish here. So hurry up because you'll have to speak French.
     Isabel (in Spanish): It's supposed to be very difficult.
     Emilia (in French, to Mme Lemonier): She says you don't have to worry. She'll learn quickly.

still speaks non-standard German (or, more precisely, non-standard Swiss German). In this scene, he comes to the aid of the immigrant, who is so overwhelmed by the amount of food available that he has shoplifted a tin opener. In contrast to Emilia, Martín does translate what the shopkeeper says, but he also adds his own commentary in order to protect his compatriot:

> Shopkeeper: Jetscht kommt er in den Rum rübere und du lascht di von mia unter-suache.
> Martín: Te van a meter en este cuarto y te van a registrar. Si lo tienes encima, tíralo, no seas gilipollas. Si te lo pillan te pondrían de patitas en la frontera y no volverías a entrar en este país. Yo voy a intentar entretenerle. Tíralo. Also. Was mach ma denn?[25]
> [01:10:00–01:10:21]

This scene illustrates in part the 'Otherness' of Switzerland, where the abundance of produce reflects its relative wealth compared to the dry barrenness of the Spain Martín and his compatriots know, but more importantly, it shows how language can be used (and manipulated) to form a linguistic and cultural bridge for the newly arrived immigrants.

In contrast to his father's still rather stilted German, Martín's son Pablo in *Un Franco, 14 Pesetas* can be regarded as an example of what is known as 'sequential' bilingualism, a phenomenon which often occurs among young migrants when exposed to a second language which they then acquire (Hoff 2009: 297–298). Born in Spain, he and his mother Pilar follow Martín to Switzerland, smuggling the ingredients for a 'real Spanish stew' past customs [50:49] – their way of cheating the 'Other'. From a screaming five-year-old who does not understand anything as his father drags him to the local Swiss school, he becomes increasingly fluent in Swiss-German and identifies himself less and less as a Spaniard. Though a discussion of the correlation between national, ethnic or cultural identity and language, particularly a second language, is far beyond the scope of this essay (see, for example, Appel/Muysken 1987: 12–16; Hu 2007: 3–7; 16), a gradual shift in Pablo's self-perception can be seen as his fluency in and exposure to Swiss-German language and culture increases. The beginning of this transition can be seen after the sharp cut following his bewildering arrival at the local school and the subtitle 'Five years later' [01:07:37]. In this scene, Pablo is shown sitting comfortably at his desk and responding to his teacher in German. At this stage, however, he still identifies himself as different from the other pupils:

> Pablo: Vielleicht kann es sein, dass die Kinder so in der Schweiz auf die Welt kommen, aber in Spanien, da geht es nicht so. Da kommen alle aus Paris und ein Storch bringt uns mit seinem Schnabel.
> Classmates: Stimmt des wirklich? Haben sie dich im Flug gebracht?

---

25   Shopkeeper (in Swiss-German): Now he's to go into that room over there and you'll let me search you. Martín (in Spanish): He's going to put you into that room and search you. If you've got it on you, get rid of it, don't be an idiot. If they catch you with it they'll send you packing across the border and you'll never get into this country again. I'll try to keep him occupied. Get rid of it! (in Swiss-German) So. What are we going to do?

Pablo: Ja. Mich und alle Spanier wie ich.[26] [01:07:53–01:08:17]

By the end of the film, however, when his parents decide to return to Spain, he no longer sees himself as different, and uses a much stronger dialect: 'Aber ich bin nicht ein Uswanderer. Mini Eltere sind. I chum zrugg'[27] [01:20:55]. Don Emilio, in ¡Vente a Alemania, Pepe!, understands this, and warns the Spanish couple whose child he has just delivered in Munich: 'Si no se van ahora, ese hijo no les dejará irse nunca'[28] [01:13:29]. In Españolas in París, however, Isabel makes a different decision, and remains in Paris with her son. Her commitment to France – possibly because she could not return to Franco's Spain with an illegitimate child – can be seen in the language she uses to talk to him, which is, perhaps surprisingly, French: 'Shh, chérie' [01:27:22].

Finding a Voice: Women, Migration and Identity

In all three films, a correlation can be traced between gaining a sense of identity as a strong or even independent woman and finding a voice, either literally in terms of acquiring a second language or metaphorically in terms of not being repressed individually or socially. Isabel's transformation from a meek maid into an independent single mother can be seen clearly over the course of the film and is reflected in Bodegas' film aesthetics. To all extents and purposes, she is the innocent country girl from Sigüenza which M. Lemonier takes her for in the breakfast scene at the beginning of the film. Though she has a voice and does use it, the fact that she cannot make herself understood and her need for a translator in the form of Emilia emphasises both her 'Otherness' and her passivity. This comes to a head when she goes for her backstreet abortion [01:20:45]. At the climax, the bird's eye angle of the camera highlights her passivity and vulnerability as she lies on her back [01:22:37]. It is, however, precisely at this point that she literally finds her voice and asserts herself by screaming and destroying the kitchen and the repressive social demands it represents [01:23:24–01:23:47]. It is no coincidence that the scene immediately afterwards shows her answering the telephone in almost perfect French [01:24:45].

With the ability to articulate herself and her needs comes the maturity of adulthood. Her growing confidence can be seen in her increasing dominance in the shot frame and the unusual, challenging frontal shots in which she looks directly into the camera [e.g. at 01:25:25, 01:27:45–01:27:47, and the final image at 01:28:45]. Her heavy, strongly defined make-up underlines the transition from a girl into a woman, while some of her last spoken lines tell the audience that she is no longer a maid but a store assistant [01:27:30]. She has thus left the domestic sphere and the kitchen with all its negative connotations and is about to start a new life as a free, independent woman.

---

26   Pablo: It might be that children are born that way in Switzerland, but in Spain it's different. There we come from Paris and a stork brings us in his beak.
      Classmates: Is that true? Did they really bring you that way?
      Pablo: Yes. Me and all the Spaniards like me.
27   'But I'm not a migrant. My parents are. I'll come back.'
28   'If you don't go now, that child will never let you go back.'

For Pilar, Martín's wife in *Un Franco, 14 Pesetas*, however, freedom comes with their return to Spain. As can be seen from the scene at the butcher's described at the beginning of the article, Pilar never succeeds at learning German. While she clearly manages to communicate adequately enough to find a flat – presumably through some form of sign language, as her landlord is deaf anyway – she is never quite settled in Switzerland. Her best friend is Mari-Carmen, Marcos' fiancée, but while Marcos, even more so than Martín, has enough mastery of the language to ingratiate himself with the Swiss managers of the factory, Mari-Carmen does not. While complaining about their respective partners, Pilar sighs: 'Por lo menos conoces a gente.'[29] Mari-Carmen, however, contradicts her: 'Yo no entiendo nada. Yo solo cocino'[30] [01:09:00–01:09:05]. Here, linguistic ability is shown to be the key to settling in, while the woman's role in the kitchen provides an excuse for – or a restriction on – the limitations of her linguistic ability and thus her freedom within the community.

When Martín, Pilar and Pablo return to Spain, the kitchen forms the focus of their new life. As his family expresses scepticism of the rather dingy-looking new flat after the lush, green spaciousness of their home in Switzerland, Martín tries to console them by saying 'pero el piso es bien grande y la cocina muy hermosa'[31] [01:29:30]. After this rather doubtful start, however, Pilar gathers strength as she feels free for the first time: from the shackles of her in-laws, with whom they lived before the move to Switzerland, and then from the language barrier. Here she has her own home and her own language, and she is clearly well in command of both. Once they start to settle back into Madrid, it is Pilar who trounces the doubts of her husband and son, calling a 'reunión familiar'[32] [01:35:49] to slate them as 'cobardes'[33] [01:36:23]. It is significant that this takes place in the kitchen: Pilar is preparing the supper as she talks, but gradually abandons it. The final spoken lines of the film, ringing with authority and triumph, are hers: '¡Va a la porra la cena!'[34] [01:38:42]. Having started the film at the beck and call of her mother-in-law, without a voice in spite of being in her home country, then finding herself free from the social aspects but shackled by her inability to communicate, she has now established her identity as mistress of her own home and the ability to express it. Her reckless abandonment of the dinner and their decision to go out for *tapas* instead is reminiscent of the final scene of *Españolas in París*, where Isabel is shown walking confidently down the street. In both instances, the women move out of the private, domestic sphere to claim the city and a voice as their own.

With the focus on Pepe in *¡Vente a Alemania, Pepe!*, the female characters play a relatively minor role. Nevertheless, it is worth noting that the image of women in the northern European countries as independent and, to an extent, sexually liberat-

---

29   'At least you get to meet people.'
30   'I don't understand anything. I just cook.'
31   'but the flat is nice and big and the kitchen is lovely.'
32   'a family meeting.'
33   'cowards.'
34   'The dinner can go to hell!'

ed or even easily available is evident in all three films, and most strongly in ¡Vente a Alemania, Pepe!. This reflected propaganda under Franco, which portrayed the women of northern Europe as promiscuous and immoral (Black 2010: 48; Cazorla Sánchez 2010: 165). The two German dancers from the boarding-house tease Pepe with champagne and sleeping tablets, while a lascivious older woman sends Pepe and Ángel garish cocktails in the night club, letting their actions speak louder than their words. Even Pepe's girlfriend, Pilar, who only remains in Munich for a very short time, has a brief taste of independence as she finds work in a bar, something she would not have been able to do under Franco's regime until just before the film was made (Grugel/Rees 1997: 134–135; 150; Black 2010: 30; 49). As already mentioned, Emilia pretends to be French when she goes on her seduction sprees in Españolas in París, donning a wig, a heavy French accent and the sexual liberation of a Parisienne. The bittersweet love affair between the two Spanish men and their attractive Swiss landladies in Un Franco, 14 Pesetas comes to an abrupt end when Pilar arrives unannounced at the guesthouse at almost exactly the same moment that Hanna, Martín's sweetheart, brings him a breakfast tray set for two. Though Pilar cannot speak any German, it is clear that she has a fairly good idea of what is – or has been – going on [56:38]. Her simple but decisive action of taking the tray out of Hanna's hands speaks volumes even if she is unable to voice her message in a language Hanna will understand [57:20]. However, despite her obviously genuine fancy for Martín, it would appear that he was not the only immigrant who attracted her attentions: when he goes to wish her goodbye and expresses surprise at her daughter's age and her Mediterranean colouring and name, Hanna laughs: 'Der Name chumt dir Spanisch vor, gäll? [...] Ja, auch Italienisch, gäll?'[35] [01:20:25–01:20:33]. All three films show the immigrant Spaniards equally overwhelmed by the relatively lax social rules on sexual behaviour in the northern European countries, represented by confident, independent women. Like the petty theft of the tin opener, they greedily take advantage of what they find, which also tends to land them in a situation where they have to explain themselves across language or culture barriers. For the Spanish women in ¡Vente a Alemania, Pepe!, Españolas in París and Un Franco, 14 Pesetas, however, coming to the northern European countries and experiencing a more liberated culture where women are emancipated from the triumvirate of Kinder, Küche, Kirche[36] opens the doors for them to assert their right to a voice.

Conclusion

Despite their very different styles, Un Franco, 14 pesetas, ¡Vente a Alemania, Pepe! and Españolas en París share a common thread: the experiences of Spaniards emigrating to northern European countries during the period of economic crisis and dictatorship. Where Franco's Spain was officially a strictly monolingual country with a

---

35   'The name sounds Spanish to you, doesn't it? [...] But it's Italian too, isn't it?'
36   'Children, kitchen, church.'

weak peseta and high unemployment, France, Germany and Switzerland were seen as countries with strong currencies and plenty of opportunities for work despite the language barriers. In these three films, we see examples of diverse ways of dealing with the language and culture contact and conflict that inevitably results. Upon arrival in the host country, migrants are faced with a barrage of unfamiliar sounds and practices, and are forced to negotiate their way through these by means of non-verbal communication or by finding someone who will mediate for them. Film aesthetics may be used to increase the impression of bewilderment, while the portrayal of strange customs emphasise the alienness of the host culture. As the immigrants settle into their new life, they begin to understand what is being said around them. While this is generally positive, minimal understanding can also result in more difficulties. On the one hand, the proximity of two languages, such as Italian and Spanish, can lead to misunderstandings, and on the other, understanding a little more or a little less than one's speaking partner supposes can result in resentment and annoyance on both sides. In the films examined, migrants with limited language skills also typically resort to code-mixing, transnationally understood cultural references such as stereotypes, and non-verbal props to get a message across, while the native speakers of the host language frequently use some form of 'foreigner talk' or 'foreigner register' in the (sometimes mistaken) belief that it will aid comprehension. In contrast, communication between Spanish-speaking emigrants is naturally shown as much freer, though not necessarily any friendlier, since animosity or disagreement can also be expressed more easily. In most cases, however, other emigrants form a lifeline for their compatriots, and they tend to form mini-communities based around their shared language (and the sharing of their language skills). Once migrants attain a certain level of fluency, they may also act as a mediator for newly-arrived immigrants. While finding a translator can ease the process of communication, however, it can also prove to be a somewhat unreliable means of understanding what is being said. With fluency comes power, and it is possible for the bilingual migrant to exploit his/her position to the advantage of his/her compatriot (even if the latter is not aware of it). As the characters find more means to communicate, they are able to develop both within and outwith their original communities. Immigrants of the second generation in particular, who have fluent command of the other language, must find a compromise between their 'home' and 'host' countries and reconcile their plural identity. For female migrants, the (re)acquisition of a voice plays a crucial role in their transition from passive young girls and kitchen-bound wives to strong, independent women, while language is also used to highlight cultural differences between the strongly Catholic home culture and the more sexually liberated women of northern Europe. At the end of the three films, several different paths are shown. In *Españolas en París*, Isabel remains in France, while in *Un Franco, 14 Pesetas* and *¡Vente a Alemania, Pepe!* the protagonists go back to Spain, Martín and his family to a new flat of their own and Pepe to his farm and girlfriend. Despite the apparent return to his old life, however, even Pepe is not quite the same as before and is shown boasting about his experiences in Germany [1:32:27–1:33:24]. Whatever the final decision of the protagonists was, the tagline from *Un Franco, 14 Pesetas* is apt: 'Emprendían mucho más que un viaje. Iniciaban el camino hacia una nueva vida.'[37] Their experiences of northern Europe have given them a new outlook on life, be it in the host or the home country, and with this new life comes, inevitably, a new voice.

Filmography

BODEGAS, R. (1971), *Españolas en París*, Spain.

IGLESIAS, C. (2006), *Un Franco, 14 Pesetas*, Spain.

LAZAGA, P. (1971), *¡Vente a Alemania, Pepe!*, Spain.

References

ANDERSON, B. (1991 [1983]), *Imagined Communities: Reflections on the Origin and Spread of Nationalism*, London/New York: Verso.

APPEL, R. & P. MUYSKEN (1987), *Language Contact and Bilingualism*, London: Arnold.

BARTHES, R. (2009 [1957; tr. J. Cape 1972]), *Mythologies*, London: Random House Vintage Classics.

BLACK, S. (2010), *Spain since 1939*, Basingstoke/New York: Palgrave MacMillan.

BOIX, E. (2006), '25 años de la Constitución española: un balance sociolingüístico desde los (y las) catalanohablantes', in: Castillo Lluch, M. & J. Kabatek (eds.), *Las lenguas de España: Política lingüística, sociología del lenguaje e ideología desde la Transición hasta la actualidad*, Madrid/Frankfurt a.M.: Iberoamericana/Vervuert, 33–61.

CAZORLA SÁNCHEZ, A. (2010), *Fear and Progress: Ordinary Lives in Franco's Spain, 1939–1975*, Chichester: Wiley-Blackwell.

FALKNER, W. (1997), *Verstehen, Mißverstehen und Mißverständnisse: Untersuchungen an einem Korpus englischer und deutscher Beispiele*, Tübingen: Niemeyer.

FERGUSON, C.A. (1971), 'Absence of Copula and the Notion of Simplicity: A Study of Normal Speech, Baby Talk, Foreigner Talk, and Pidgins', in: Ibid. (selected and introduced by A.S. Dil), *Language Structure and Language Use: Essays by Charles A. Ferguson*, Stanford: Stanford U.P., 277–312.

FREUD, S. (1992), *Der Witz und seine Bedeutung zum Unbewußten/Der Humor* (originally published as two separate works, 1905 and 1927 respectively), Frankfurt a.M.: Fischer.

GASS, S.M. & L. SELINKER (2008), *Second Language Acquisition: An Introductory Course*, London/New York: Routledge.

GRUGEL, J. & T. REES (1997), *Franco's Spain,* London/New York: Hodder & Stoughton.

HEISS, C. (2004), 'Dubbing Multilingual Films: A New Challenge?', in: *Meta*, vol. 49:1, 208–220.

HOFF, E. (2009), *Language Development*, Belmont: Wadsworth.

HU, A. (2007), 'Mehrsprachigkeit, Identitäts- und Kulturtheorie: Tendenzen der Konvergenz', in: De Florio-Hansen, I. & A. Hu (eds.), *Plurilingualität und Identität: Zur Selbst- und Fremdwahrnehmung mehrsprachiger Menschen*, Tübingen: Stauffenburg, 1–23.

KREFELD, G. (2004), *Einführung in die Migrationslinguistik: Von der Germania italiana in die Romania multipla*, Tübingen: Narr.

---

37 'They took on much more than just a journey. They took the first step on the way to a new life.'

MARSH, S. (2006), *Popular Spanish Film under Franco: Comedy and the Weakening of the State*, Basingstoke/New York: Palgrave Macmillan.

ODLIN, T. (1989), *Language Transfer: Cross-linguistic Influence in Language Learning*, Cambridge: Cambridge U.P.

REINART, S. (2004), 'Zu Theorie und Praxis von Untertitelung und Synchronisation', in: Kohlmayer, R. & W. Pöckl (eds.), *Literarisches und mediales Übersetzen. Aufsätze zu Theorie und Praxis einer gelehrten Kunst*, Frankfurt a.M.: Lang, 73–112.

SHOHAT, E. & R. STAM (2006), 'The Cinema After Babel: Language, Difference, Power', in: Shohat, E., *Taboo Memories, Diasporic Voices*, Durham/London: Duke U.P., 106–138.

VILAR, J.B. & Mª J. VILAR (1999), *La emigración española a Europa en el siglo XX*, Madrid: Arcos Libros.

Voices Against the Silence:
Polyglot Documentary Films
from Spain and Portugal

Verena Berger

Polyglot Documentary Film

The era of globalisation is not only embodied in multilingual and pluralistic societies – the European Union, for example, is a multicultural and plurilingual geographical region composed of many nations – but is also reflected in cultural productions such as literature, music, visual art or film. In contemporary cinema, the number of fiction and non-fiction films in which communication takes place in more than one language has increased substantially. Although this tendency has become more relevant recently, even early cinema was plurilingual to a certain extent, as it was targeted at audiences with different linguistic backgrounds (see Bock et al. 2006). In his essay *Der Geist des Films*[1] first published in 1930, Béla Bálazs draws attention to the presence of foreign languages in filmic dialogues of early cinema, underlining the fact that the acoustic-sensual effect is as important as the content. He concludes that it is therefore not disturbing to hear foreign languages without understanding what is being said while the story continues to be clear. Mentioning the example of *Die Nacht gehört uns*[2] (1929) directed by Carl Froelich and Henry Roussel where Italian peasants speak their mother tongue, Bálazs refers to the image as a 'Originallandschaft'[3], an acoustic and natural shooting, a 'Sprachlandschaft'[4] (Bálazs 2001: 127). By maintaining foreign languages in contemporary cinema dealing with migrants' integration into their host societies, film-makers are not only creating a distinctive 'spoken landscape', but also uncovering hegemonic discourses while allowing the immediacy of 'subaltern voices' (Spivak 1988) to be heard. Their filmic texts thus maintain the linguistic habits of the speakers in order to confer authenticity on the multicultural societies being visualised.

---

1   *The Spirit of Film.*
2   *The Night Belongs to Us.*
3   'original landscape.'
4   'spoken landscape.'

As Hamid Naficy points out, the 'accented style' of migrant cinema (made by migrant film-makers) is often characterised by bilingual, multilingual, multivocal or 'multiaccented' films (Naficy 1999: 138; 2001: 24). However, the filmic depiction of a variety of languages is not restricted to migrant film-makers, but can appear in any film dealing with the topic of migration. Due to its plurilingual character, this cinema requires multiple modes of filmic representation in order to address its audiences. While fictional film has already been studied extensively in order to highlight the use of multilayered dialogues, dubbing and subtitling (e.g. Chaume 2003; 2004; Bleichenbacher 2008; Egoyan/Balfour 2004; Goldstein/Golubović 2009; Heiss 2004; Wahl 2005a; 2005b; 2008; Whitman-Linsen 1992), the genre of documentaries is still an object of marginal research. However, it is precisely the non-fiction film which can depict the 'polyphonic play of voices' (Stam 1991: 255) that characterises the topic of migration. With respect to the extensive discussion about the 'blurred boundary' between fiction and nonfiction in relation to this genre (Nichols 1994: 43; Rhodes/Parris Springer 2006: 9), we postulate the hypothesis that these documentaries offer filmic texts which confront their audience directly with the migrant protagonists' voices and not by acting or re-enacting as is guaranteed in fiction film. By articulating their situation in their own words, the genre combines storytelling with the claim to truthfulness. Since the documentary is classified as an informative genre (Agost 1999: 87), it is seen to portray 'real life, using real life as [its] raw material' (Aufderheide 2007: 2). According to Bill Nichols, a documentary grows out of events which have already happened or are currently taking place, which in turn should be supported by the structure, the editing, image and sound (Nichols 1991: 18–23; 2001: 26–32). In terms of style, the narrative is marked by voice-over, interviews and interpretation carried out by real people, archive material and on-location sound recording. The non-fiction film therefore grows from the protagonists, the *mise-en-scène*, or some form of intervention in reality. Nevertheless, even documentary is a carefully composed production which (re)constructs the truth.

Among the polyphony of voices in films focusing on migration the audience is presented with a multitude of languages. Film-makers must consider several strategies when creating their films to make these comprehensible. In contrast to fiction film, spoken language in documentaries consists largely of spontaneous speech in 'real-life-scenarios' (Ward 2005: 34) where speakers of different languages come together in a context considered as a situation of language contact (Thomason 2001: 1–14). To make polyglot films accessible to their audiences, it is important to decide which methods of translation, if any, will be employed. George Steiner argues that every translation has to be considered an interpretation regarding decisions relative to the meaning and character of the original (Steiner 1975: 28). While fiction films in particular tend to be dubbed, 'given our desire to believe that the heard voices actually emanate from the actors/characters on the screen' (Shohat/Stam 1985: 49), the protagonists in documentary films are mainly subtitled in order to maintain the authenticity of their narratives. Dubbing is generally considered a loss of information and 'a reduction of a film's polyphonic, profilmic event into a univocal sound track' (Betz 2009: 86). By maintaining the original voices, the documentary genre offers the possibility of representing the real use of different languages and sounds: '[...] while words are socially shared and therefore more-or-less translatable, voices are as irreducibly individual as fingerprints. [...] each voice imprints a special resonance and coloring' (Shohat/Stam 1985: 49–50). Subtitling furthermore converts film into a hybrid medium combining aural and visual messages by integrating the written word and the activity of reading to the cinematic experience.

Besides dubbing and subtitling, there are several other less common strategies which can be spotted in relation to the representation of foreign languages in fiction films, as Frederic Chaume and the TRAMA Group point out in their essay in this volume: self-translation, liaison interpreting, voice-over, and non-translation. While most European countries such as France, Germany, Italy or Spain generally use full-cast dubbing, both in films and TV, Portugal differs from this model, using subtitles only and producing dubbed versions exclusively for children (Media Consulting Group 2007; Reinhart 2004: 75). In the following analysis, we will determine by means of a close-reading of six documentaries from Portugal and Spain whether this classification is also valid for these and to what extent the different strategies are used. Documentaries, in contrast to fiction films, are generally not widely released, since they have traditionally played a secondary role in cinema (Payán 1999: 59). This essay therefore examines the films to which the author was able to gain access, in some cases thanks to the generosity of the film-makers and producers. While an analysis of the complete corpus of polyglot documentary from Spain and Portugal remains a future project, the films studied here can be considered representative of the genre. All shot in the first decade of 21st century, they offer an insight into the use of plurilingualism and the way in which film-makers approach it in non-fiction film.

'Spoken Landscapes' in Spain: *Extranjeras*[5]

Helena Taberna's *Extranjeras* (2003) is classified as a documentary film dedicated to the experiences of female migrants of diverse backgrounds who live in Spain and generally have less access to any means of public expression. The film-maker succeeds in painting a portrait of the hybrid spaces of migration: encounters and relationships between people from every continent, their nostalgia, integration and racism, and the contact and exchange of cultures. This gives rise to 'un relato caleidoscópico, algo así como un mosaico de rostros, biografías y culturas'[6] (Bermejo 2003). Taberna rejects the classic 'arrival scene' identified by Bill Nichols in which the Spanish director establishes a relationship between the filming subject and the filmed object and identifies the physical space in which the filming takes place (Nichols 1991: 222). In fact, in contrast to classical documentary, Taberna is

---

5   *Foreign Women.*
6   'a kaleidoscopic tale something like a mosaic of faces, biographies and cultures.' (Translations by the author.)

never present in the filming, but rather applies what Stephen Mamber defines as 'the ethics of non-intervention' (Mamber 1974: 145). She uses interviews without a visible or audible interviewer/observer and there is no point at which the encounter with the interviewee/observed can be seen. Moreover, the film-maker not only eschews the arrival scene and the standard form of interview, but also any form of commentary, voice-over or introduction of the female migrants. Only in the very last sequences of *Extranjeras*, which are filmed in a bar frequented by many of the interviewees, is Taberna visible for a couple of seconds. The protagonists thus stand at the heart of the film. By using the camera to focus on both the migrants and the urban landscape of Madrid and Alcalá de Henares (the Lavapiés district, the Gran Vía, Retiro Park, metro stations, markets, shops and bars), the director concentrates on characters and locations which exist in the pre- and post-filmic reality. Edited as a choral film, *Extranjeras*' structure consists of mini-biographies and mini-reports which are presented to the camera by the migrants themselves, who come from China, Bangladesh, Rumania, Poland, the Ukraine, Morocco, Algeria, Iraq, Syria, Senegal, the Sudan and several Latin American countries. They narrate the process of adaptation to their new lives in Spain directly to the audience while still keeping the customs inherited from their respective cultures alive. The camera draws the audience into the subjectivity of the migrants by using close-ups, converting their faces into 'el lugar privilegiado para la filmación'[7] (Rodríguez 2003: 6). By breaking with the tradition of shot-countershot, the director brings the protagonists literally to the centre of the film.

Taberna's documentary is strongly marked by non-standard immigrant Spanish, including the incorrect use of grammar, phonetic interferences and poor syntax. An example is the presentation of a Chinese school girl, a second-generation immigrant: 'Me llamo Surinha. Y me he nacido en español' [04:05]. The subtitles in English and French try to translate non-standard Spanish: 'My name is Surinha and I was born 'in Spanish'/Je m'appelle Surinha. Et je suis née en 'espagnol'.' Taberna also uses subtitles in Spanish so that the audience can understand the Bengali of a woman who only speaks a few words of Spanish: 'Aún no soy capaz de hablar español. Me gusta aprender español pero no he tenido tiempo porque he tenido un hijo'[8] [09:02–09:14]. Meanwhile, the different migrant groups are depicted in their community life, as can be seen in the sequences in a Chinese school, an orthodox mass in Rumanian, an Arabic language class in an Islamic community centre, the prayers in Chinese in a Buddhist centre or in Arabic in a mosque, as well as songs by African immigrant musicians, where the original languages are maintained without any translation. Furthermore, Taberna also films shop signs, such as those of the 'Flor de la Canela' bar and the 'Kakitanda' hairdressing salon in order to draw attention to the 'Otherness' of the scene. Through the combination of a personal narration

---

7   'the place privileged for filming.'
8   'I am still not able to speak Spanish. I like learning Spanish, but I have not had time because I had a baby.'

and the written language of the signs, image and sound reinforce the authenticity of the African and Latin American women portrayed. Finally, by integrating the voices of women from the Dominican Republic, Ecuador, Peru, Colombia and Venezuela, *Extranjeras* also presents its audiences with several varieties of Spanish. This documentary therefore uses not only the multiplicity of a single language as well as foreign languages, but also different translation strategies in order to offer various levels of comprehension.

'Spoken Landscapes' in Mediterranean Contact Zones: *Paralelo 36*[9]

The main theme of *Paralelo 36* (2004), directed by José Luis Tirado, can be seen in its subtitle 'Documento y ficción en la frontera sur de Europa'[10]:

> El *Paralelo 36* es una línea imaginaria en un mapa, a la vez que un espacio real en el que transcurre el viaje de la emigración clandestina en el Estrecho de Gibraltar. En *Paralelo 36* los protagonistas son los emigrantes: documento y ficción, gestos y palabras, sueños y deseos. *Paralelo 36* es un relato, un cruce de micronarrativas que cartografían la frontera sur de Europa.[11]

Dedicated to the constant flux of Africans who arrive clandestinely in open boats along the coast of Cadiz, this film bases its narrative on the testimonies of those who have succeeded in crossing the Mediterranean as well as the difficulties of their legalisation and integration. *Paralelo 36* falls into the category of a 'docufiction', i.e. a hybridisation of fiction and images taken from reality:

> Docufictions stand [...] at the blurred boundary between fiction and documentary, questioning the possibility of a clear distinction [...] between the codified but increasingly outmoded idea of a stable division between fiction and nonfiction in film and media. (Rhodes/Parris Springer 2006: 9)

While a possible border between fiction and reality in the other filmic texts analysed here may not seem obvious at first sight, being secondary to factors relating to the directors' subjectivity (the choice of topic, protagonists and location, frame, sound, editing etc.), in *Paralelo 36* the hybridisation of the elements of documentary and fiction are intentional:

> Docuficción [...] (n)o es una representación ficcionada de una realidad, sino la realidad ficcionada mediante recursos del lenguaje cinematográfico, o literario, etc. La emigración en el Estrecho es un fenómeno tan complejo, que con imágenes documentales sólo no es posible aprehender. Hace falta recurrir a otros lenguajes, como la literatura, en este caso, para completar el mosaico de su complejidad.[12]

---

9   *Latitude 36.*
10 'Testimony and fiction on the southern border of Europe.'
11 '*Latitude 36* is an imaginary line on a map, which is simultaneously a real location in the Straits of Gibraltar where irregular emigration takes place. In *Latitude 36* the protagonists are the emigrants: testimony and fiction, gestures and words, dreams and desires. *Latitude 36* is a tale, a crossroads of micro-narrations that map the southern border of Europe.'
12 'Docufiction [...] is not a fictional representation of reality, but reality fictionalised through a language which is cinematographic, literary etc. The emigration on the Straits is a phenomenon which is so complex that it cannot be understood only with images depicting the reality. It is necessary

The film is mainly set at the Port of Tarifa in Spain. The story, starting from the first sequences, is told in the form of a diary which begins on the 21st of June and finishes on the 23rd of October, telling the story of the permanent arrival of boats filled with exhausted migrants. By inserting the date, time and location of the images being filmed, Tirado aims to underline the authenticity of what the audience is seeing. Using a documentary style more frequently seen in television, the camera captures the first images of migrants disembarking from their small boats or the bigger launches of the Red Cross where they receive first aid, but also their immediate detention by the authorities and their subsequent removal in buses. The images of these incessant arrivals are constantly mixed with the 'micro-narrations' of the migrants themselves who put forward their experiences much as they do in *Extranjeras* by means of an interview without an interviewer.

As in *Extranjeras*, the spectators of *Paralelo 36* are also confronted with many testimonies in non-standard Spanish. In some sequences, irregular migrants again express themselves in their mother tongue – the majority Arabic – offering translation by subtitles which can be selected from English, French and German. The immediate testimonies of the migrants themselves are complemented by fictional texts (*Vengo buscando a Driss/Looking for Driss*, *La isla de las Palomas/The Isle of Doves* and *Historia de Raïs/Raïs' Story* by Juan José Téllez, and *Hicham el Invisible/Hicham the Invisible*, by Nieves García Benito) and non-fictional texts (*Carta a mis padres/Letter to My Parents*, by Khalid Ezzamani, and *Extractos de entrevistas en Tánger/Extracts of Interviews in Tangiers*, from the Colectivo Aljaima).[13] These narratives are interwoven with real scenes of what happens at the Port of Tarifa and with sequences where the diverse protagonists speak directly into the camera in their mother tongues or non-standard Spanish. In this way, José Luis Tirado holds the audience at a distance, giving it the same feeling of alienation which the immigrants experience when faced with the language of the country in which they have just arrived – in this case Spanish. In *Vengo buscando a Driss*, the audience is confronted with the voice-in-off of a mother who, as red clouds billow behind her, asks in Arabic about her son who has disappeared: 'Vengo buscando a Driss, que cuando era niño olía a primavera y a duraznos'[14] [07:54–08:00]. Her voice is accompanied by images showing lists of the dead, empty migrants' boats on the beach and cemeteries with tombstones marking the resting place of an 'Inmigrante de Marruecos, 16 Mayo 2001'[15] who could be Driss [07:30–09:13]. Similarly, images of the city of Tangier are shown while a polyphony of Arabic voices-in-off relates the reasons why Moroccans decide to emigrate. Thus Arabic is present at an auditory level, with the meaning transmitted through subtitles

---

to resort to other languages, such as literature, in this case, in order to transmit the mosaic of its complexity.' J. L. Tirado, quoted from an e-mail to the author on 4th of June 2008.

13   See the credits at the end of *Paralelo 36*. However, in a personal letter to the author, the director confirmed that only *Looking for Driss* is a real literary text, whereas he classifies all the others as testimonies, based on 'real texts by the protagonists'.

14   'I am looking for Driss, who, when he was a child, smelled like spring and peaches.'

15   'Immigrant from Morocco, 16 May 2001.'

[13:56–15:07]. In the documentary text *Cartas a mis padres*, the voice-in-off of a Mauritanian is directed at his family, relating his experiences as an irregular migrant. Here the translation strategy changes, since the Arabic voice-in-off is dubbed into another voice-in-off speaking in Spanish, while the Arabic script of the letter is superimposed on the images of the city [15:56–18:40], which represents the most striking example of the strategies used by any of the film-makers analysed, combining the exoticism of the original 'spoken landscape' with the possibility of comprehension.

'Spoken Landscapes' in Catalonia: *Si nos dejan*[16]

Si nos dejan (2005) is a film directed by Ana Torres, an Argentine resident in Barcelona and an example of migrant cinema. The documentary collects the testimonies, subtitled in Spanish and English, of migrants from four continents who have chosen to start their new lives in the Catalan capital. As a result, as well as portraying the plurilingualism which is self-evident in polyglot cinema, in this case the film is also set in a community which is bilingual – Spanish and Catalan. The complexity of the language contact in the film is therefore deepened by the setting.

In fact, *Si nos dejan* represents a subjective and reflexive documentary (Nichols 1991: 57) on the topics of immigration and emigration from several points of view. Again, the film mainly deals with the non-standard Spanish of migrants from Poland or even the USA, subtitled in English, breaking with the dominant stereotype of migration from Third World countries. It also integrates non-standard English from Ghanaian migrants, subtitled in Spanish, and varieties of Spanish spoken in Latin American countries like Argentina and Venezuela. In addition, the inhabitants of Barcelona are interviewed about their opinion on immigration, sometimes answering in Catalan subtitled in English.

Due to the bilingual context of Barcelona, it is not surprising that speaking about language use and identity is a particular focus of this documentary. This is brought into sharp relief by a Venezuelan woman: 'Yo no me siento catalana, yo no me siento española. Yo me siento sudaca. Y mientras más racismo..., más sudaca me siento'[17] [18:46] and 'Ya saben que aunque tu familia sea catalana, aunque hables catalán perfectamente, eres una inmigrante'[18] [19:13]. Catalan only interferes in the language of the local population, and many of the city's inhabitants switch over to Spanish when directly confronted with their opinion on migration to Barcelona. Against its inherently bilingual setting, *Si nos dejan* presents the transnational character of a European metropolis at the beginning of the 21st century through a polyphony of voices. While Ana Torres' documentary breaks with the conventional image of the migrant from the Third World, it nevertheless employs traditional modes concerning the use of language and its translation by subtitling.

---

16 *If They Let Us.*
17 'I don't feel Catalonian, I don't feel Spanish. I feel 'sudaca'. The more racism I see, the more I feel 'sudaca'.' ('Sudaca' is a colloquial expression for 'Latin American' and has a pejorative connotation.)
18 'They know that, though your family is Catalan and you speak Catalan perfectly, you're an immigrant.'

'Spoken Landscapes' Between Western and Eastern Europe: *À espera da Europa*[19]

The documentary *À espera da Europa* (2006) by Christine Reeh, a German film-maker living and working in Portugal – another example of migrant cinema – was shot in Portugal, Spain and Bulgaria. The film deals with emigration from a woman's point of view and the dream of a Bulgarian couple, Vania and Ivo, to migrate to Western Europe before the accession of the Eastern European country to the European Union. The first 20 minutes take place in Lisbon, with Vania Nikolova explaining her reasons for emigration to Portugal in non-standard Portuguese [03:17–04:10]. The sequence is followed by a statement from her parents in Bulgarian, explaining that the situation is equally difficult for Bulgarian migrants in foreign countries and for Bulgarians who remain in their home country. The second part of *À espera da Europa* takes place in Spain, when the protagonists move to Alcalá de Henares. Although they have left Portugal, in the following sequence Vania mixes non-standard Portuguese and non-standard Spanish during her conversation with a butcher:

> Butcher: ¿Eres de aquí?
> Vania: Sí...
> Butcher: ¿Dónde vives?
> Vania: Aquí en Alcalá.
> Butcher: Ah, en Alcalá. ¿Llevas mucho tiempo?
> Vania: Estou aqui as nove meses.
> Butcher: Aja. Pues hablas muy bien español, digo, para llevar poco tiempo.
> Vania: ¿Qué?
> Butcher: Hablas muy bien español, digo yo, para llevar poco tiempo.
> Vania: Não, no hablo muito espanhol.
> Butcher: Sí, hablas bien, mujer, hablas bien.[20] [24:10–24:36]

Language acquisition is also an important topic in this documentary. Vania continues to explain in non-standard Portuguese that in her case it was difficult to learn Spanish because she could not obtain a job and stayed at home, her only real language contact being Bulgarian [24:45–25:19]. In the following sequences she meets a waitress in a bar who is also Bulgarian. Once aware of their common mother tongue, the dialogue switches entirely to Bulgarian subtitled in English. The waitress, who has already lived in Spain for 15 years and speaks standard Spanish, warns Vania that being an immigrant is difficult due to problems with language and legal status. She even recommends

---

19 *Waiting for Europe.*
20 Butcher (in Spanish): Are you from here?
    Vania: Yes...
    Butcher: Where do you live?
    Vania: Here in Alcalá.
    Butcher: Ah, in Alcalá. And for how long?
    Vania (Portuguese): I have been here for nine months.
    Butcher: But you speak Spanish pretty well for someone who has just arrived.
    Vania: What?
    Butcher: You speak Spanish very well, really. For someone who has been here for a short time.
    Vania (mixing Portuguese and Spanish): No, I don't speak Spanish very well.
    Butcher: Yes, you do, you speak well...

that Vania return to Bulgaria and search for work there instead of in Spain because there are already too many irregulars working for a very low income [26:20–28:50]. The importance of language acquisition is underlined once again by the next sequences where Vania tries to improve her Spanish by listening to sentences and repeating them in order to improve her pronunciation [28:59–29:21]. The following interviews with Giurgana Kirolova, another female Bulgarian migrant [29:22–30:52], and Letchezar Mertchev Stoitchev, Ivo's brother, [30:53–31:45] are marked by the same characteristic use of language by migrants: Giurgana speaks non-standard Spanish, while Letchezar expresses himself in non-standard Portuguese, but without any translation of their errors in the English subtitles.

The third part of the documentary is dominated by Bulgarian with English subtitles due to Vania and Ivo's journey home for Christmas. Using direct speech as well as voice-over accompanying film images of Vania still in Spain, Sashka Petrova, Ivo and Letchezar's mother, explains the reasons for the emigration of her sons as well as her own sense of their absence [34:06–36:02]. The soundtrack of the movie is also marked by Bulgarian music, songs as well as dances, in order to unite image and sound to authenticate the locality. While the conversation of Bulgarians is in Bulgarian, Vania and Ivo continue to speak in non-standard Portuguese in order to be accessible to the Portuguese audience. The end of the film is summarised by an insert in Portuguese: 'Vania e Ivo regressaram a Espanha. Ainda não sabem quando volarão definitivamante para a Bulgária. Vania está grávida'[21] [53:23]. À espera da Europa is a documentary in three spoken languages subtitled in English: Portuguese, Spanish and Bulgarian, structuring the language use in the filmic text by images of geographical areas. Again, foreigners mainly speak their mother tongues or non-standard Portuguese and Spanish, and subtitles are applied as the mode of translation.

'Spoken Landscapes' in Lisbon: Lisboetas[22]

The analytic and descriptive documentary Lisboetas (2004) by Sérgio Tréfaut, a migrant film-maker born in Brazil and living in Portugal since 1977, depicts the difficulties of migrants from several countries like Brazil, the Ukraine, Lithuania, Russia, Romania, Moldavia, India, Pakistan and China as well as from former Portuguese African colonies such as Angola, Equatorial Guinea or Cape Verde in search of a better life in the capital of Portugal. One main focus of the documentary is the difficulty of getting residence visas, for which they have to queue at the Serviço de extrangeiros e fronteiras (immigration authorities) in order to be interviewed by officials in Portuguese despite the fact that most of them have no mastery of the language. Again, the filmic topics focus on language acquisition, integration, adaption to a different culture, various religious practices (e.g. Muslim and Christian Orthodox), the search for a job and everyday life. Despite living as foreigners in

---

21   'Vania and Ivo returned to Spain. They still don't know when they will come back to live in
     Bulgaria. Vania is pregnant.'
22   Lisboners.

Lisbon, the protagonists are presented as 'lisboetas' by adoption in an ironic way, as the movie title already indicates.

Spoken languages in *Lisboetas* are standard and non-standard Portuguese, non-standard English, Romanian, Ukrainian, Russian, Bengali and Mandarin. While all dialogues in standard and non-standard Portuguese are not subtitled, spoken foreign languages are subtitled in Portuguese. The target audience of this documentary is therefore mainly Portuguese speakers. The lack of subtitles in English or French consequently acts as a self-imposed barrier to the broad reception of *Lisboetas* as it excludes spectators who have no knowledge of Portuguese.

Sérgio Tréfaut also frequently uses voice-over to integrate the polyphony of different languages in this documentary. One example is the sequence where a masculine voice begins a radio emission in Romanian while the content is translated in the subtitles:

> Bună ziua domnilor ascultători! Bună ziua cititoarea jurnalului Luso-Romănu diaspora! Au fost prins și una această dimineață în Lisabona în timpului operațiunea poliției 53 destrăini fără documente. Aceasta avut loc în Campo Grande în această piață neagra a munci unde după cum se știe început cu ora cinci de dimineață responsabila ai construcților civile vie să căut de mîne de lucru disponibilă și ieftină principal formată dîn imigranți ilegal. Marea parte din indiviziei reținuțea astăzi erau de naționalitate ucraniană însă se numără printre 7 brasilieni, 5 moldoveni, 3 romăni, 2 indieni și 1 nigerian. La această oră încă nu se știe ce se va întămpla cu ăcești străini arestați de poliție.[23] [22:19–23:15]

As *Lisboetas* represents a realistic image of the cultural and linguistic diversity in Lisbon at the beginning of the 21st century, the polyphony of modern society is portrayed by maintaining original languages made understandable by subtitles in Portuguese. The film therefore consists mainly of real dialogues between migrants, telephone calls to family members in their home countries as well as interviews in foreign languages with subtitles. The plurilingualism of the migrant population even mixes with tourism, as can be seen in the sequence where a Pakistani man tries to sell his flowers to German tourists in the restaurants of nocturnal Lisbon: 'German? English? Sprechen Sie Deutsch?'[24] [36:50]. At the same time, the short conversations in the streets with his fellow Pakistanis remain without any subtitles, giving the spectators a similar feeling of foreignness to that experienced by the migrants as they find themselves unable to comprehend ordinary dialogue [37:09–38:18].

As in *À espera da Europa*, the necessity to speak the local language turns out to be an important issue in *Lisboetas*. This fact is illustrated by a long sequence dedicated to a Portuguese class where migrants, mainly from Eastern Europe, are practising

---

23   'Hello, dear listeners. Hello readers of the Luso-Rumanian newspaper Diaspora. This morning 53
      foreigners without documents were imprisoned by the Lisbon police. The detention took place at the
      Campo Grande, a black market, where every morning starting at five o'clock employers involved
      in civil construction search for cheap and available casual labourers, mainly illegal immigrants.
      The majority of the detained individuals are Ukrainian. But seven Brazilians, six Moldavians, three
      Rumanians, two Indians and one Nigerian have also been imprisoned. At this moment it is still
      impossible to know what will happen to these foreigners.' (With thanks to Zsuzsa Gaspar for the
      transcription of the Rumanian original.)
24   (in German) 'Do you speak German?'

basic conversation rules and being trained in the conjugation of Portuguese verbs and phonetics [25:07–30:22]. This example of a Portuguese class furthermore takes place above an orthodox church, which suggests that the migrant community itself has taken the initiative for organising language teaching for their members. Interestingly, at the end of the mass which takes place in the following sequence, migrants leave their contact details and messages on a board outside the church in Cyrillic letters, thus integrating an example of written foreign language. Finally, Sérgio Tréfaut's documentary underlines the fact that migration waves to Portugal are a new phenomenon by interviewing children who were mainly born in Eastern Europe and Asia and therefore still express themselves primarily in their mother tongues. The birth of a baby from a migrant mother in Lisbon at the end of the film certainly indicates that the second generation of migrants – probably bilinguals who will no longer speak only their mother tongues like their parents, but standard Portuguese after school enrolment as well – will reinforce the polyphony of Lisbon in the future.

'Spoken Landscapes' on the Way to Europe: *Bab Sebta*[25]

The origins of *Bab Sebta* (2008), shot by Frederico Lobo and Pedro Pinho, rely on the events of September 2005 when Sub-Saharan migrants carried out massive attacks on the borders of the Spanish enclaves Ceuta and Melilla, producing the death of an indeterminate number of people. The documentary is therefore no longer located in Europe, but takes the audience on a journey through Northern Africa in order to investigate the reasons for migration. The film is shot in the Moroccan cities of Tangier and Oujda, on the border with Algeria, in Nouakchott, the capital of Mauritania, and in Nouadhibou, a city with a sea port in the north of the country. *Bab Sebta* depicts the hope, aspirations and desperation of Africans willing to undertake dangerous journeys as irregular migrants in order to enter Europe. The narration is centred on migrants' stories related in the first person, introducing the audience to their everyday life in Africa, their families and their migration routes. As the plot advances, the expression of protest against the living conditions in Africa and the behaviour of European countries towards Africans becomes increasingly stronger.

In *Bab Sebta* the audience is once again confronted with a polyphony of languages in the filmic narration: standard and non-standard Portuguese, non-standard English, French, several Nigerian dialects, Wolof, Creole from Guinea-Bissau as well as Hassānīya Arabic, a variety of Arabic spoken by inhabitants of Algeria, Morocco, Mauritania, Mali, Niger, Senegal and the Western Sahara. In contrast to the other documentaries presented in this essay, *Bab Sebta* frequently uses inserts in order to give the audience a sense of orientation [01:33; 24:52; 35:34]. These inserts are in Portuguese without any subtitles: 'Nouadhibou. Cidade portuária junto à fronteira

---

25   In Arabic 'Bab Sebta' means 'the door to Ceuta' and refers to the frontier between Morocco and the Spanish enclave of Ceuta.

com o Sahara Ocidental. Principal porto comercial da Mauritânia. Situada a 900 km do Arquipélago das Canárias'[26] [59:16].

In Tangier the audience is not only confronted with the exotic landscape of the outskirts of the city, but also with Morocco as a reception centre where migrants from all over Africa are stranded. While the soundtrack reflects the Arabic voices of playing children, the first part of *Bab Sebta* is marked by a narration in non-standard English and Nigerian dialects subtitled in Portuguese. Migrants are depicted in the precarious conditions they experience as irregulars in Morocco, complaining about their existence in the Arabic countries, their failed intents to cross the Mediterranean in boats, being rescued and returned to Oujda, the difficult travel conditions crossing the desert and their hope to reach Europe one day in the future. *Bab Sebta* thus shows that Africa itself is heavily affected by migration routes and people crossing the continent to reach the points of access in their attempt to breach the Fortress Europe. The stops in Oujda and in Nouakchott are presented in the introductory inserts in Portuguese as 'ponto do passage obrigatório para quem vem do deserto argelino'[27] [24:52] with the distance to the Canary Islands [35:34]. Curiously, in the parts set in Mauritania, the audience is not confronted with the official language Arabic, but instead is aware of several African languages as well as French as a result of the country's post-colonial heritage.

Reflecting Africa's ethnic diversity, *Bab Sebta* involves migrants who speak different native languages such as Wolof, but also official languages like French and English. However, these official languages are rarely spoken in their standard form, as can be seen in the following statement by a Black African whose sons already live in Europe and America: 'I will to nationalise in America. I will nationalise in America. America, Italy, London...' [16:10 – 16:20]. Although the filmic strategies used to integrate the polyphony do not differ from other documentaries discussed above – in this case mainly subtitles in Portuguese – *Bab Sebta* stands out as the film with the greatest diversity of languages among those studied. The fact that the protagonists express themselves in non-standard English/French or their mother tongues underlines the relevance of a former colonial language as a 'lingua franca', while simultaneously giving voice to a variety of native African languages rarely present in European cinema.

Conclusion

The tension of the film text as a linguistically and aesthetically coded object comes to the surface when dealing with transnational, cross-cultural and polyglot cinema, challenging both national cinemas as well as their audiences. This is even more complex in the case of documentaries as a genre which claims to be both informative and realistic. The common denominator of the filmic corpus analysed in this essay lies in the polyphony of migrants' stories which question stereotypes normally transmitted by the

---

26 'Nouadhibou. City with a sea port on the border with the Eastern Sahara. Main commercial port of Mauritania. Located 900 km from the Archipelago of the Canary Islands.'
27 'obligatory point of passage for those who come from the Algerian desert.'

mass media. Film-makers dedicated to this topic therefore aim to deconstruct critical attitudes towards migrants by giving them a voice. Allowing the migrants to express their situation with the use of their mother tongues reaffirms their existence: 'Languages can serve not only to oppress and alienate but also to liberate' (Stam 1989: 84). In doing this, however, film-makers are confronted with the inherent polyphony of the acoustic track of their documentaries. Therefore, they have to decide whether the original languages are to be maintained and how to make them accessible to audiences, if at all. While fiction films are usually dubbed due to the importance of being able to identify with the characters and follow the plot, in documentaries the subtitling mode is dominant in order to preserve the individuality of the original voices.

In the films studied, the globalisation of modern visual culture is evident in the fact that languages are no longer bound by geographic borders. Instead, migrants from all over the world leave their mark by spreading their mother tongues into Europe. While films shot in mainly urban areas like Lisbon, Madrid or Barcelona focus on Spanish and Portuguese as the dominant languages (*Extranjeras*, *Si nos dejan*, *Lisboetas*), they also tune into the soundtrack of European metropolises by combining official and foreign languages with non-standard Spanish/Portuguese. Others, like *À espera da Europa*, *Bab Sebta* and *Paralelo 36,* which are mainly or partially shot in the migrants' countries of origin, even integrate both the acoustic landscapes of the home countries and the countries of reception.

With regard to the strategies used, six approaches could have been employed: dubbing, subtitling, self-translation, liaison interpreting, voice-over, and non-translation. Dubbing has been rejected in all films, while subtitling has been applied as a dominant strategy due to the fact that it makes the content more accessible for audiences while maintaining the veracity of the original. Non-translation is used in many cases, such as in *Extranjeras* or *Lisboetas*, although it is not a dominant strategy. The use of non-translation is generally restricted to sequences which are intended to evoke a particular atmosphere, creating a 'spoken landscape' which is aesthetically relevant, but less important in terms of content. Nevertheless, although non-translated speech can be considered background sound, the audience excluded from the reception of a part of the documentary can themselves experience the disturbing sensation of non-understanding. Whereas the strategies of self-translation and liaison interpreting have not been applied by the film-makers, voice-over is present in *Lisboetas* and *Paralelo 36*. In the latter, the use of this strategy is particularly noticeable when the narrative is given in two different languages – Arabic and Spanish – at the same time. By employing this method, the documentary offers the audience both the 'spoken landscape' and the possibility of understanding, as subtitling does, but only at the acoustic level. While this represents an interesting approach to the film-makers' dilemma of portraying plurilingualism, it would not be a sustainable solution for a feature-length text to be received in two languages simultaneously.

Polyglot documentaries not only highlight the migrants' geographical and linguistic distance from their origins, but also try to confront spectators with the feeling of foreignness experienced once in the host country. Thus, the films discussed make it clear that the zones of language contact, as was the case during the era of colonisation and even during the process of decolonisation, are no longer geographically bound. Moreover, they depict Portugal and Spain as areas of intense language contact at the beginning of the twenty-first century. As a result, contemporary film-makers are engaging with a new form of 'glocal' plurilingualism which makes their documentaries especially challenging to audiences at both a cultural and linguistic level.

Filmography

LOBO, F./PINHO, P. (2008), *Bab Sebta*, Morocco/Portugal.

REEH, Ch. (2006), *À espera da Europa*, Portugal.

TABERNA, H. (2003), *Extranjeras*, Spain.

TIRADO, J. L. (2003), *Paralelo 36*, Spain.

TORRES, A. (2005), *Si nos dejan*, Argentina.

TREFAUT, S. (2004), *Lisboetas*, Portugal.

References

AGOST, R. (1999), *Traducción y doblaje: palabras, voces e imágenes*, Barcelona: Ariel.

AUFDERHEIDE, P. (2007), *Documentary Film. A Very Short Introduction*, Oxford: Oxford U.P.

BÁLAZS, B. (2001[1930]), *Der Geist des Films*, Frankfurt a.M.: Suhrkamp.

BERMEJO, A. (2003), 'Voluntad de supervivencia', in: *Metrópolis*, 21 November, URL: http://www.lamiaproducciones.com/extranjeras/textobermejo.htm (06 April 2010).

BETZ, M. (2009), *Beyond the Subtitle: Remapping European Art Cinema*, Minneapolis: University of Minnesota Press.

BLEICHENBACHER, L. (2008), *Multilingualism in the Movies: Hollywood Characters and their Language Choices*, Tübingen: Francke.

CHAUME, F. (2003), *Doblatge i subtitulació per a la TV*, Vic: Eumo.

CHAUME, F. (2004), *Cine y traducción*, Madrid: Cátedra.

BOCK, H.-M./JACOBSEN, W./SCHÖNING, J. & J. DISTELMEYER, (ed.) (2006), *Babylon in FilmEuropa: Mehrsprachen-Versionen der 1930er Jahre*, Munich: Text und Kritik.

EGOYAN, A. & I. BALFOUR (eds.) (2004), *Subtitles. On the Foreignness of Film*, London: MIT.

GOLDSTEIN, A. & B. GOLUBOVIĆ (eds.) (2009), *Foreign Language Movies – Dubbing vs. Subtitling*, Hamburg: Kovač.

HEISS, C. (2004), 'Dubbing Multilingual Films: A New Challenge?', in: *Meta*, vol. 49:1, 208–220.

MAMBER, S. (1974), *Cinema Verité in America: Studies in Uncontrolled Documentary*, Cambridge: MIT Press.

MEDIA CONSULTING GROUP (2007), *Study on Dubbing and Subtitling Needs and Practices in the European Audiovisual Industry*, *Final Report*, Paris/London, URL: http://ec.europa.eu/information_society/media/overview/evaluation/studies/index_en.htm (23 February 2010).

NAFICY, H. (1999), 'Between Rocks and Hard Places. The Interstitial Mode of Production in Exilic Cinema', in: Ibid. (ed.), *Home, Exile, Homeland: Film, Media, and the Politics of Place*, New York: Routledge, 125–147.

NAFICY, H. (2001), *An Accented Cinema. Exilic and Diasporic Filmmaking*, Princeton: Princeton U. P.

NICHOLS, B. (1991), *Representing Reality*, Bloomington: Indiana U.P.

NICHOLS, B. (1994), *Blurred Boundaries: Questions of Meaning in Contemporary Culture*, Bloomington: Indiana U.P.

NICHOLS, B. (2001), *Introduction to Documentary*, Bloomington: Indiana U.P.

PAYÁN, J. M. (1999), *El cine español de los 90*, Madrid: JC.

REINART, S. (2004), 'Zu Theorie und Praxis von Untertitelung und Synchronisation', in: Kohlmayer, R. & W. Pöckl (eds.), *Literarisches und mediales Übersetzen. Aufsätze zu Theorie und Praxis einer gelehrten Kunst*, Frankfurt a.M.: Lang, 73–112.

RHODES, G. D. & J. PARRIS SPRINGER (eds.) (2006), *Docufictions. Essays on the Intersection of Documentary and Fictional Filmmaking*, Jefferson: McFarland.

RODRÍGUEZ, M. P. (2003), 'El nuevo documental: Julio Medem y Helena Taberna', in: *Pérgola*, 5 December, 6.

SHOHAT, E. & R. STAM (1985), 'The Cinema after Babel: Language, Difference, Power', in: *Screen* 26/3–4, 35–58.

SPIVAK, G. C. (1988), 'Can the Subaltern Speak?', in: Nelson C. & L. Grossberg (eds.), *Marxism and the Interpretation of Culture*, Urbana: University of Illinois Press, 271–313.

STAM, R. (1989), *Subversive Pleasures*, Baltimore/London: John Hopkins U.P.

STAM, R. (1991), 'Bakhtin, Polyphony and Ethnic/Racial Representation', in: Friedman, L.D. (ed.), *Unspeakable Images: Ethnicity and the American Cinema*, Urbana/Chicago: University of Illinois Press, 251–276.

STEINER, G. (1975), *After Babel: Aspects of Language and Translation*, New York: Oxford U.P.

THOMASON, S. G. (2001), *Language Contact*, Edinburgh: Edinburgh U.P.

WAHL, C. (2005a), *Das Sprechen des Spielfilms. Über die Auswirkungen von hörbaren Dialogen auf Produktion und Rezeption, Ästhetik und Internationalität der siebten Kunst*, Trier: WVT.

WAHL, C. (2005b), 'Discovering a Genre: The Polyglot Film', in: *Cinemascope – Independent Film Journal* 1, URL: http://www.madadayo.it/Cinemascope_archive/cinemascope. net/articolo07_n1.html (6 March 2010).

WAHL, C. (2008), ' 'Du Deutscher, toi français, You English: Beautiful' – The Polyglot Film as a Genre', in: Christensen, M. & N. Erdŏgan (eds.), *Shifting Landscapes: Film and Media in European Context*, Newcastle: Cambridge Scholars Publishing, 334–350.

WARD, P. (2005), *Documentary. The Margins of Reality*, London: Wallflower.

WHITMAN-LINSEN, C. (1992), *Through the Dubbing Glass: The Synchronization of American Motion Pictures into German, French and Spanish*, Frankfurt a.M.: Lang.

VI. LOCAL AND GLOBAL: POLYPHONY IN ITALIAN CINEMA

Dialect and the Global: A Combination Game

Camille Gendrault

In Italy, territorial affiliation is much more powerfully marked by dialectal forms than it is in other countries that have long been heavily centralised. Depending on period, region, and genre, cinema has either exploited such forms or glossed over them. The cinematographic fortunes of the Neapolitan dialect, for example, have varied widely over the years, although the city of Naples has always featured heavily in Italian film. Indeed, Naples has a place all its own in Italian collective representations. Witness the many movies in which the city appears: Naples is, after Rome, the second most frequently filmed city in Italian cinema (Fofi 1993: 67; Aprà 1994: 77; Bruno 2005: 492).[1] The pages that follow take an interest not only in the more or less strongly marked presence of Neapolitan dialect in various films, but also in the languages with which Neapolitan is brought into contact in the period between Massimo Troisi's *Ricomincio da tre*[2] (1981), where Neapolitan appears side-by-side with standard Italian, and Matteo Garrone's *Gomorra* (2008), where it appears alongside languages from other continents.

'Those born in Naples know the city somehow belongs to a Third World that is mythic, Mediterranean, and seductive, yet a Third World, after all,' the writer Raffaele La Capria noted in the late 1990s; 'one need think only of the misery and suffering found there. People from Naples also know that, although the city belongs to Europe culturally and by tradition, it is considered an unhappy member of the European family, one confined to its margins – a second-class European' (Schifano 1992: 290). It is precisely because the collective imaginary makes Naples over into a marginal space that we have chosen to examine films bearing on this space, with a view to determining what the phenomena of plurilingualism reveal about it, more distinctly than they do elsewhere. To what extent does plurilingualism, given the way it has changed in the course of the last three decades, lead us to redefine this margin as it draws our attention to major shifts in migratory flows? Above all, to what extent does it help us grasp the dynamic that progressively reconfigures the geographic frame of reference responsible for organising representations?

---

1 Translation of this essay by Geoffrey Michael Goshgarian.
2 *I'm Starting from Three.*

A Specific Language

1981 saw the release of the movie that made Neapolitan comedian Massimo Troisi one of the most popular directors, actors and screenwriters in the Italy of his day: *Ricomincio da tre*. The film was very successful throughout the country, although dialect is used in most of the dialogues in it, especially the lines put in the mouth of the film's protagonist, Gaetano. Played by the director, Gaetano is a young Neapolitan who tires of his everyday surroundings and decides to strike out for Florence, only to discover that, as soon as he has set foot outside Naples, he is constantly asked the same question: 'È emigrante?'[1] The question is purely rhetorical and those who ask it are not looking for an answer. They pay little attention to Gaetano's denials: 'No, no... cioè, ci avevo pure un lavoro a Napoli, na cosa... normale, proprio, come tutti quanti... No, so'partito così, pe viaggià, pe cunoscere nu poco...'[2] [14:24]. But how can a Neapolitan, once he is identified as such, be perceived as a young person like any other, or, at least, a young person who is not necessarily fleeing poverty and unemployment, but just wants to 'see something of the country'? Gaetano learns by personal experience that, in Italy's collective imaginary, 'o napulitano nun pò viaggià, pò sulamente emigrà!'[3] [01:09:45]. He is the South come North, in a country where representations are profoundly shaped by the cleavage between these two poles and the Neapolitan incarnates everything southern *par excellence*.

Italian cinema thus exploits the game of pitting North against South to the full. To cite just one more example from the same period, *FFSS cioè... che mi hai portato a fare sopra Posillipo se non mi vuoi più bene?*[4] (Renzo Arbore, 1983) confronts the most shopworn clichés associated with the South on the one hand and the North on the other. Dialect is one of the elements it employs, in the most outrageous fashion, to make fun of Neapolitan peculiarities: the city is portrayed as a communitarian enclave held together by primitive practices that are fundamentally foreign to the Italy to its north. For comic effect, it transforms Neapolitan dialect into a strange, semi-Arabic idiom. From time to time, the story line is interrupted so that an 'Islamic commentator' can intersperse, in a sort of Arabo-Neapolitan, summaries of the plot for an audience made up of 'our Arab brothers' [07:54]. These plot summaries are nevertheless always comprehensible for the film's Italian audience, not least because they are accompanied by certain gestures which, presented in their turn as characteristic of the local language, are part of what the film mocks.

Massimo Troisi's film *Ricomincio da tre*, for its part, does not play on this facile opposition. As the dialogues mentioned above show, the film limits itself, rather, to bringing out its significance in the collective imaginary. By the same to-

---

1   'Are you an emigrant?'
2   'No. I mean... I even held a job in a Naples... completely normal... just like everyone else who has a job... No, I just left, to travel, see things...'
3   'A Neapolitan can't travel... all he can do is emigrate!'
4   The title is hardly translatable into English: The first part, *FFSS*, would be the acronym of 'Federico Fellini South Story' but also refers to the initials of the national railway (*Ferrovie dello Stato*); part two cites the refrain of a famous Neapolitan song of 1923: *L'Addio* (Libero Bovio and Nicola Valente).

ken, Troisi's film does not treat dialect as a heavily stereotyped motif exploited for comic effect; rather, it employs dialect authentically, as a systematic mode of expression. The same holds for *Non ci resta che piangere*[5], a 1985 movie co-directed by Troisi and Roberto Benigni. *Non ci resta che piangere* features an encounter between two dialectal worlds, Neapolitan and Tuscan. In *Ricomincio da tre*, the vernacular is never foregrounded. Although Gaetano's language often proves incomprehensible to people who are not from Naples, inasmuch as it shifts constantly back and forth between regional Italian and dialect thanks to the play of various linguistic interferences[6], the other characters, who, for their part, speak standard Italian, never draw attention to this fact and are not in the least troubled by it. Moreover, the protagonist's use of dialect forms is never calculated to produce an effect. This is so clearly the case that it is disconcerting. For this character's subdued gestures and introverted attitude fly in the face of the cliché which has it that exuberance is the inevitable register of Neapolitan expressivity and that dialect is necessarily accompanied by emphatic gesticulation. Here, on the contrary, 'the gestures of the hands and arms and even facial expressions are directed inward rather than outward; they seek to contain and control rather than project and dramatize' (Quaresima 1985: 123).

Dialect is, nevertheless, a rarity in the cinema of this period, with the exception of a handful of films such as Troisi's; the great majority of the movies of the day may well incorporate it as a motif, yet they make no use of it in dialogues. Overall, films produced in the 1980s which are set in Naples tend to restrict themselves to sprinkling standard Italian dialogues with words and accents that evoke Neapolitan in order to create a sense of authenticity. Only in the opening years of the next decade did Neapolitan dialect return to the screen in full force.

Thus, in the early 1990s, Naples witnessed the nearly simultaneous emergence of a number of new directors whose first films now caught the public eye – Antonio Capuano, Mario Martone, and Pappi Corsicato –, who were soon followed by others. While each of these directors has his own distinctive style and cannot be reduced to the category of 'new Neapolitan cinema', which has sometimes been unjustifiably mobilised to cast all of them in the same mold, they have, undeniably, at least one trait in common: all three privilege dialect in their dialogues. In some cases, the dialect used is so thick that subtitles are needed to make it comprehensible to a national audience. This applies, for example, to certain sequences of Antonio Capuano's *Vito e gli altri*[7] (1991) or, again, to Giuseppe Gaudino's *Giro di lune tra terra e mare*[8], which was produced several years later, in 1998; here dialect is employed from one end of the film to the other. It should no doubt be added that, while Neapolitan films of the day utilise dialect, it is far from being homogeneous. The different varieties

---

5   *Nothing Left to Do But Cry.*
6   See Stromboli (2000) for an extremely rigorous and clear analytical description of the language used in the film.
7   *Vito and the Others.*
8   *Round the Moons Between Earth and Sea.*

of dialect to be heard in them are rich in nuance for viewers capable of perceiving them. In *L'amore molesto*[9] (1995), Mario Martone makes particularly subtle use of such varieties to highlight not only sociocultural differences between the characters, but also recent sociological shifts as they are manifested between two generations of the same family. Thus the oldest members of the family speak a somewhat dated dialect that evokes the pre-war era, whereas the next generation speaks a dialect that has been 'contaminated and vulgarized by television' (Martone 1995: 174). Far from purveying an image of rigid identity, therefore, dialect presents itself in these films as a living language subject to constant change. It is this living language, far more than standard Italian, which confronts the new immigrants who begin to appear in films from the early 1990s on.

The New Immigrants: How Visible Are They? How Audible Are They?

The 1990s were not only the decade in which Neapolitan cinema reappropriated dialect. These were also the years in which new types of characters began to appear in Neapolitan films: the immigrants for whom the Italian language has created the unambiguous term *extracomunitari*, which means, literally, 'those who do not belong to the European Community'. To be sure, this is not a strictly Neapolitan phenomenon; it takes in much of the rest of Italy and Italian cinema as well.[10] Yet it assumes special significance in Naples, marking as it does a reversal in the city's status. Once a city of emigration, Naples now becomes a space of immigration.

Initially, immigrants are nothing more than a diffuse, anonymous presence in these films. Perceived more or less furtively in the course of a sequence, the immigrants of various origins make up part of the urban landscape without playing any real role in the plot. From the front credits onward, Stefano Incerti's camera happens upon large numbers of Africans in *Il verificatore*[11] (1995) as the film's main character wanders through the city. However, in these eye-level shots in semi-documentary style, the gaze does not linger over a single detail or the face of a single African. Yet the presence of these extras does help characterise the neighbourhood in which most of the movie unfolds, in a way that, deliberately and from the outset, undermines the picturesqueness of the stereotypes associated with the city. In these first shots, the sky is overcast and the urban setting is an immigrant neighbourhood. It is precisely because neither aspect corresponds to the usual iconography that the viewer does not understand, until he hears the Neapolitan dialect, that the film is set in Naples, albeit in neighbourhoods that had previously very rarely been filmed: the quarters near the main train station where much of the immigrant population lives, as it does in many other cities as well. Yet this immigrant population still plays only a very limited, accessory role in Incerti's movie. One sequence does, it is true, take us into the home of some of these Africans along

---

9   *Nasty Love.*
10 See Durante (1996: 343–348) for an overview of the films on this theme dating from the first half
    of the 1990s.
11 *The Gas Inspector.*

with the protagonist, a gas-meter reader, whose professional visits offer, throughout the film, a sort of vertical cross-section of society. Yet this sequence is quite brief, lasting forty seconds at most, and does not give rise to any real verbal exchange between the Neapolitan and the Africans. After walking into a shared mezzanine apartment, sparsely furnished with mattresses spread out on the floor, the meter-reader listens silently, against a backdrop of animated discussions he cannot understand, as one of the occupants aims a vulgar play on words in Neapolitan his way. The camera pans across the apartment, where everyone has burst out laughing [23:29].

Mario Martone's 1998 release *Teatro di guerra*[12] testifies to the same effort to integrate the new fact of immigration into the general picture. The role played by the new immigrant populations is sharply limited in this film as well, however, and does not lead to any verbal exchange. We see the Filipino community this time. Shot on site, the film follows rehearsals for a theatre performance by a small theater company in the Teatro Nuovo, located in a very old working-class neighbourhood downtown. Disturbed by music during one of their rehearsals, the director and several other members of the company throw open the door of the adjoining hall, only to discover, to their stupefaction, a throng of Filipinos waiting to hear a concert that has been organised for them. The camera lingers over the crowd, and yet the Filipinos remain extras; we come no closer to them [25:26–26:10].

In Antonio Capuano's *Pianese Nunzio, quattordici anni a maggio*[13] (1996), the new figure of the immigrant makes an even more fleeting appearance: the camera pans across several immigrants before coming to rest on the protagonist. Like him, they are filmed close-up as they speak in a telephone booth, but we cannot hear their conversations, because the sound of traffic drowns out the audio [01:35:08–01:35:17]. Thus these new residents are shown very briefly, only just long enough to evoke their presence, which the director nevertheless intended to invest with greater significance. So he claimed, at any rate: 'Un fallimento è però stato non riuscire a convincere nessun extracomunitario a fare la comparsa nel film: si sono rifiutati, tutti'[14] (Capuano 1996: 12).

It seems that Gianfranco Planta did not come up against the same problem: a sequence in his 1990 film *C'è posto per tutti*[15] shows several immigrants being questioned by the owner of a boxing club after being 'fished off the streets' near the central train station and up and down Naples' main shopping strip, the Via Toledo. One identifies himself as an architecture student from Lebanon; another says he is a business student from Gabon [29:10–31:26]. Like the movies discussed above, albeit more explicitly, *C'è posto per tutti* in no way attempts to contrast impoverished immigrants with a reputedly wealthy Italian host society, or, at any event, a society displaying signs of affluence, but simply narrates the trials and tribulations of young Neapolitans con-

---

12 *Rehearsals for War.*
13 *Pianese Nunzio, Fourteen in May.*
14 'One problem was that we failed to convince a single emigrant to participate in the film. They all refused.'
15 *There's Room for Everyone.*

demned to the dole. We are shown that the new immigrant population will soon swell the ranks of the poorest of those living in the downtown working-class neighbourhoods; that is, we understand that it will eventually come to share a situation that, while certainly harsh, can hardly be called marginal, let alone marginalised. Vincenzo Marra's *Tornando a casa*[16] (2001) pursues and develops the same theme.

Marra's movie deserves to be analysed in greater depth here, especially because it assigns a much more important role to the figure of the immigrant, given a central place in the story and thus endowed with the status of a full-fledged character. To be sure, the character in question, Samir, remains somewhat in the background, as his status as an illegal Tunisian immigrant suggests he should. Yet he fully shares the life of the other fishermen in his little crew, who boldly cast off from the small port of Pozzuoli north of Naples to take their chances working illegally in the more promising Tunisian waters off the Sicilian coast. *Tornando a casa* thus revolves around the narration of two contrasting movements, both illegal: while the Neapolitan fishermen head south in pursuit of more profitable working conditions, people seeking a better life travel north from Africa.

Although it is evident from the first sequence of the movie that the oldest members of the crew maintain a racist attitude towards Samir, the next sequence shifts the focus to the bond between the Tunisian and the youngest fisherman, Franco, by showing us a discussion between them on the edge of the quay [05:29–08:20]. In their conversation, made more intimate by a series of rapid shot and countershots, Samir describes the difficulties of his situation as an illegal immigrant and talks about his homesickness. Franco, for his part, reveals that he wants to emigrate to the United States and is actively preparing to leave. By a kind of mirror effect, the film thus associates the motif of immigration, currently bound up the Naples region, with that of emigration, which evokes the region's past and surfaces in somewhat anachronistic fashion here.

Linguistic practices further reinforce this parallelism. The first thing to be noted is that Samir, who says that he left his country five years earlier, has adopted the inflexions and expressions of the Neapolitan dialect, and fits very naturally into the context of the unusually thick dialect presented by the film (so thick, in fact, that non-Neapolitan Italian viewers have trouble understanding the dialogues). However, the French that is part of the colonial heritage also leaves its mark on what Samir says, spontaneously resurfacing ('Putain de merde!'[17]) when he curses [06:28] and, in a later sequence, slipping (in the form of a 'Ça va?'[18]) into a dialogue conducted entirely in Arabic between Samir and one of the students, also immigrants, with whom he shares an apartment [26:43]. On the other hand, Neapolitan and Arabic never interfere with one another. Heard in alternation throughout the soundtrack and always kept distinct, they correspond to one or the other of the two worlds in which Samir evolves. One exception does occur in the dialogue between Franco and Samir discussed above: here Samir teaches the young Neapolitan the right pronunciation of the most common greeting in

---

16 *Back Home.*
17 'Fucking hell!'
18 'How are you?'

his native language [07:42–07:59]. It is precisely this formula that Franco repeats at the end of the movie [01:21:29], when, distraught by the brutal death of his fiancée and, as it were, taking his friend's place, he returns to his own country, although he had previously dreamed of setting out for America. Fished from the water along with an illegal immigrant whom he tried to rescue when the latter fell overboard, Franco slips his Italian identity card onto the corpse and takes his place among the undocumented North-African immigrants who have welcomed him aboard their makeshift boat. He is turned back by the Italian authorities, just like his new compatriots, although he cannot understand their language. The decision to subtitle part of the Arabic dialogues [01:09:36–01:19:07; 01:20:53–01:22:03] might be questioned, since it seems to run counter to the realism that the movie otherwise embraces, undermining the viewer's identification with the foreignness that Franco feels among his new companions. Yet this choice appears altogether apt when it is recalled that the director's intention is not to stress the differences between the two shores of the Mediterranean, but, rather, to forge a symbolic link between them, bringing them into dialogue by means of a mirror effect that is also a crisscrossing of the one with the other.

To be sure, Marra's film sets out to portray the new migratory flows toward southern Italy and does so far more thoroughly than earlier movies set in Naples, which contented themselves with registering, more or less in passing, the new immigrants' presence. However, by linking the southern metropolis to northern Africa, the film inscribes this new fact in the framework of a venerable topos: that of Naples as the gateway to Europe for Africa and the gateway to Africa for Europe. Thus the plurilingualism that associates Arabic and the Neapolitan dialect in *Tornando a casa* [01:15:00–01:16:02; 01:18:42–01:19:50] does not fundamentally alter the frame of reference.

Cinematographic descriptions of the city have often chosen to spotlight its eastern character, using the soundtrack, in particular, to this effect. For example, in *Libera* (1993), Pappi Corsicato twice utilises the beginning of a famous song by Egyptian singer Oum Kalsoum [59:10; 01:20:32]. Yet his use of the soundtrack produces an effect of surprise. The reason is that the music is not associated, in Corsicato's movie, with images of the city's central neighbourhoods, that dense network of narrow little streets that the collective imagination likes to consider a Casbah. Rather, a very different space is shown, namely, the suburbs of Naples, presented as gray and anonymous. Were it not for the use of the local vernacular in the dialogues, these suburbs would evoke generic suburbs, like the suburbs of untold other major cities, devoid of any particular territorial features. The landscape of apartment blocks is, however, easily identified by viewers familiar with Naples, the more so as it quite often appears in films that consider the city's suburbs, of which it is generally held to be sadly emblematic. Indeed, this neighborhood is identifiable as the 'Vele' ('Sails') in Secondigliano, in the Scampia district (it owes its name to some of the buildings on its skyline). The dismal reputation of these suburbs is now international, thanks to the enormous success of Matteo Garrone's movie Gomorra[19], most of which was shot in them.

---

19   *Gomorrah.*

Dialect and Globalisation

Matteo Garrone, taking up a position between documentary and fiction, has shown an interest in Italy's immigrants ever since shooting his first short film, *Silhouette* (1996). This theme also forms the central axis of his first full-length movie, significantly titled *Terra di mezzo*[20]. The film brings three episodes together under the key rubric of immigration. The first of them is the earlier short film *Silhouette*, which is about Nigerian women who prostitute themselves by the side of the road. The second, *Englan & Gertian*, portrays young Albanians looking for work as day-labourers in the construction sector. The protagonist of the third and final episode, *Self-Service*, is an elderly Egyptian who mans the pump at a gas station. Thus Garrone is perfectly familiar with the plurilingual dimension. Plurilingualism explains much of the appeal of *Silhouette* in particular, as the dialogues spoken by the young prostitutes are a brisk blend of their native language, French phrases, and an off-the-cuff Italian with markedly Roman inflections. This makes for very funny exchanges with the prostitutes' customers, who come from a still rural region on the outskirts of the city. With *Gomorra*, however, the Roman director Garrone delves into yet another acoustic universe: that of the Neapolitan region.

The movie pursues five parallel story-lines, set in five different locations, some suburban and others rural; all confront us with the Neapolitan dialect, which is occasionally so thick that *Gomorra* had to be subtitled in Italian before it could be shown nationwide. The best-selling book on which the movie is based does not take this very special linguistic dimension into account; it contains very little dialogue (and few dialectal formulas are used in such dialogue as there is). By contrast, the movie itself, resting on the performances of local actors (professional and amateur), most of whom have a background in theatre, brings the linguistic dimension fully to the fore. The sounds of dialect are central to the carefully crafted soundtrack[21], which artfully combines particularly harsh vernacular speech with music that likewise reflects the local dimension: contemporary Neapolitan songs. These songs, always diegetic, resound in space like the equally peculiar lilt of the voices that call out or answer each other between buildings. Thus language here serves as a very powerful regional marker identifying the action with a specific place. By contrast, there is virtually no localisation at the visual level. Not only is the film set mainly in nondescript spaces; Garrone, with his fondness for close-ups, does not show us much of them. Most importantly, he never falls back on the kind of stereotyped images that might serve to signify them. The use of dialect notwithstanding, the soundtrack contributes to this blurring of clear markers, inasmuch as the dialogues include whole sentences, without subtitles, in other, even less familiar languages.

This holds for a sequence that shows two characters, Marco and Ciro, on their way into an abandoned villa on the coast where a little group of Africans engages in

---

20   *Middle Ground.*
21   Created in Los Angeles by 'sound designer' Leslie Shatz, who has worked with Francis Ford Coppola and Gus Van Sant, among others.

various kinds of trafficking [12:15 – 15:07]. Garrone disorients the viewer by opening the sequence with a close-up of one of these Africans, accompanied by French dialogues. The ensuing verbal exchanges are placed under the sign of linguistic contamination: dialogues blend the Neapolitan dialect with African languages and French, thereby suggesting a context of relative intercultural familiarity.

This is a far cry from those scenes in the movie in which Chinese is spoken. Approached in poor Italian by Xian, who runs a Chinese textile workshop, the tailor Pasquale (played by Salvatore Cantalupo), himself a worker in the local informal sector, agrees to pass his *savoir-faire* on to Xian's foreign apprentices in return for a generous financial reward. Pasquale finds himself face-to-face with an absolutely foreign environment, one that produces an almost comic effect despite the harshness characteristic of the film as a whole. When he is introduced to the workers in the workshop, he is applauded, and then treated to a long introductory speech of which he, as spectator, understands only a single word – his own first name [51:40]. 'Cin Ciun Cian', he repeats to himself that night before falling asleep, reproducing his perception of the sounds that accompanied his bizarre first night as an instructor [54:23]. The large, well-equipped Chinese workshop, employing no fewer than eighty people, represents a foreign microcosm within the film, so that Pasquale needs an interpreter whenever he goes there. 'Ma che, so'stat'a Cina...'[22], the tailor tells his wife, speaking in dialect, when he goes back to his village at dawn [53:04].

Garrone does not, however, juxtapose different languages in order to underscore the possibility of conflict between communities or cultures. The main reason is that the director focuses, intermittently but to good effect, on the bonds of sympathy that spring up between Xian and Pasquale on the basis of non-linguistic cultural codes. For example, Pasquale explains that he practices Tai Chi. He also discovers and develops a taste for Chinese cooking; it inspires an unmistakable tribute from him, as in his remark that 'hanno fatto una spigola che era proprio buona'[23], a fish that holds a privileged place in Neapolitan cuisine. Most strikingly, the one space in which dialect is spoken to the exclusion of all other languages is the *vele* neighbourhood, a space ravaged by the war between clans and divided up into zones with strict borders, or even into mini-zones consisting of single buildings within the same complex of apartment blocks (at one point, a character points out the buildings that he must avoid [01:10:57], at the risk being shot if he doesn't: 'Sette Palazzi, Case dei Puffi, Case Celesti...'[24]). Thus people speaking different languages draw closer in the film, even as others who share the same culture (even the same local culture, in the strictest sense of the word) and speak the same dialect clash in an internal conflict governed by a powerful territorial logic. The disintegration of local bonds manifest in this notion of territory can be

---

22 'You'd have thought you were in China...'
23 'They cooked a sea bass which was really good.'
24 These buildings are named after certain of their salient features. The name 'Case celesti', for example, derives from the blue color of the buildings, while 'Case dei puffi' refers to the fact that the buildings in question are of no great height, so that they are associated with the houses of smurfs (*puffi* in Italian).

heard in the film's dialogues; we are made particularly sensitive to it by the space that (de-)composes the film. Rapid cuts force the viewer to switch abruptly from one story-line to another; the disorienting effect of this technique is intensified by the fact that many sequences open with close-ups that prevent the viewer from identifying the set-ting. Indeed, the staccato editing cuts the world of the movie up into a sort of spatial patchwork that resists articulation as a coherent whole. This confusion is compounded by signs of a diffuse globalisation, such as the jerseys bearing the words 'England' or 'Scotland' in bold letters sported by the young Totò, Secondigliano's son, while one of the Africans in the sequence mentioned above wears a jersey bearing the word 'Italy' and the corresponding national colors. A remark uttered by Xian in his clumsy Italian is another case in point: 'E poi, come in Cina, adesso tutte le città, la mattina quan-do esco, vedere questo giardino, pieno di persone, più di anziani, più di cinquant'anni, tutti fa tai chi'[25] [01:32:54]. The film thus forges a complex combination of territorial and global logics and dialectal and plurilingual levels.

In this context, in which dialect is brought face-to-face with globalisation at its most frenetic, standard Italian is very rarely heard in the film's dialogues. Yet it serves as the *lingua franca* for globalised exchanges. Xian speaks standard Italian when communicating with his collaborator Pasquale, who speaks dialect. In much the same way, Franco (played by Toni Servillo), an unscrupulous businessman spe-cialising in the disposal of toxic waste, drops his dialect when talking business in Italy's industrial north. Standard Italian is thus presented as the language proper to the passage from illicit to licit, from the underworld to the official world on view. The dialogue carefully reinforces this impression, in a way that is the more signifi-cant because it is repeated, when it has Franco's interlocutor from the Venetian re-gion use a term borrowed from the standard language used to discuss undisguised globalisation: 'Ma è tutto *clean* come dicono negli Stati Uniti?... A me interessa che tutto sia *clean* come dicono in America.'[26] Standard Italian is used again later in the film, and to the same effect, in the sequence that brings Pasquale's story to an end. This time, the 'speaker' is a TV set. In this sequence, a stupefied Pasquale recogni-ses – along with the viewer – one of the items he last worked on in the sweatshop: a *haute-couture* creation worn by the American star Scarlett Johansson at the *Mostra internazionale* fashion show in Venice and discussed at length by the TV journal-ists! [01:56:00]. With its glamorous images and standard Italian, national television, at the end of the day, lends a sleek air to what is in fact anything but sleek. Above all, it belies all the complexity of a globalised economy that the movie, in contrast, suc-ceeds in bringing to light – by situating itself on the level of the local and dialectal.

---

25 'And then, just like in China, all the cities, in the morning when I leave the house, see this park, full of people, more old people, more than fifty years old, everyone does Tai Chi.'
26 'But is everything *clean*, as they say in the United States?... All I care about is that everything be *clean*, as they say in America.'

Conclusion

In the three decades examined, Italian cinema has gradually reappropriated the Neapolitan dialect, exploiting it in increasingly radical forms. In the process, it has brought it into contact with languages of increasingly remote provenance. By means of the various phenomena of plurilingualism thus put to work, the very nature of the space organised by cinematographic representations is progressively and profoundly transformed. Throughout the 1980s, dialect, whenever it is included in a soundtrack, is confronted with standard Italian, above all, or with linguistic forms associated with other regions of Italy. The frame of reference here is the national space, marked by the north-south divide and the evocation of internal migration. In later representations, however, this frame of reference appears less and less appropriate. This is especially true of *Tornando a casa*, which, linking the two shores of the Mediterranean by following the new migratory flows, ignores national divisions in order to delineate a space that cuts across borders. Within the space that the film thus invites its viewers to consider, located on the confines of the West, Tunisian Arabic presents itself as a vernacular form with the same status as the Neapolitan to which it is juxtaposed in the dialogues. The same might be said about the linguistic practices from sub-Saharan Africa or China that appear in *Gomorra*. If only by juxtaposing idioms corresponding to widely separated geographical worlds, the film makes the space it forges not simply a transnational, but, rather, a trans-territorial space.

Thus what Garrone manages to make us feel by means of the languages heard in his film and the blurring of spatial markers is less the articulation between, than the telescoping of, the global and local. In this perspective, the notion of the margin that the collective imagination associates with the world of dialect proves obsolete. As many of those working on the new forms of mobility and the space they delineate have emphasised by paraphrasing Pascal (Abélès 2005: 20; Augé 2009: 23), henceforth 'the centre is everywhere and the circumference nowhere.'

Filmography

ARBORE, R. (1983), *FFSS cioè... che mi hai portato a fare sopra Posilippo se non mi vuoi più bene?*, Italy.

BENIGNI, R. & M. TROISI (1985), *Non ci resta che piangere*, Italy.

CAPUANO, A. (1991), *Vito e gli altri*, Italy.

CAPUANO, A. (1996), *Pianese Nunzio, quattordici anni a maggio*, Italy.

CORSICATO, P. (1993), *Libera*, Italy.

GARRONE, M. (1996), *Silhouette*, Italy.

GARRONE, M. (1996), *Terra di mezzo*, Italy.

GARRONE, M. (2008), *Gomorra*, Italy.

GAUDINO, G. (1998), *Giro di lune tra terra e mare*, Italy.

INCERTI, S. (1995), *Il verificatore*, Italy.

MARRA, V. (2001), *Tornando a casa*, Italy.

MARTONE, M. (1995), *L'amore molesto*, Italy.

MARTONE, M. (1998), *Teatro di guerra*, Italy.

PLANTA, G. (1990), *C'è posto per tutti*, Italy.

TROISI, M. (1981), *Ricomincio da tre*, Italy.

References

ABÉLÈS, M. (2005), 'Preface', in: Appadurai, A., *Après le colonialisme: Les Conséquences culturelles de la globalisation*, Paris: Editions Payot & Rivages, 7–23.

APRÀ, A. (1994), 'Naples et ses alentours dans le cinéma sonore (1930–1993)', in: Aprà, A. & J. Gili (eds.), *Naples et le cinéma*, Paris/Milan: Centre Georges Pompidou-Fabbri Editore, 77–129.

AUGÉ, M. (2009), *Pour une anthropologie de la mobilité*, Paris: Editions Payot & Rivages.

BRUNO, G. (2005), 'Naples', in: Jousse, T. & T. Paquot (eds.), *La Ville au cinéma*, Paris: Cahiers du cinéma, 492–499.

CAPUANO, A. (1996), 'Vita e malavita; Dentro la Sanità', in: *Linea d'ombra*, 118, 9–12.

DURANTE, C. (1996), 'Extracomunitari', in: Sesti, M., *La "scuola" italiana: Storia, strutture e immaginario di un altro cinema (1998–1996)*, Venice: Marsilio, 343–348.

FOFI, G. (1993), 'Contro lo stereotipo, il vecchio come il nuovo', in: *Dove sta Zazà*, 1, 67–68.

MARTONE, M. (1995), 'Itinerario di una voce: conversazione con Mario Marton', in: *Filmcritica*, 454, 172–186.

QUARESIMA, L. (1985), ' "A ff'a tenevo." Le avventure linguistiche di Massimo Troisi', in: Bernardi, S., *Si fa per ridere... ma è una cosa seria*, Florence: La Casa Usher, 122–127.

SCHIFANO, J. N. (1992), 'Raffaele La Capria: les faux départs', in: Ibid., *Désir d'Italie*, Paris: Gallimard, 286–294.

STROMBOLI, C. (2000), 'La lingua di *Ricomincio da tre* di Massimo Troisi', in: *Rivista italiana di dialettologia*, 24, 125–166.

Biographies

MICHAËL ABECASSIS graduated from the University of St. Andrews/UK. He is a Senior Instructor and a college lecturer at the University of Oxford/UK. He has published widely on French linguistics and cinema and is currently researching language and symbols of war in Iranian cinema.

SALIH AKIN is a lecturer in general linguistics at the University of Rouen/France. His research concerns the linguistic and sociolinguistic description of Kurdish, discourse analysis, the typology of languages, onomastics, the languages of immigration and the representation of foreigners in French media.

VERENA BERGER teaches Spanish and Latin American Studies at the University of Vienna/Austria, with a focus on theatre and film. She is the co-editor of *Montreal-Toronto. Stadtkultur und Migration in Literatur, Film und Musik* (2007) and *Escenarios compartidos: Cine y teatro en España en el umbral del siglo XXI* (2009). Her current research includes a publication on Latin American Cinema.

KARINE BLANCHON is a French researcher working at the Centre d'Études et de Recherches sur l'Océan Indien Occidental (CEROI) in Paris/France. She obtained her PhD about *Malagasy cinemas between images and imaginary* in 2007 at the National Institute of Oriental Languages and Civilisations (INALCO, Paris), published in 2009 as *Les Cinémas malagaches, 1937–2007* (Paris: L'Harmattan).

FREDERIC CHAUME is Professor of Audiovisual Translation at the Universitat Jaume I/Spain and Honorary Professor at Imperial College London/UK. He is author of *Doblatge i subtitulació per a la TV* (Eumo 2003), *Cine y Traducción* (Cátedra 2004), and *Teories Actuals de la Traductologia* (Bromera 2010). He has co-edited a number of *Perspectives*: *Studies in Translatology* (1999) and two collective volumes on audiovisual translation (*La traducción en los medios audiovisuales* and *La traducción audiovisual: investigación, enseñanza y profesión*). For the past 22 years he has also been working as a professional translator for different dubbing and subtitling companies.

CAMILLE GENDRAULT teaches Film Studies at the University of Bordeaux 3/France. A trained historian with a doctorate in film and media from the University of Paris 1 – Panthéon Sorbonne/France, she defended her thesis on *Depictions, Images and Imaginations of Naples in Italian Film from 1980 in 2003* (forthcoming in 2010, Editions L'Harmattan). Her research is dedicated to the relationships between urban space, collective identity and film aesthetics.

ALEC G. HARGREAVES is Director of the Winthrop-King Institute for Contemporary French and Francophone Studies at Florida State University/USA. His recent publications include *Multi-Ethnic France: Immigration, Politics, Culture and Society* (London/New York: Routledge, 2007) and *Memory, Empire and Postcolonialism: Legacies of French Colonialism* (Lanham, MD: Lexington, 2005).

IRENE DE HIGES ANDINO graduated in Translation and Interpreting at the Universitat Jaume I/Spain in 2007. She has worked as a Production Manager Assistant in Soundub (Madrid/Spain). From 2007 to 2009 she also was a professional freelance translator specialised in the translation of cinema articles, voice over for TV and subtitling for film festivals. She is presently working on her PhD thesis on multilingual movies and translation and as a full-time researcher in the TRAMA Group.

LESLIE KEALHOFER is a preparing a PhD dissertation at Florida State University/ USA. Her research compares the ways in which literary, cinematographic and other sources mediate the voices of first-generation North African women in France.

MIYA KOMORI is a lecturer at the WU Vienna University of Economics and Business/Austria. She did her undergraduate degree in Spanish and German at the University of Cambridge/UK and her postgraduate degree in Romance Languages at the University of Vienna/Austria, focusing on the semiotics of food in film and literature. Her main research interests are language and culture contact and intercultural communication.

CRISTINA JOHNSTON teaches French culture and language, and European cinema in the School of Languages, Cultures and Religions at the University of Stirling (UK). Her research interests lie in contemporary French cinema ('minority' cinemas in particular – *cinéma de banlieue*, gay cinema, etc.) and in cinematic exchanges between the US and metropolitan France, as well as on notions on citizenship. She is currently working on a monograph on French minority cinemas to be published by Rodopi.

JOSÉ LUIS MARTÍ FERRIOL obtained a Bachelor's Degree in Industrial Chemistry from the University of Valencia/Spain in 1985, and earned his PhD degree in audiovisual translation at the Universitat Jaume I/Spain in 2006. For 21 years, he combined his professional activity in several chemical process production companies with his education in Translation Studies. Since 2007, he has been a full-time lecturer and researcher at the Universitat Jaume I. His main research field is audiovisual translation and he recently published the book *Cine independiente y traducción* (Tirant Lo Blanch, 2010).

CRISTINA MARTÍNEZ-CARAZO is a professor at the University of California/USA. She received her Bachelor's degree at the University of Salamanca, Spain and her PhD at the University of California/USA. Her publications include *De la visualidad literaria a la visualidad fílmica: La Regenta de Leopoldo Alas 'Clarín', Twentieth Century: Spanish Fiction Writers* (with M. Altisent), *Hispanismo y cine* (with J. Herrera), *Spain's Multicultural Legacies* (with A.L.Martin) and *Contra el olvido. El exilio español en Estados Unidos* (with S. Faber). She is currently working on a volume about Pedro Almodóvar.

JUAN JOSÉ MARTÍNEZ-SIERRA is a lecturer of Audiovisual Translation and Specialised Translation in the Department of Translation and Interpreting of the University of Murcia (Spain). Besides his PhD in Translation Studies (Universitat Jaume I/Spain, 2004), he holds a BA in English Language and Culture (Universitat Jaume I/Spain, 1995) and an MA in Intercultural Communication (University of Maryland/USA, 2001). He has published several articles dealing with audiovisual translation, humour, and culture as well as a book (*Humor y Traducción. Los Simpson cruzan la frontera*) on the translation of humour in audiovisual texts from an intercultural and discursive perspective.

CAROLIN OVERHOFF FERREIRA is professor of Contemporary Film at the Federal University of São Paulo (UNIFESP)/Brazil. She holds a PhD from the Free University of Berlin/Germany and was Post-Doctoral Senior Fellow at the University of São Paulo after holding positions at the Portuguese Catholic University in Porto, the University of Coimbra and the University of Arts and Design in Hannover. She is the author of *Identity and Difference – Postcoloniality and Transnationality in Lusophone Films* (forthcoming, University of Manchester Press), *Neue Tendenzen in der Dramatik Lateinamerikas* (Vistas, 1999) and the editor of *O Cinema Português através dos Seus Filmes* (Campo das Letras, 2007) and *Dekalog: On Manoel de Oliveira* (Wallflower Press, 2008).

GAËLLE PLANCHENAULT is a professor of French Applied Linguistics at Simon Fraser University/Canada. In her research, she has been interested in studying cultural and social representations occurring in media texts, with a focus on representations of otherness and linguistic differences, especially in films. Among her recent publications she has written an article on the subtitling and dubbing in French of the American movie *Rize* (published in *Glottopol* N° 12, 2008) and an article on French stylisation in the *Poirot* TV series (to appear in a special issue of *Sociolinguistic Studies*).

ANA M. PRATS-RODRÍGUEZ holds a BA in English Language and Literature (University of Valencia/ Spain, 2002) and a BA in Translation and Interpreting (Universitat Jaume I/Spain). She was a Teaching Assistant at the University of Georgia/USA (2002–2004), where she obtained a Master in Spanish Literature with a dissertation on the evolution of the Cuban post-revolutionary documentary. She is presently writing her PhD on the language of dubbing and participates as a full-time researcher in the TRAMA Group at the Universitat Jaume I.

JOHN D. SANDERSON is a Senior Lecturer on Film and Theatre Translation and on Film and Literature at the University of Alicante/Spain. He has published articles in the fields of screen translation, theatre translation and film studies with a particular focus on translation strategies and Shakespeare. He is the editor of four volumes on screen translation and three on film studies. Three of his translations of Shakespeare's plays have been published and staged in Spain, and he is the author of the book *Traducir el teatro de Shakespeare: Figuras retóricas iterativas en Ricardo III* (2002).

HÉLÈNE SICARD-COWAN teaches at Dawson College in Montreal/Canada. She holds a PhD in French and Francophone Literatures and Cultures from the University of California/USA. She has taught at the University of California, the University of Virginia/USA, McGill University/Canada, as well as the French Cultural Institute in Vienna/Austria. Her current research interests are: colonial and post-colonial studies, immigrant literatures and cinemas, transculturality and intermediality, literature and cinema from and about the Brittany region.